"I'm not **mad,** I just hate you!"

"I'm not mad, I just hate you!"

A New Understanding of
MOTHER-DAUGHTER CONFLICT

Roni Cohen-Sandler, Ph.D.,
and Michelle Silver

VIKING

VIKING
Published by the Penguin Group
Penguin Putnam Inc., 375 Hudson Street,
New York, New York 10014, U.S.A.
Penguin Books Ltd, 27 Wrights Lane,
London W8 5TZ, England
Penguin Books Australia Ltd, Ringwood,
Victoria, Australia
Penguin Books Canada Ltd, 10 Alcorn Avenue,
Toronto, Ontario, Canada M4V 3B2
Penguin Books (N.Z.) Ltd, 182–190 Wairau Road,
Auckland 10, New Zealand

Penguin Books Ltd, Registered Offices:
Harmondsworth, Middlesex, England

First published in 1999 by Viking Penguin,
a member of Penguin Putnam Inc.

10   9   8   7   6   5   4   3   2

LIBRARY OF CONGRESS CATALOGING-IN-PUBLICATION DATA
Cohen-Sandler, Roni.
    I'm not mad, I just hate you! : a new understanding of mother-daughter
  conflict / Roni Cohen-Sandler and Michelle Silver.
        p.   cm.
    ISBN 0-670-88343-3
    1. Mothers and daughters.   2. Parent and child.   3. Conflict of generations.
  I. Silver, Michelle.   II. Title.
  HQ755.85.C624   1999
  306.874'3—DC21   98–39724

This book is printed on acid-free paper.
∞

Printed in the United States of America
Set in Bembo
Designed by Mark Melnick

DEDICATION

Dedicated with great admiration to my mother, Arleen Cohen, who has taught me by example about courage, dignity, and the power of love—as well as extraordinary commitment to mother-daughter relationships.   —R.C.-S.

For my mother, Bobbi Silver, who has taught me the value of being true to myself, retaining an adventurous spirit, and indulging in the occasional "hit of chocolate." You continue to be my best friend.
                                        —M.S.

ACKNOWLEDGMENTS

We are most grateful to Loretta Barrett, our agent, who believed in us, nurtured this project from its inception, and continues to teach us to navigate through the world of publishing. Also, thank you to Laura Van Wormer, who was kind enough to read our proposal enthusiastically and introduce us to Loretta. Janet Goldstein, our editor, saw the potential pearl and somehow worked her magic in getting us to find and polish it. Molly Dolan, Jennifer Suitor, and others at Viking have been wonderful.

Roni Cohen-Sandler: This book is an outgrowth of many treasured relationships. My peer study group provides astute insights, inspiration, and camaraderie: Caren Glickson; Orla Cashman; Karen Alter-Reid; Debra Hyman and Debbie Eisenberg, who read early chapters; and Lyn Sommer, whose thoughtful reading of the final manuscript and incisive suggestions were invaluable. Barbara Vinograd not only read the initial manuscript but provides the candor, affection, and reality checks that I rely upon regularly. Jodi Susser's friendship for more than half my life has given me more than I can express. Vicki Schonfeld's legal expertise is most appreciated; her warmth and wisdom are cherished. Jill Sharfstein's enthusiasm about this project and valued thoughts contributed to this project from the very beginning. Mary Einzig and I have discussed at great length the travails of raising teenage daughters. I am also especially grateful to the many women and adolescent girls with whom I have worked over the years. By sharing their experiences and reflections, they have taught me a great deal about many things, especially mother-daughter relationships.

I am most fortunate to have a family whose love and support truly make everything possible. My parents, Arleen and Larry Cohen, have exemplified nurturance and generosity of every kind. My in-laws, Rose and Sam Sandler and Jodi and Steve Ogen, have always been there eagerly to pitch in and to cheer. My daughter, Laura, and son, Jason, not only tolerated admirably the time I spent on this book but have given happily and sweetly of themselves, in their own ways. My husband, Jeff, is simply incomparable; this book would have been impossible without his unflagging confidence in me, his vital input at even the most uncivilized hours, and, despite his own busy practice, his essential and game takeover of the kitchen duty.

Michelle Silver: I would like to thank my mother, Bobbi Silver, my stepfather, Jules Spotts, my brother, Eric, and my sister-in-law, Kathleen, for their uplifting humor and continued encouragement. Extra thanks go to Lisa Frattini and Peter Flynn for their unwavering support and open ears.

CONTENTS

Part 1

Understanding Your Worlds

Chapter One

You and Your Daughter

I don't know what's gotten into my daughter lately. The other day some out-of-town friends called to say they were in town and asked if they could stop by for dinner. So of course I said yes, and I called home to ask Melanie, who's fifteen, to give me a hand by straightening up the kitchen and setting the table. When I rushed home from work, I found the kitchen in disarray and Melanie upstairs in her room, door shut, sorting through a stack of CDs. When I asked, quite calmly, why she hadn't done as I had asked, Melanie said she'd forgotten. She shrugged and just kept rearranging the CDs. I could hear my voice beginning to shrill when I demanded that she help me . . . NOW! She said okay but didn't budge. So I promptly started screaming at her to get off her duff and get downstairs. She had the nerve to ask me why I was making such a "big deal"! But I knew we had hit rock bottom when she muttered under her breath that I wasn't "exactly Mrs. Reliable." I said the first thing I could think of: that she was grounded . . . until further notice.
—Alice, age forty-six

My mother is ridiculous. I was in the middle of talking to my best friend, who had a really bad problem. She thought her boyfriend might be getting ready to break up with her, so of course she was upset, and I had to help her. And then my mother goes and calls on the other line and makes me hang up on my friend. It's like my phone call isn't even important. Just when I got done calming down my friend, my mother came home, barged into my room, and screamed at me about the stupid kitchen. What was I supposed to do? If I didn't clean up my CDs, she'd yell at me 'cause my room is a mess. No matter what I do, it's wrong. She's never happy!

—Melanie

Is it any wonder mothers almost universally fear their daughters' adolescent years? Like the majority of mothers of teenage (or nearly teenage) daughters, you may be wondering how your relationship suddenly became so complicated. How did the simplest, most mundane situations become so highly charged? When did you and your daughter stop seeing the world through the same lens? And, most important, what became of your delightful, agreeable "baby" girl?

Perhaps during her early childhood you heard the warnings: "Just wait till she's a teenager" or "You'd better enjoy her while you can." You were told your relationship would begin to unravel, if not explode, just around the time your daughter got a training bra. But adolescence seemed a lifetime away. Besides, it wouldn't happen to you and your daughter. You had developed a close relationship with her, more like the one you'd always longed for with your own mother. You'd cherished those morning cuddles in bed, the giggles you'd shared, and all the precious drawings and heartfelt poems she'd ever given you.

Then, in the blink of an eye, everything changed between the two of you. Out went the easy chats, holding hands on walks, and keeping her secrets. In came slammed doors, exasperated sighs, sullen moods, and rude comments. There are still plenty of whispered confidences, but now they're only to her friends. As soon as you even approach the vicinity, the whispering stops abruptly; eyes get rolled. You are clearly unwanted, excluded from the adolescent sanctum. These days, if your daughter is not overtly blaming you for "ruining" her life, she's avoiding you, yelling at you, or demanding that you stay out of her room and mind your own business. You've been made painfully aware that your every gesture "annoys" her. This is not the mother-daughter relationship you had in mind.

As Mary-Jo, mother to fifteen-year-old Jeannie, described it, "I'm walking on eggshells all the time. Everything I do is 'ridiculous'; everything I say is 'wrong.' I don't even like to be around my daughter anymore, especially if she has friends over; she sighs disgustedly every time I even open my mouth. And if I have the nerve to ask one of her friends a simple question, forget it! I'm supposed to be the adult, but instead, I find I'm afraid to say a word."

Welcome to the world of parenting a teenage daughter, a task more arduous, frustrating, and exhausting than any you ever imagined. Where did you go wrong? You were committed to being open, emotionally available, honest, and consistently supportive of your daughter. She would know that she could come to you with any problem, question, or concern and you would answer her calmly, without patronizing or judging her. These strategies would ensure the building of a strong, close, and trusting mother-daughter relationship, and if you were fortunate, this plan worked—at least for the first decade of her life.

Along with the onset of puberty, however, came the intense and unpredictable moods, the temper tantrums you hadn't seen since age two, and the tendency to bristle over any and all perceived slights. Terry, the mother of a fourteen-year-old, related this classic example: "I was driving in the car with my daughter on the way to her high school orientation. We were sitting there quietly, in what I'd call companionable silence, when all of a sudden she startled me by saying, 'Be quiet, Mom!' But I hadn't said a single word!"

When you hear another woman complain of these absurdities, it may seem humorous, but it couldn't be any less funny when it's happening to you. In fact, your own once-respectful and affectionate daughter may now be telling you to "shut up," making fun of you, or withdrawing into her room for days on end. You might feel like the forty-year-old mother who described her oldest daughter's sudden transformation upon entering middle school: "It seemed like one day my little sweetheart moved out and some angry stranger who hated me moved in." Or like the mother of a thirteen-year-old who explained, "It's like I've suffered the loss of someone very dear to me."

At times you are relieved, if not ecstatic, to see vestiges of your daughter's old self. As she proudly shows you an accomplishment, you glimpse the broad grin and unguarded affection of her younger days. Or you hear from another parent about what an "especially lovely, polite child" visits her home. "We must be doing something right," you think. You are especially delighted to overhear her, incredibly, bestowing advice or kind words to her younger sibling and think, "Maybe, just maybe, she'll be all right after all." Then, in the next moment, and for a reason apparent to no one—perhaps not even to your daughter herself—she transforms again, shouting, "I hate you!" and huffing and stomping off to her room, leaving a trail of accusations in her angry wake.

These changes are mystifying and devastating to mothers. Are you really as out of touch with her life as she accuses? Worse yet, is it possible she sees in you some of the traits you abhorred in your own mother and swore you'd avoid? Just what is it that makes you the prime target of your daughter's wrath?

Unquestionably, teenage girls bristle and rage about nearly everything—from minor disappointments to undeniable tragedies—with nearly equal intensity. It is well known that adolescents perceive the most innocuous of comments as slights or even major insults. Many a mother has commented that she has only to look at her daughter to be accused of criticizing her or thinking she is "fat"! Paradoxically, because your unquestioned love makes your daughter feel safe, she feels free to direct much of her frustration and hostility toward you, regardless of whether you are remotely involved. You have likely joined the ranks of mothers who are tired of feeling they can never say or do anything right.

At times your relationship with your daughter may deteriorate further. As Ann, a thirty-five-year-old single mother, put it, "I'm dealing with a level of conflict I never imagined. Since she was thirteen, Morgan pretty much decided she didn't need to listen to me or respect me. She treats me with nothing but contempt. I'm devastated by what our relationship has become and frightened by what lies ahead. If we're constantly at each other's throats, how can I hope to help her through these next years? How can I keep her safe from alcohol and drugs and all the rest?"

Not only do mothers despair over feeling that their relationships with their daughters have been lost, but they become terrified about surrendering any lingering threads of control they may have held.

Yet again, you may be reading this from the perspective of the unaffected. Perhaps your daughter is still asking you to French braid her hair, give your opinion on social matters, and accompany her on long nature walks. She may still confide in you the details of her day: who said what to whom, which girls are on the outs, who got into trouble in music class. You may be seeking to preserve the closeness you now share with your daughter and especially to prevent future struggles you may anticipate or worry about. "Frankly, I'm petrified," said Fran, the mother of a teenage son and a ten-year-old daughter. "I look around, and all I see are the problems lurking ahead. Every day I hear about drugs, teenage pregnancy, date rape, AIDS. My friends whose daughters are already teens tell me how horrible it is. I want to know what I can do right now to ensure these problems don't hit us in a few years.

What I want, most of all, is for my daughter and me to continue as we are now."

Whether you're still anticipating the teen years, reeling from the rockiness of your ever-changing adolescent, or struggling with a mother-daughter relationship that's deteriorating by the day, this book is written for you. While there are books that discuss such parenting topics as the adolescent girl's physical development, body image, peer relations, substance abuse, and sexuality, this book focuses specifically on the evolving and challenging mother-daughter relationship during the teen years. We speak to mothers who are desperate for help in handling conflicts with their teenage daughters more effectively ("I can't stand another minute of this arguing!" "I've about had it!") and to those who experience painful self-doubt about their mothering skills ("Am I making the best decisions?" "Should I be doing something differently?"). It is important to note that while we acknowledge that fathers play a pivotal and ever-growing role in raising teen daughters, we have deliberately chosen to focus on the unique dynamics of the mother-daughter connection.

Because of our distinct careers and experiences—one of us a clinical psychologist working intensively with mothers and daughters, the other a senior editor of a national girls' magazine—we are able to portray the needs, concerns, and viewpoints of both mothers and adolescent girls. We clarify the concerns of teenage girls and specifically what they are seeking when they say their mothers "just don't understand" them and are "always butting in" or saying "all the wrong things." We shall also help you by describing what typically distresses daughters, why they are so quick to blame their mothers, and how they can better handle negative emotions. In the chapters that follow, we'll show you many ways to connect with your teenager or to restore previous closeness and to find more gratifying ways of interacting. At a time when your own daughter may be withdrawn and secretive, this information can be invaluable.

Mothers nearly always wonder if what they're going through is normal. The balance of voices throughout this book will help you put your experiences with your own daughter in perspective. As you will see, there is an enormous variation of predictable struggles that are influenced by your daughter's age, genetic endowments, family background, and experiences. At any given moment your relationship will be affected by these factors, as well as by your teenager's notoriously mercurial moods and inconsistent behavior. Your relationship with your daughter, like all relationships, will have its ups and downs. But when you establish a solid connection with her and keep your long-term goals clearly in focus, you can be confident of your relationship's withstanding these inevitable turbulent periods.

What is normal is also broad because adolescent maturation is hardly uniform and rarely linear. Whereas one mother swears she "barely survived" her daughter's thirteenth year, another claims age sixteen is "positively the worst." If there is one thing we can assure you of, it's that there are no givens. Occasional backsliding into behavior characteristic of earlier developmental stages (what therapists call regression) in response to stress, heightened demands, or life circumstances is to be expected as well. For example, your staunchly independent daughter, who has embraced each new school year with the barest of waves good-bye, may at thirteen suddenly cling to you like Velcro when she is introduced to junior high school teachers. Or, out of nowhere, you may find your fifteen-year-old five-foot-tall baby girl on your lap—a not so subtle message that she needs some extra TLC.

Your relationship with your daughter is also highly determined by your own goals and expectations for raising her. No one can tell you what kind of daughter you should raise or the nature of the relationship you want to have with her. Whereas one mother may find her daughter's exclamation "I hate you!" unacceptably disrespectful, another may take comfort in her teenager's ability to express strong negative feelings. Similarly, while some mothers are so primed for confrontation that every piece of lint on their daughters' carpets is an impetus for a major battle, others may overlook red flags signifying serious problems in order to avoid conflict at all costs.

Recognizing the uniqueness of every woman and teenage girl, this book prescribes few absolute solutions. Instead, we invite you to participate actively in the process of learning more about yourself and your daughter as well as about how to strengthen your relationship. The first part of this book helps you examine the respective issues each of you brings to the mother-daughter relationship. As you explore the intense feelings and challenges intrinsic to mothering today's teenage girl, we ask you to reflect on your own particular attitudes, strengths, and formative experiences.

Similarly, you will view from the perspective of adolescent girls the developmental, interpersonal, and social challenges they commonly face, thereby gaining a better understanding of your own daughter's likely wishes, fears, hopes, and frustrations. Empathy for your daughter's emotional experiences, and appreciation for what she brings to the relationship, are at the heart of your connection with her. You will have the chance to examine what you have learned from your own family and the larger culture in which you live and how these lessons influence your relationship with your daughter.

The second part of this book provides the practical know-how, the tools to improve and strengthen your relationship and to stay connected with her in spite of daily challenges. You will learn to choose your battles wisely, to be clear on what you hope to accomplish, to respond more pragmatically when your daughter expresses her anger, and to communicate effectively about important issues. The empathy you develop will then guide you in interpreting her everyday communications, both verbal and nonverbal. You will better decipher what she is really saying when she screams, "I'm not hungry," and stomps away from the dinner table, when she "forgets" the errand you desperately needed her to take care of, or when she leaves to catch the school bus in the very same ripped jeans you told her not to wear. You will see the myriad possible messages that can be communicated by the universal slammed bedroom door. You will also learn how to stay the course during your conflicts with your daughter, remaining fast to your beliefs and values even when your most valiant efforts bring less than optimal immediate results.

Mothers typically ask, "What do I say?" and "What do I say when my daughter says——?" Hearing from dozens of mothers what they've learned from their teenage daughters will give you both effective strategies and much-needed words. Because people often learn best by realizing what *not* to do, we offer dialogues illustrating common but unproductive ways to communicate with adolescents. We will set you at ease by anticipating worst-case scenarios and teaching useful ways to recognize and handle them.

By the close of this book it is likely you and your daughter will still have your struggles. On occasion you may even battle intensely. But you will be convinced that conflict is not necessarily dangerous or to be avoided at all costs. In fact, you will have discovered that you and your daughter not only can stay connected in the presence of conflict but can grow from it. You will come to appreciate that strong emotions such as anger can be powerful tools used to improve your relationship (and life in general), rather than to harm or ruin it. Your repertoire of effective communication and conflict resolution skills will increase your confidence in many other areas of your life.

Not only will you be empowered by this knowledge, but so will your daughter. In the third part of this book you will learn to help her apply these new skills to other areas of her life. When teenage girls clash with friends, teachers, and boyfriends, mothers are often hard pressed to figure out their own roles. In these chapters we show you how the tools you've acquired in resolving mother-daughter conflict can be put into practice as your adolescent moves beyond the home and into the adult world.

Girls, now more than ever, must learn to handle conflicts with employers, college professors, coaches, peers, and even themselves. Daughters need both permission and know-how to take a stand against many potential threats; they must learn to tolerate anxiety and even to risk rejection by their friends when it is in their best interest or safety to do so. This is not merely an issue of "just saying no." Recently a sixteen-year-old told her therapist that the previous Saturday evening she had had sex with four boys. When the therapist asked, "Did you want to?" the girl replied, "No, but I didn't want to hurt their feelings."

These are the times when women and girls must discard politeness, even feminine concern for others, in order to protect themselves. In fact, these are the times when you want your daughter to know how to speak up and wage a good fight.

By hanging in there in the face of conflict with your daughter, you will teach her, by example, these vital life skills. By your plugging along and demonstrating your commitment, she will realize how worthy she is and how well she deserves to be treated. In this process you will accomplish your ultimate goal: developing and maintaining a close, enriching, lifelong connection to your daughter.

Chapter Two

Being a Mother

As teenage girls are forging identities, their mothers often undergo an almost parallel process of struggling with what kinds of mothers they are—and what kinds they hoped to be. This is no coincidence. Your daughter merely needs to sulk, threaten, or accuse you of being the "absolute worst mother ever" to provoke that unsettling spasm of self-doubt: "What did I do wrong?" The sting of one well-aimed barb is all it takes to make you question, "Am I really as bad as she says?" To avoid being thrown off-balance by your daughter's challenging virtually everything you say and do for the duration of her adolescence, it is crucial that you understand and feel confident of who you are and that you be certain of your values and goals.

This chapter is intended to help you step back and regain some much-needed trust in yourself as a mother by encouraging you to think through these important issues. As a preliminary step in strengthening your connection to your teenager, you will be asked to consider what you bring to the mother-daughter relationship. As you read about the myriad emotions women typically experience, as well as various messages about mothering they get from their families, you can reflect on where your own attitudes and values come from and determine what changes, if any, you would like to make in raising your daughter. In the course of your self-examination you will also meet three women, who share their own various struggles with their teenage girls. Each of these women found herself questioning in a profound way what defined a good mother and whether she was in fact the kind of mother she had always wanted to be.

WHY IT FEELS DIFFERENT NOW

Until she hit the teen years, it is likely you too found a satisfying way to nurture your daughter, to provide the basics, and to rise to whatever challenges she presented—in short, to be a capable mother. During her infancy you probably consulted family members, books, and pediatricians about feeding, teething, rashes, and other health questions. During toddlerhood you and your daughter may have participated in a play group or preschool, where she learned to socialize with her peers and you got welcome suggestions (and reassurance) from other mothers dealing with tantrums, sibling rivalry, napping, and other "terrible two" behaviors. During elementary school you may have participated in school activities, parent-teacher meetings, or child development lectures and read up on fostering achievement and self-esteem.

Sure, you two had your spats. But you made up, and then it was as if nothing had ever happened. In general, you thought you did many "right" things. You felt prepared for the onset of puberty, the chats about menstruation; you were ready to shop for the first bra, to administer first aid for the first pimple . . . so what went awry? Now that your daughter has entered her teenage years, why does being her mother make you somehow question your sensibilities, your words, and your very self?

Actually, considering the staggering developmental challenges that your daughter encounters, which will be described from her perspective in the next chapter, it is not in the least bit surprising that she evokes equally powerful responses in you. As she grows and evolves, your daughter induces corresponding changes in her relationship with you. As an integral part of this relationship you cannot help being affected. Understanding why mothering an adolescent feels different will help you put your own emotional reactions in perspective. Consider these reasons:

The Entire Family Is Stressed

The first thing to keep in mind is: It's not just you. When your daughter hits puberty, each member of the family feels the dramatic effects of her changes and is forced to adapt. Your family, no matter how well functioning, is necessarily shaken up. Typically everyone reverts to earlier ways of behaving and relating with one another. Relationships may get closer or more distant. Alliances shift. There is pressure on the marriage. Or in cases of divorce the ex-spouses' ability to coparent effectively may be severely challenged. Your adolescent's younger siblings feel the stress, often resenting the amount of attention given to the new teen. For example, asked in school to describe his middle school sibling, an observant eight-year-old boy wrote, "I have a changing sister. She's all my parents ever talk about."

Perhaps more important, the teenager reawakens in her mother and father feelings from their own respective adolescent years, particularly their desires to rely on their parents. Much to their dismay, whatever struggles they may have had with their own families seem to be replaying themselves. When such "hot" issues are stirred up, they often have a ripple effect throughout the family. A mother of four, Carmen was surprised by her reaction to her oldest child's becoming a teenager: "I expected big changes in my daughter, but I was caught off guard by how she affected all of us. For a while it was as if all hell broke loose. We lost our footing as a family."

While this can be an uncomfortable, unsettling time for everyone, in general this process is both temporary and adaptive. Each family member is prompted to step back and take stock of what is going on within his or her daily life. Mothers and fathers are compelled to deal with the impact of past issues and feelings on their present families. As a result of this reflection, adults can potentially become more empathic with their teens. This may engender greater mutual understanding between parents and children; adolescent growth is facilitated. In fact, if all goes well, each member develops further as an individual, and the family becomes stronger and closer as a unit.

Mothers Take the Brunt

As the emotional caretakers of the family mothers typically sit at the helm throughout this process, anxiously steering the family's course through the maelstrom of the adolescent years. As such they often feel responsible for ensuring that each member survives and even thrives. Consequently, mothers often feel a dramatically increased burden during their daughters' adolescence.

Mothers today have enough concerns. Whether by choice or economic necessity, the number of women in the workforce has skyrocketed. There are ever-increasing numbers of single-parent families. Mothers, most often custodial parents, struggle to balance child rearing, work, and social demands. Margaret, forty-four, said, "I'm always feeling pulled in different directions. I can't do everything well or even give one hundred percent of myself to anything." Unlike previous generations, modern extended families often live far apart and are no longer available as sources of support to mothers or daughters. These changes in family structure, the workforce, and prevailing societal problems not only don't assist mothers but significantly exacerbate the difficulties they face with their teenagers.

In addition to all of the above, there is far more going on that contributes to the undeniable intensity facing mother and daughter. Mothers often reel from powerful memories and emotions evoked by their daughters' adolescence: unresolved issues with their own mothers and fathers, regrets, glories, mistakes, hurts. The shared gender between women and girls, which permits the mother to identify more easily with the daughter, can also result in unparalleled intensity. Whereas fathers can empathize with what their daughters are going through, mothers sense that they feel exactly what their daughters are feeling.

Through their various adolescent experiences, ranging from fantastic to devastating, each adult comes away with certain attitudes and beliefs. Unless you consciously reflect on what you learned from your family, these ideas can insidiously permeate your relationship with your own daughter. For example, how you respond to your daughter's mistakes, complaints, and demands is shaped in part by how you were treated by your own mother as a child.

Similarly, unless you purposefully reflect on your notions of what is best for your daughter, you may have trouble distinguishing her desires and feelings from your own. A mother who as a teen struggled to make friends and be included in the "popular" crowd may desperately encourage her daughter to achieve what she could not. This is fine, unless the mother's desires interfere with her judgment, say, if she promotes her fourteen-year-old's going to unsupervised coed parties or if the mother is pressuring her child to have many friends in spite of the daughter's contentment with just one or two close pals.

Consider the case of Marie, a thirty-eight-year-old with two children: "My mother was an incredibly gifted dancer, and she could have toured nationally with a company, but she had to take care of her brothers and sisters when her parents got divorced. She wanted me to be a great dancer, and she invested a lot into making that happen, but I couldn't do it. I wasn't talented the way she was, and I didn't love dance the way she did. It caused a lot of unnecessary friction between us."

It is crucial to define these boundaries between mothers and daughters, for when they are blurred, it is often difficult to understand, much less to resolve, the antagonism that erupts between them.

Her Development Affects You

It is far from easy to live with someone who is undergoing rapid changes in how she looks, thinks, and feels. On the most obvious level, girls' maturing bodies, vitality, and burgeoning sexuality tend to make their mothers uncomfortable. Developmentally this makes sense. Just when girls are blossoming into shapely young women, beginning to menstruate, and exploring their appeal to males, their mothers, often in or approaching midlife, are facing the indisputable and unwelcome effects of aging: wrinkling, sagging skin, decreased muscle tone, weight gain, and perimenopausal or menopausal symptoms.

For women whose appearance has been important in their lives, it may be difficult to live with adolescent daughters who remind them of their ever-diminishing youth. It may be hard for some mothers to watch their daughters get male attention when they themselves feel their attractiveness waning. This may be particularly problematic for mothers who are dating at the same time as their daughters.

At another level mothers often react to their daughters' growing independence. For those who prided themselves in their ability to care for their daughters, being told she doesn't "need your help" can be a significant blow. In fact, adolescence brings complex circumstances and problems that mothers, no matter how devoted, simply cannot solve. The process of relinquishing control, of giving up the sense of being able to guide their daughters through tumult, is difficult, to say the least. Moreover, as girls reach late adolescence, when they prepare to leave home, mothers can be profoundly affected by the imminent sense of loss. Throughout this period you will feel forced to adapt to your daughter's changing needs; your role as a mother will shift dramatically.

> *Adolescents have to refight many of the battles of earlier years, even though to do so they must artificially appoint perfectly well-meaning people to play the role of adversaries.*
> —Erik H. Erikson

It Is Impossible to Please Her

Mothers constantly report feeling confused about exactly what their daughters want from them. While their adolescents desperately struggle for independence, at times they seem to demand that their mothers take care of them. The fifteen-year-old who insists she is old enough to go backpacking for a week with a friend will in the next breath whine that she can't wear her favorite shirt until her mother does the laundry. The teen girl's simultaneous messages to "Let me grow up" and "Baby me" cause constant chafing with her mother.

Similarly, because the adolescent uses her mother as the standard to which she both aspires and struggles against, mothers are frequently called upon to be sounding boards for their daughters. You are the vehicle through which your daughter tests out her shaky opinions and practices expressing her thoughts. You can hardly expect her to say, "Gee, Mom, I'm a little confused. I need to hear what you believe so I can figure out how I feel." Instead, she will likely instigate fights and herd you into battles, poking, prodding, and provoking you so she can ultimately hear your reasoning.

There are therefore a few sure and disappointing bets during this time. If you like certain music, your daughter is apt to loathe it. Whatever your political leanings, your daughter will be inclined to advocate an alternative position. Although you may be determined to agree with your daughter, she knows precisely which buttons to push to compel you into debate: "It's so awful having Grandma here. I think you should put her in a nursing home." "Chrissy's mother is the best. She trusts her, even to go to parties when the parents aren't home." "You always tell me to be honest, so why did you lie to Dad's boss today?" Through discussion, and argument, teens glean their mothers' logic in order to integrate and distinguish mothers' beliefs and values from their own.

It Feels Personal

Mothers typically describe feeling scrutinized by their teens. As one woman put it, "Living with my daughter is like having my own personal X-ray machine." This is because your daughter's effort to develop her own individuality, as well as refine her likes and dislikes, motivates her to examine your every action, belief, trait, and mannerism. Moreover, she does not hesitate to express her disdain for your "inferior" and ill-formed choices. This is a far cry from her early child-hood, when you frequently could do no wrong, when you were described enthusiastically as the "prettiest," "nicest," or "best mother in the world."

Now your daughter is becoming a keen observer, sharing in a bru-tally honest manner everything she concludes about you. It is hard not to become defensive and only too easy for you to take her feedback and critiques personally. A mother returned from taking her fourteen-year-old to the doctor and reported this conversation: "First, my daughter looked horrified and pointed out that my slip was showing. So I tugged my skirt over the offending patch of white and thanked her. Next, she said 'Mom, you have fuzz in your hair!' so again I said thanks and found whatever was bothering her. But not two seconds went by before she whispered furiously to me that there was something on my nose. I must've sounded annoyed because she then asked, 'Why are you saying it like that? I'm only trying to help.' "

Is your daughter aghast about your new haircut, refusing to be seen with you in public? Does she cringe when you laugh, begging you to "keep it down"? Has your daughter graciously appointed herself to be your new, indispensable adviser, telling you how, what, and when to do almost everything? Perhaps you're able to keep in mind that she is studying you to figure out what she wants to emulate. It's just that you can't help feeling in your heart that she's tearing you apart.

It is also true that sometimes girls provoke arguments not to refine their belief systems but simply to take out their frustration and anger on their most available and prized targets, their mothers. During this time when emotional turmoil is high and control over impulses is low, ado-lescents are likely to use mothers as scapegoats for whatever goes wrong in their lives. For this reason as well, mothers often say they are con-tinually dodging their daughters' sarcasm, rudeness, nastiness, insults, accusations, and thrown objects. Is it any wonder that these daily skir-mishes feel "personal"?

Dealing with Conflict Is Particularly Hard

In general, women have a tough time handling conflict and anger. They therefore regard their teenage daughters' challenging behavior or outright hostility as particularly unwelcome. Thinking back to when your daughter was a little girl, you probably expected her to get into squabbles with her peers and siblings. You knew there would be the struggles over who would use the red crayon, receive the bigger piece of cake, or wear the princess costume. You often anticipated fights over who got to pick the activity during a play date, or who was invited to which birthday party, and you were also prepared to teach her how to resolve these situations effectively.

Now that your daughter has reached adolescence, you, like many mothers, may believe that your daughter should be beyond all that. She should know how to get along with people—especially with you.

But for the reasons described above, you two are probably experiencing more rather than less conflict. You may be finding that the least little disagreement will escalate into a screaming match. You'd rather get along with your daughter. You prefer peaceful times. In fact, you'd like simply to get through one day without an episode of belligerence, a disgusted sigh, or a slammed door.

Reminding yourself of these sentiments, and thinking of all the reasons why mothering a teen is so challenging, can feel a bit overwhelming. So before you explore what conflicts typically stir up for mothers, take a deep breath. For the next few minutes, set aside your own emotions while you hear from Bess, a forty-five-year-old woman whose daughter's adolescence sparked intense self-questioning and reevaluation of her expectations about motherhood.

BESS

Bess's curly hair, heart-shaped face, and freckled complexion gave her a youthful and somewhat innocent appearance. The moment she sat down at the edge of her chair, however, she began to speak animatedly about her daughter, her intense dark eyes and rapid gestures betraying her sense of urgency. "I don't know how we got to this place or where I went wrong," she said. "As a matter of fact, I'm not even sure there *is* anything wrong. But every day has become sheer torture. This can't be normal. Maybe what I'm feeling is abnormal. I don't even know who I am anymore." At that she began to sob. What was clear right then was that Bess was in anguish.

Since her only child, Rachel, started junior high school the year before, Bess had felt "shaken to the core" by what she perceived as her daughter's sudden and total rejection of her. Contemplative by nature, Bess reported spending hours upon hours trying to make sense of what had gone wrong. She was insightful. She knew that Rachel's adolescence and transition to junior high were causing dramatic changes for the entire family, herself especially. Despite this recognition, however, she could not shake an increasing sense of emptiness and sadness.

For Bess, the most pivotal incident in their relationship had occurred in the fall of the previous year. Eager to volunteer in her daughter's new school, Bess had signed up to be a chaperon at the first dance. Rachel was appalled and refused to attend the dance if her mother was anywhere near school property. Bess was devastated. As she said, "I was incredibly hurt. What had I done that made her that ashamed of me? Somebody's parent had to chaperon, so I figured it might as well be me. I couldn't understand what the big deal was, but Rachel was adamant."

Like a domino effect, this dynamic continued. When Rachel quit her Girl Scout troop, Bess as the leader felt "abandoned," as if the rug had been pulled out from under her. "I definitely took it personally," Bess admitted, "even though she seemed to lose interest in many activities, all at the same time. Why was I suddenly so unwanted?"

Bess had always made it her business to be involved in her daughter's day-to-day life. When Rachel was born, she took a leave of absence from her teaching position but never returned. Instead, Bess was the class mother, the scout leader, the field trip chaperon, the PTA treasurer, and the mother in charge of dance costumes. She said, "I enjoy being a hands-on parent. I don't want to miss these years with Rachel; they go by too fast." In this way Bess described herself as very much like her own mother, with whom she had been close until her mother's death six months before.

Bess became tearful while describing her despair about Rachel's attitude. "She's become unbelievably nasty," Bess complained, shaking her head, as if incredulous that this could be happening. "No matter what I say or do, she's so remote. She hardly ever looks at me, or when she does, it's to give me a dirty look. I'm trying so hard to get things back on track for us, but nothing works. She has absolutely no interest in doing the things we used to do together. Forget breakfasts out, malls are only for her friends, and tag sales have become 'boring.' I'm so worried we'll get farther and farther apart."

Fortunately, where she wasn't directly involved, Bess was able to be more objective about her daughter. She could say that Rachel had adjusted well to junior high, had made friends, and was getting good grades. Her teachers had nice things to say about her. She was a fine soccer player on a travel team. "Actually, Rachel seems okay. I'm the only one with the problem," Bess concluded. But as she continued speaking, it appeared her relationship with her husband was affected as well.

Bess and Michael had dated in high school and married right after college graduation. Although they initially decided to "be a couple" and work for a while before starting a family, it then took them several years and considerable medical intervention to get pregnant. Both parents were thirty when Rachel, their "wonder baby," was born. Although they subsequently endured costly and painful procedures to try to have more children, they gave up when they felt the strain on their marriage and became resigned to Rachel's being an only child. Michael often speculated that because Rachel was that much more precious, Bess probably babied her and was "too involved" with her.

Bess therefore felt blamed for the family's disharmony. "It's just one more thing that's making me doubt myself," she explained. "I feel discarded by my daughter and criticized by my husband. I don't think my mother ever felt like this, but I'm not sure, and now I can't even ask her. I just don't know if this is normal. Do you think we need help?" she asked.

It was understandable that Bess felt bewildered and overwhelmed. Still grieving the death of her own mother, she was remembering the best aspects of their relationship, which had been established as she grew up and had a family of her own. Bess very much wanted and even expected to enjoy the same ideal relationship with her own teenager. Bess's sadness resulted as well from the loss of Rachel's early childhood, particularly the easiness and camaraderie they previously enjoyed. As Rachel matured, Bess reluctantly had to figure out new ways of relating to her. Moreover, as she progressed through her forties, this adjustment coincided with other life changes.

THE EMOTIONAL FALLOUT OF CONFLICT

It is not mere unpleasantness that women like Bess fear when they think of conflict with their daughters. For you too, a whole host of undesirable images may come to mind. However inevitable, conflict rarely makes mothers feel good about themselves or satisfied with their relationships. Instead, every skirmish between your teenager and your-self is likely to leave you struggling with a multitude of feelings you hadn't anticipated, what could be called the emotional fallout of conflict. Below are some of the negative reactions mothers report most frequently.

Self-doubt

Mother-daughter conflict sorely tests a woman's self-esteem. A new theory of women's psychological development provides insight into why mothers almost universally feel unsure of themselves as a result of clashing with their daughters. According to Janet L. Surrey, a researcher from the Stone Center, Wellesley College, women's growth is achieved through their connections with others. She suggests that the mother-daughter relationship is one important vehicle through which women acquire positive feelings about themselves. There is no doubt that mothers often work hard to relate to their children. In fact, they may take particular pride in developing and maintaining close relationships with their daughters. This process through which women strive for mutual understanding—to understand and to be understood—is thought to be crucial for establishing self-acceptance.

Enter the teenage girl. When daily interactions are transformed into constant bickering or harsh exchanges, mothers understandably feel threatened. After years of your attempting to be sensitive to your daughter and to stay in tune with her emotions, to be told you "don't have a clue" about her is devastating. Even when you know deep down that her accusations aren't particularly rational, when she tells you that you failed horribly as a mother and slams the door in your face, it is difficult not to second-guess yourself. Your very sense of self-worth is at stake.

Of course, adolescent girls are on to the scent of their mother's insecurities as efficiently as drug-sniffing police dogs. They are only too eager to pin the blame for whatever they can on their mothers. Nan, age thirty-eight, told of informing her preteen daughter, Nina, of a stormy forecast and the possibility that a pool party to which she had been invited would be canceled. Nina yelled sarcastically, "Thanks a lot!" Nan remembered momentarily wondering if she had indeed been at fault.

This is where the maybes kick in: Maybe I haven't been the best mother. Maybe I haven't given her enough freedom. Maybe I've given her too much freedom. Maybe I haven't listened to her enough. Maybe I should set more limits. Maybe she's correct; I should be able to make everything all right.

Vera, the mother of a sixteen-year-old, put it well: "I think I know better, but I can't help it. Every time we have a hateful moment, I tell myself I should be more understanding and doing a better job with her. Every time we have words, I feel I must be awful. When my daughter and I have a really big blowup, I think, 'You must be the worst mother.'"

What mother *hasn't* thought that?

Hurt

The most prevalent of mothers' reactions to increasing or escalating conflicts with daughters is hurt. Many report feeling wounded, or even devastated, by their teenagers' snippiness or snide comments, not to mention the more overt and extreme expressions of hostility. For example, Shaileen, thirty-seven, says her fifteen-year-old daughter "constantly makes me cry. I know it drives her crazy, and I try not to, but I can't help feeling unbelievably hurt when she's insulted me." Like many mothers, Shaileen finds it hard to tolerate her daughter's animosity. She knows that she is vulnerable to feelings of rejection: "I have to remember that she's just a kid and I'm the adult and that just because we argue doesn't mean she doesn't love me."

No matter how much mothers steel themselves, their teenagers can cause immeasurable pain. Because they are often so tuned in to their mothers, girls easily discern and exploit their mothers' weaknesses. As one woman put it, "My daughter knows exactly what to say, as well as how and when to say it, to inflict the greatest possible hurt."

Recognizing hurt feelings accomplishes two things. First, it allows mothers to address their reactions separate from what their daughters said and did. Maybe your daughter's anger was valid, but to make her point, she was unnecessarily vicious. In this case you may need to teach your daughter to express herself while also considering the feelings of her listeners. Second, your awareness of hurt feelings will make it less likely you will react in a reflexive or retaliatory manner—for example, by condemning her, insulting her, or punishing her inappropriately.

Worry

Mothers have all sorts of worries about conflicts with their daughters. They become alarmed that their teenagers' inappropriate expressions of hostility will accompany them for life. Molly, fifty, says, "Aggie's rudeness and tantrums remind me of my crazy aunt Phyllis, who's become the albatross of the whole family. What if she turns out just like her?" Perhaps your daughter does need to refine her ways of dealing with conflict. But catastrophizing her present behavior into permanent character flaws is unhelpful and possibly even self-fulfilling. You can and will soon learn to shape your daughter's self-defeating style into more acceptable and useful patterns.

The more basic fear, however, is that the conflict you have with your daughter is the antithesis of love and connection. For many mothers, the very notion of conflict brings to mind tremendous inner pain and ruined relationships. When hurtful words are exchanged in the heat of conflict, many women fear the damage will be irreparable. Whether from an accumulation of petty disagreements or from one enormous battle, they believe the relationship will completely disintegrate. Mothers simply cannot understand how they can stay connected to their daughters after being assaulted with insults or accusations they would neither expect nor tolerate from their own worst enemies. To put it simply, they equate conflict with loss.

As a result, these mothers worry when their daughters push their buttons, provoke arguments, and challenge their decisions. They are afraid of nasty words and scornful accusations. When daughters rail, "I hate you!" mothers may believe their relationship is forever doomed. Conversely, when daughters withdraw for days on end, mothers worry that "She doesn't care about me anymore."

To counteract these worries, it is reassuring to hear from mothers who not only weathered their daughters' adolescence but emerged stronger because of working through it. May, fifty-five, offers helpful perspective: "When my daughter was sixteen, I didn't think I could survive one more day. I used to tell my husband, 'One of us has to go.' We were at each other's throats all the time. Annie was awful to me, and I couldn't stand to be around her. I never thought we'd get through that, But, you know, what I thought was impossible really happened: She's in her twenties now, and we're actually friends." Although it is difficult to envision your daughter as a young adult, and even harder to imagine enjoying a better relationship with her in the future, you can be assured this goal is within your reach.

Guilt

If someone hurts you, you're likely to feel angry. When that someone is your daughter and the hurting occurs on an almost daily basis, complications arise. Why? Because for mothers, the quintessential nurturers, it seems unnatural, against their instincts to protect their daughters, to feel hostility. In the course of conversation, a thoughtful, intelligent professor who was the mother of two teen daughters once asked, "Do you ever get mad at your children?" That a mother would even ask this question indicates just how difficult it is for women to accept having such feelings toward their offspring. In fact, mothers often express tremendous guilt when they confess, "It's hard for me to say this, but sometimes I really don't like my daughter." You can imagine how horrified they are to admit, "Sometimes I feel like smacking her."

Feeling guilty about your own negative thoughts or feelings is bad enough. But many mothers feel guilty about any and all conflicts that arise with their daughters—whether or not they were to blame. Linda, age forty-three, had a typical example: "My daughter, Lauren, who's in seventh grade, came out of her room after doing about a half hour of homework after school one day. 'I'm so mad at you!' she screamed at me. When I asked why, she told me that she had forgotten her science book. Now she couldn't study for her test the next day, she would fail the course, and her teacher would be mad at her. Maybe she would get a detention and be kicked off the soccer team too. Of course, it was all my fault. I was flabbergasted. What could all this have to do with me? Well, it turns out that at the end of the day, just before she went to her locker, there was an announcement about the school dance scheduled for the next night. According to Lauren, she was too busy worrying about whether I would let her go to both the dance on Friday night and her baby-sitting job on Saturday night. It was my 'unfair rule' about being out on only one weekend night that caused her to forget her science book. A part of me thought this made no sense, but I started to feel bad anyway. Maybe I had put too much pressure on her to decide between a dance and a job. The sad thing is, I actually felt guilty."

Being aware of guilt is important. Women can feel overwhelmed when they belabor guilt, which further erodes their self-confidence. In addition, when mothers want to assuage their guilt or compensate for their perceived mistakes, they may inadvertently cave in to daughters' unreasonable requests. Regrettable decisions can result. Perhaps most important, you may feel guilty about perfectly normal angry feelings that arise in the course of everyday conflict with your daughter. You may feel awful about being upset with her. Your guilt about having such feelings probably gets in the way of your telling your daughter when she's done or said something that bothered you. Keeping such feelings inside is not only unsound but also prevents you from resolving legitimate disagreements.

Shame

Some mothers go to the other extreme. When they believe they've mishandled situations with their daughters, especially when they have failed to exercise appropriate self-control, they often report feeling ashamed. "I lost control with my daughter," confessed Rhona, forty. "I know I shouldn't ever raise a hand to her. But I came home from work and found out she'd been in trouble at school, she'd tortured her sister all afternoon, and she then had the nerve to start in with me. She got so fresh I couldn't stop myself from slapping her. Then I felt horrible. I still do."

Many mothers feel bewildered about how they could lose self-control. Some have ongoing struggles. "I called my daughter a bitch," "I pushed her a little," and "I wished some horrible things for her" are a few of their confessions. Recognizing the shame you might feel when you express strong feelings through inappropriate words or actions is the first step in gaining self-control. This is precisely what prompted Audra, the forty-eight-year-old woman whose story appears below, to seek help for herself and her daughter. If you are apprehensive about arguments with your daughter getting out of control, or if you are in the thick of such episodes, you may relate to her shame, frustration, and worry. Perhaps you will connect with the replay of Audra's own family dynamics between her and her daughter.

AUDRA

One look at Audra is enough to deduce her nonconformity. Despite her conventional job as a legal secretary, this mother of two appears striking in a somewhat offbeat way. All-black attire, studded broad belt, and high heels are set off by waist-length, wavy red hair and bright lipstick. Seeking therapy for her fifteen-year-old daughter,

Kyle, Audra came for an initial consultation. She was furious. "I'm at my wit's end!" she exclaimed. "My daughter is totally out of control. She has no respect for me, and I won't have this kind of relationship with her."

Audra described how their relationship had deteriorated into constant yelling, threatening, and, most recently, physical fighting. Their differences of opinion—in fact, their diametrically opposing ways of viewing everything—prevented these two from ever agreeing. But what especially set off Audra was Kyle's insistence on going out with friends. "She feels entitled to go wherever she pleases, whenever she pleases, until all hours of night. I know she's never where she says she's going. Plus, I don't like the looks of some of those friends she has. I've heard that some of them are into drugs. I'm sure Kyle's sneaking around doing God knows what, so how can I trust her?" As Audra went on, it became clear that the situation with Kyle had become exactly what she feared most.

The youngest of four children, Audra had left home as soon as she could, mostly to escape her mother's caustic comments and constant denigration. "I was never her favorite," Audra said bluntly, "but after my brothers went away, she was really awful to me. By then my parents had divorced, and my mother had gotten really bitter." Audra paused, then added quietly, "Maybe she blamed me, 'cause she sure acted like she hated me."

Audra spoke of how she had always wanted a different relationship with her own daughter. Until she and her husband divorced, just before Kyle's twelfth birthday, Audra felt they were on their way. "But Kyle went downhill after that. I know she's not happy about her father and me. It's not just the divorce. For the past three years my ex-husband and I have been at each other's throats. He's always trying to change our agreement, or else he decides he's not going to give me what he's supposed to. So one way or another we're back in court." Audra realized that Kyle, as the only child still at home, was taking the brunt of the ongoing anger and blame reverberating between her parents, but she was at a loss about how to change this situation.

Because of the divorce, Audra also had been forced to work more hours at her job to pay expenses for her and Kyle. Feeling guilty about not being home for Kyle after school only fueled her determination to fight her ex-husband for more support. Essentially on her own in the afternoons, Kyle floundered. So when Audra returned from work, she felt doubly anxious to find out where Kyle had been, what she was up to, and whether she had done her homework. She felt that she had little time with Kyle to make up for all the hours lost.

"I know she thinks I'm on her back, but what am I supposed to do?" Audra asked. "Am I just supposed to let her do whatever she wants and not care? Half the time she lies about having her homework done, or else she does it halfway. No wonder her grades are horrible." Audra and Kyle were locked into a vicious cycle: The more Audra tried to assert her authority, the more Kyle rebelled. Eventually Audra was coming home from work to an empty house. When Kyle returned, Audra, feeling helpless and enraged, would demand to know where she had been and threaten her with punishment. In response Kyle would either offer monosyllabic answers or retaliate by screaming insults at her mother. Whenever Kyle used profanity or vulgarity, Audra became further enraged, "and then I hear myself say things I know I'll regret. I say some horrid things. Once or twice I even pushed her. I swore I'd be nothing like my mother, and here I am."

Already overwhelmed by the changes brought on by her divorce, as well as battling continuously with her ex, Audra had few emotional resources to deal with a hurt, angry, and challenging teenager. Under the best of circumstances, her intention to be a different sort of mother from her own would have been difficult to achieve. Although Audra did not hesitate to confront her daughter, the unproductive manner in which she did so succeeded only in teaching Kyle to tune her out and alienating her further. In part this enabled Audra to avoid getting to the heart of the issues. If she learned what Kyle truly was doing, she would be opening up a Pandora's box, which she felt incapable of coping with in her present, overwhelmed state. As Audra put it, "I've about had it. I can't deal with one more thing right now."

To reassure herself that she was not like her own mother, Audra was ambivalent about how strict and demanding she wanted to be. "I want her to grow up right, but I don't want to ruin her teenage years. Plus, when I discipline her, she's even more miserable, and then we really fight. I just want us to get along." Audra did not recognize how her mixed messages encouraged Kyle to test her mother's limits continuously. Fighting thus became, for Audra and Kyle, the only way they communicated with each other. For this reason, perhaps, as much as conflicts were painful for Audra, she was also comfortable and familiar with them. Fighting was their way of interacting, of being close. She had experienced this dynamic firsthand with her own mother.

LEARNING FROM YOUR OWN MOTHER

Part of reflecting on what you bring to the relationship with your daughter is taking a closer look at where your attitudes, expectations, and style of mothering come from. Your relationship with your own mother is a logical place to start, for she has undoubtedly fashioned many of your present ideas. If you were fortunate, you received nurturance, encouragement, guidance, soothing, teaching, healing, and a host of other crucial ingredients of mothering. You may have learned from your mother how to be courageous, gentle, and kind. You might have emulated her quick wit or ability to find the humor in adversity. Since she undoubtedly was, like all mothers, imperfect, you probably also learned about what you do not want to repeat with your daughter. Perhaps you are determined to avoid being judgmental or overly controlling of your daughter, dismissing her worries, or undermining her initial, precarious steps toward autonomy. Examining your relationship with your own mother up close will help you decide what qualities you want to bequeath to your daughter and which ones you will happily discard.

Clinical experience suggests, however, that relatively few women speak of their mothers without going to extremes. Some, like Bess, describe mothers as wonderful, while others, like Audra, believe their mothers to be terrible. When women assign their mothers to one of these polar extremes, they frequently attempt either to emulate the ideal mother or to avoid being even remotely similar to the evil mother. This tendency to idealize or devalue our mothers is hardly unique. According to feminist psychologist Nancy Chodorow, each is the opposite side of the same coin, a prevailing myth of the all-powerful mother induced by a male-dominated society, inequalities in the marriage, and political issues. In this line of thought, mothers are assumed to be totally responsible for how their children turn out.

Subscribing to this philosophy, many women overgeneralize their mothers' good and bad tendencies, often developing their own parenting styles as a direct result of these attributions. As you will see below, however, adhering blindly to these notions, without taking a careful and realistic look at your relationship with your own mother, is often unproductive, if not destructive.

The Monster Mother

In some cases women's early mothering was truly neglectful and abusive. In such situations women often consciously and understandably attempt to be the exact opposite of their mothers: warm when mothers were rejecting; close when mothers were distant; protective when mothers were cruel. Ginny, a forty-three-year-old woman, grew up with a mother who could not tolerate her individuality. "It wasn't even like we had fights," she said. "I couldn't so much as disagree with her. Just my wearing something she wouldn't have picked out threatened her. Whenever I did something she considered inappropriate or not like her, she'd stop speaking to me. That was her way. I can't tell you how many times I had to go stay with my aunt for a while." Ginny learned early on that being her own person—much less having any sort of conflict with her mother—risked losing her mother's love.

The majority of women looking back on their teenage years, though, remember their mothers' less extreme failures of empathy and resources. Perhaps your mother had no idea how to communicate with you. You thought she had no understanding of what it felt like to be scorned by a first love, pressured into drinking at a party, or ostracized suddenly by a group of friends. Or, alternatively, she had no way of talking to you about these things. She was unable to show you that she understood your fears, insecurities, or rage, so you decided to become a completely different kind of mother.

Maybe this experience made you determined to demonstrate to your daughter that you are completely interested in her, eager to hear the most minute details of her daily life. You avidly await her descriptions of each and every date, any argument in her group, the stories about who's on the outs and who said what about so-and-so. But this may not be *her* idea of a mother-daughter relationship. What if your daughter's personality does not incline her to be self-disclosing or talkative? Worse yet, what if she resents your attempting to learn all about her life by asking questions?

As another example, perhaps you blame your mother for many of your disappointments in growing up. She may have seemed insensitive to the depth of your pain or failed to guide you in ways you would have liked. You may have felt alone and disconnected from her.

Connie was the second oldest of six children in a family with limited means. "My mother stayed home to care for us kids but was always too busy to pay attention to us. We had to do things on our own. If we wanted something, we had to get it ourselves."

Consequently, Connie was determined to do the opposite: to be closely connected to her children, to give them every chance and advantage she possibly could. But driven to compensate for the paucity of opportunities in her own childhood, Connie has, by her own admission, "gone overboard. People tell me I'm a bit obsessed. I'm the mother who's volunteering to be on the board of the basketball association and buttering up the coach so my daughter makes the A team. I know I'm going to have to chill out, as my daughter tells me."

The Cleaver Complex

More rarely, perhaps, it is the other way around. Instead of aiming to be the exact opposites of their mothers, women feel they'll never live up to them—rivals only to June Cleaver, who always had everything under control, took everything in stride, and handled every little trouble. Abby, a forty-year-old mother of two, said, "I don't remember my sisters and me ever giving my mother a hard time. Somehow we just respected her. She had three more children than I do, and I don't seem to do half as well as she did. Every time she visits, she asks how I can let my daughters act up. It makes me feel like a failure." Similarly, a thirty-nine-year-old mother of three lamented: "I feel so inadequate compared with my mother. She had six children in nine years and never lost her temper. I never remember us being angry at one another." Comparing themselves with such "perfect" models, many women feel hard pressed to do anything but devote their lives solely to their children and, even then, having done that, sometimes feel they come up short. Bess is a perfect example.

Such comparisons to "ideal" mothers, regardless of how accurate, further erode women's confidence in their mothering skills. Moreover, what worked for your mother may not work for you. Your daughter is different, and her world is different. Although there are certainly time-less issues faced by mothers and adolescents, mothers today do have new challenges because of unique circumstances inflicted on daughters. The challenge of ensuring safety while allowing daughters appropriate autonomy has never been greater. It is almost impossible to compare mothering now with mothering then.

Even the Perfect Mother "Stinks"

Many women, regardless of their age, still long for the "perfect" mother. Some can name dozens of ways in which they would have liked their mothers to have been different, and they spend a lifetime blaming them for the way they turned out. Persisting in this harangue, however, is not only exhausting; it is unconstructive. The truth is, women who throughout adulthood continue to blame their mothers do a disservice both to their mothers and to themselves.

It is important to recognize that motherhood is a two-way street. It is almost never an issue of *just* a mother and a daughter but rather an evolving relationship between the two. This is as true of you and your daughter as it was of you and your mother. Each child presents her own special needs and wishes. Research on temperaments in infancy has demonstrated that enormous differences in sensitivity, distress, and soothability exist from birth. Moreover, as therapists know, at times there may simply be an unfortunate match between a mother and her child's temperament. For some children, nothing the mother does ever seems to be enough. Perhaps these daughters' demands are impossible for mothers to fulfill.

The particular circumstances in which girls are raised also has an enormous impact upon mothering. The size of the family presents one obvious example. Compared with women raised in smaller families, those from large families often report having developed different sorts of relationships with their mothers, in part because of the sharing of time with siblings. Other considerations affecting your mother's ability to parent include the cultural and religious conventions of your family, financial pressures, the need to care for elderly relatives (e.g., grandparents), or hardships such as serious illness.

Taking the Best, Leaving the Worst

If you are wise, you have made peace with your mother—even if this accord was accomplished solely in your own head. You may have come to appreciate circumstances beyond her control that shaped your upbringing. Unless she was truly abusive, you have recognized that she probably did what she could with the resources she had available. This reflection has enabled you, as your daughter might say, to "cut her some slack." That is precisely what you wish your daughter to do for you someday. In this process you may have discovered attributes your mother had that you can now draw upon. You also can point to your mother's shortcomings. But rather than fixate upon them, an activity that is immobilizing, you are motivated to channel this knowledge into making changes in your own mothering style. Like many mothers, you will use this awareness to emulate your mother's best qualities while trying to avoid making some of the mistakes she made. Without question, you will make different ones; this is the responsibility of every generation.

By reflecting upon your mothering style and its origins, you avoid unconsciously perpetuating old, unsatisfying patterns. You clarify your own thoughts, expectations, and needs and, by extension, those of your daughter. You thereby ensure that your parenting is not simply a reaction to past history—how you were mothered and your own adolescent experiences—but rather a thoughtful, purposeful approach that considers appropriate current issues, such as who your daughter really is and her particular circumstances. For Elizabeth, a bright but reticent, not psychologically minded fifty-two-year-old mother of two daughters, avoidance of such reflection had serious repercussions. As you read her story below, you will appreciate her underlying struggle: to preserve her family's outwardly successful image or to delve into her daughter's more troubled inner life.

ELIZABETH

Wearing a tailored suit that flattered her tall, slim build, with her medium-length blond hair perfectly coiffed, Elizabeth gave the impression of effortlessly looking well put together at all times. She seemed mildly uneasy as she sat down, however, gazing for several minutes at the diplomas on the wall beside her as if to buy time before speaking. Elizabeth had made an appointment because her seventeen-year-old daughter, Kirsten, had asked to speak to a therapist. Elizabeth first wanted to find out more about psychotherapy and how it could help Kirsten.

This family was well known in the small community in which they lived for their active participation in youth sports, their church, and local politics. The parents were thought of as caring, intelligent individuals who were extremely committed to their children. Kirsten's older sister, who was then a sophomore at an Ivy League college, had been a star athlete and scholar while in high school. No one in the family had ever seen a mental health professional. Other than what she'd seen in the movies, Elizabeth didn't know what to expect.

After taking a deep breath, she plunged into her thoughts on what could be prompting Kirsten to see a therapist. Elizabeth described her daughter as a happy, well-adjusted girl who had never caused her parents trouble. Quieter and not as feisty as her sister, Elizabeth found Kirsten easier to enjoy. She described their relationship as quite good. In fact, the only time Elizabeth showed any emotion was when she talked about why Kirsten might want to see a therapist. "I thought she would have felt she could come to me and talk to me about anything," Elizabeth said, her voice tremulous. "I can't even understand what could possibly be bothering her now. She's just started to get a figure. She's beautiful; she's smart; she's a great athlete and has lots of friends."

Asked what was going on their lives, Elizabeth looked perplexed. "Nothing that I can think of," she said. "Everything's fine." This was not a woman being withholding; she was genuinely baffled. She didn't know what else to say. She and her husband were happily married. Their families were healthy. Elizabeth enjoyed her own mother, whom she met for lunch once a week. On the basis of what really mattered, the major things, Elizabeth felt, Kirsten should have been content. She didn't have a boyfriend, but that wasn't a concern to either of them. So why was she asking for therapy?

Answering questions about Kirsten and the rest of the family was uncomfortable for Elizabeth. She was not by nature inclined to dwell on emotional matters or to disclose what she considered private matters. She felt at sea in a process that was ambiguous and, at least initially, lacked clear goals. "But I'll do whatever I have to help Kirsten. We have only one more year left, and I don't want her to go off to college next spring unless she's fine," Elizabeth stated. Then she added, "How many sessions will she need?"

Before that question could be addressed, the issue of Kirsten's leaving home and what that meant to Elizabeth had to be discussed. Surprising information emerged. Elizabeth said, "It was hard for me when my older daughter left for college, but this is different. I don't know if I should let Kirsten go because she may not be ready." When asked about her specific concerns, Elizabeth replied, "Well, for one, I won't be able to keep an eye on her." And after a pause: "The other night . . . I think she might have vomited after dinner." Oh? Had she spoken to Kirsten about her suspicion? "Yes," she said. "She said she did it only once. She felt too full after the big meal we had that night. And she said lots of girls are doing that stuff, that it was like an epidemic."

As if she were anticipating the question, Elizabeth immediately volunteered that she doubted Kirsten actually had any difficulties with eating. In fact, she explained, "I think it's good that she's become more conscious of her body. She used to be a little chubby, but now she's slimmed down and looks better than she's ever looked." As she made this statement, Elizabeth looked away, as if closing off the subject.

Elizabeth herself had never had a weight problem. The women in her family were naturally slim, she said. Elizabeth's mother could still fit into her size six wedding dress, which had also been worn by Elizabeth and her sister. "I never said anything about Kirsten's shape," she said, "because I never wanted her to feel bad or become self-conscious. She seems to take after her father's side of the family. I don't know why this would suddenly become a problem for her."

It was clear from Elizabeth's comments that her daughter's request for therapy had caught her completely off guard. At least on the surface, using the standards she knew, academically and socially, Kirsten was doing well. She considered herself close to Kirsten and noted that they never fought. Elizabeth found it unsettling that something that she didn't know about might be wrong with her daughter. Despite her own discomfort with the process of therapy, however, she bravely agreed to participate as needed to support Kirsten. Elizabeth's last comment, spoken as she walked out the office door, poignantly hinted at her own vulnerability: "If there's anything I'm doing wrong, just let me know."

TAKING STOCK OF YOUR ASSETS

Like Elizabeth, many women agonize that they may unwittingly be causing vast and irreparable damage to their daughters. Consequently, when women reflect on their mothering, there is an unfortunate tendency to think primarily about their shortcomings and limitations. To many mothers, greater self-awareness is often synonymous with self-condemnation. "I'm not great at this" and "I know I've really got a problem with that" are all too common confessions. Less often do mothers remember to reflect on their assets, on the inherent strengths they have to offer their daughters or others with whom they have relationships. Along with identifying what weaknesses you would like to improve, make it a priority to consider your skills: Are you especially tolerant? A good listener? Are you described by others as fair-minded? Are you well organized, creative, resourceful, a good manager? What interests or talents do you bring to relationships?

Equally important are the characteristics of your personality— neither good nor bad, perhaps, just "you." For example, you were born with a particular, inherent temperament. You may be energetic, calm, high-strung, or patient. You may be anxious, easygoing, even-tempered, or irritable. Knowing yourself, and the likely effects of your personality on others, will help give you invaluable insight into the dynamics between you and your daughter.

Thinking of yourself as a whole person, not just as the mother of a teenage girl, is crucial while you're raising your daughter. Rather than see yourself exclusively as someone raising an adolescent, you will keep this role in perspective among other areas of your life. No doubt you have had many other significant roles: daughter, sister, aunt, grand-daughter, niece, student, girlfriend, volunteer, wife, cousin, friend, em-ployee. Each of these relationships taught you essential life experiences and skills. Within each, you developed connections, worked out differ-ences, and sustained varying degrees of closeness.

Take a moment to consider these relationships. Are you a caring friend, an emotionally available partner, a loyal employee? What have you contributed to make relationships work? Have you developed expertise in listening, understanding, and showing empathy? You may have learned when to speak and when to hold your tongue, as well as how to be tactful. In these ways the relationships you have developed over time are a powerful resource for you in raising your daughter. Not only will you continue to focus on the activities and relationships that bring you joy, satisfaction, and confidence during your daughter's teenage years, but you will use these assets to strengthen your connec-tion with her.

In addition, your ties both within and outside the mother-daughter relationship provide your teenager with powerful lessons about women's roles. As you negotiate within the complex web of relationships with your spouse, friends, employers, and parents, you are your daughter's role model. As she is closely watching, she is learning much about her own capacities and expectations for relationships. She is acquiring key ideas about how to think through and handle conflicts. Consider, then, your ability to communicate to your daughter the following vital messages.

"Take Good Care of Yourself"

Unless your daughter sees you actively protecting yourself in relation-ships, your encouragement that she do so will fall on deaf ears. After a string of abusive relationships with boyfriends, Anessa, a twenty-year-old college student, sought therapy to become more assertive. She was looking for actual words to say no to her current boyfriend, a magical phrase or charm that would permit her to wangle out of his demands, sexual and otherwise. At first Anessa had no idea that she was repeating a pattern of relating to men that she had learned in her own home. Asked to describe her homelife, she said, "My mother is a slave to my father. She does whatever he makes her do. Even though she works full-time too, she'll run out at night to get him more soda if that's what he wants." Anessa did not expect young men to treat her as an equal, to value her opinions, or to comply with her wishes. As she told it, "You just have to put up with it; that's just the way it is," her voice a ghost of generations past.

Girls don't want their mothers to be passive, resigned to emotional or physical abuse. Instead, they want their mothers to combat these injustices, to take a stand and fight for themselves. A mother's demon-stration of good self-care is more important than anything she says to help her daughter protect herself in her own relationships.

"Relationships Are Give-and-Take"

Girls need to learn that setting limits is permitted and even encouraged in relationships. It is not necessary for women to allow themselves to be taken advantage of or exploited. Walking the fine line between giving of themselves and giving too much is difficult for many women. There are always women who cheerfully volunteer to take on all the responsi-bilities, committees, and chores others zealously refuse. Every commu-nity needs such treasures. But when women drop everything in their own lives to fill in for those who "couldn't do it," including rescuing daughters from the consequences of forgotten responsibilities, they communicate that relationships require women to sacrifice themselves. When daughters see their mothers constantly trying to please everyone, they learn that this is what women do. Although they may take full advantage of their mothers, they also feel guilty about the imbalance in their relationship. Kerry, twenty-five, called her mother a doormat. "She just can't say no. Just this week she canceled something she had planned to do because I needed to do errands and couldn't take time off from work." When you communicate to your daughter that you will not allow anyone to exploit you, she learns to set similar limits in her own relationships, and you are setting the tone for give-and-take in the mother–daughter relationship.

"Be Yourself"

Does your daughter see you giving up who you are, your natural self, to appease others and maintain relationships? Some women relegate important life decisions about working, hobbies, and friendships to spouses or mothers or friends instead of contending with the choices themselves. Rather than model a mutual relationship in which they seek and consider others' input along with their own, these women feel compelled to relinquish their identities for the sake of relationships. It is important that your daughter see you holding on to your sense of self. She needs to see you demonstrate that women can persist in being themselves in a healthy relationship. Of course, nowhere will this be more apparent than in your relationship with your daughter. She needs to see you remaining firm in your principles, rather than caving in to her every demand in fear of losing her love.

"Conflicts Can Be Addressed"

Remember, your daughter has sensitive radar for hypocrisy. She learns far more about relationships from what you do than from what you say. If she sees you avoiding injustices, she will learn to do the same. When women are loath to address grievances directly with others, however, they may unconsciously get others to do it for them. This phenomenon, for example, is all too common in divorced families. Natalie, twenty-one, spoke of feeling in the middle of her still-warring parents: "My mom said all this stuff about my dad, how he didn't give her any alimony this month, so she couldn't pay her rent or get the new tires she needed. Naturally that made me pretty angry, so when my dad and I got together for dinner, I started yelling at him." When your daughter sees you effectively confront people who mistreat you, she will feel entitled to do the same. You are giving your approval of her right to express anger and take a stand. She will then feel more permission to communicate her feelings and handle conflict within your relationship.

"Relationships Can Endure"

You want your daughter to get the message that disagreements in relationships are not only normal but eminently workable. Relationships don't have to end merely because people get upset. Unfortunately some women have intensely unstable relationships with friends and spouses. Bonnie, twenty-three, said this of her mother: "My sister and I make fun of her, but it's really not funny. We ask each other, 'Who's the friend of the week?' She's always got to be mad at someone." When girls see their mothers ending friendships because of angry feelings, they may come to believe, and fear, that this will be the outcome of the mother-daughter relationship. Girls may become apprehensive about being "dropped" exactly as they perceive their mothers have rejected others.

Conversely, when your daughter sees that you expect to work through difficulties and value sustaining relationships, you are acing her test of constancy. You will not abandon her just because of a conflict. You will always be there for her. Your daughter will thereby be convinced of the stability of your love for her and your commitment to the mother-daughter connection.

Along with this commitment, you now bring to the mother-daughter relationship a better sense of your own contributions. You are clearer about your ideas about mothering, more aware of the myriad feelings elicited by your interactions with your daughter, and more convinced of the powerful positive lessons she will learn through your relationship—all assets as you begin to look at and handle conflict in new ways.

Chapter Three

Being an Adolescent Girl

Before you can begin to resolve conflicts more effectively with your daughter, it is necessary to refine your understanding of what she brings to the relationship. This is no easy task. Far from being straightforward, the teenage girl is a study in startling contradictions and inconsistencies. From one moment to the next she will be stirred by an emotion, wowed by a different perspective, and moved to a complete change of heart. What she adamantly detested yesterday will be today's passionate craze—be it an idea, a style, an activity, or a person. While this is what makes the teenage years so stimulating and exciting, the average girl will admit that at times she herself is completely baffled by what she is thinking and feeling. No wonder you, her mother, are confused as well.

But to strengthen your relationship to your daughter, you must be willing to hone your empathic connection. You must become adept at discerning nuances in her attitudes, moods, and behavior and capable of deciphering her communications, both verbal and nonverbal. When she comes to you with sweeping accusations or announcements of catastrophes, you have to determine first what she is feeling, even when she isn't sure herself. This process is similar to solving a cryptogram; you need to see the most frequently occurring patterns in order to figure out a message based on few clues.

A WHOLE NEW WORLD

To interpret your daughter's motivations and behaviors, you must understand her most common adolescent experiences and appreciate the world she lives in. Of course, you can remember what it was like being a teenager; it wasn't *that* long ago. Or can you? Many mothers question whether they are truly able to comprehend their daughter's experiences. Some wonder if they can possibly relate to their daughters when they have no idea why MTV and body piercing have somehow become captivating. Mothers' own doubts about their understanding are compounded by teenage daughters' repeated refrain "You just don't understand what it's like!" As a result, mothers are always asking, "Are today's problems truly new?"

It's a valid question. The most accurate answer is yes—and no. Many teen issues are age-old, but with a new twist. Today's girls definitely face these challenges at ever-younger ages. A generation ago, for example, girls often were aware of boys potentially pushing them to be more physical than they wanted. Maybe it wasn't called date rape, but the phenomenon did exist. On the other hand, back then girls certainly did not have to worry about somebody "slipping a Roofie" into their sodas or contracting the deadly AIDS virus. Drugs were probably not a mere impulse away: You couldn't sign on to the Net to find out where to buy drugs, how to cultivate marijuana plants, and even how to replicate the chemical formula for methamphetamine (speed) from your own bedroom. Taking these developments into consideration, this chapter will highlight for you what is truly different for your daughter.

The good news is, the dangers of your daughter's adolescent years will probably be balanced by meaningful friendships, first love, discovering skills and talents, finding wonderful mentors, and experiencing successes of which she can be proud. Being a teen still involves studying for tests, dreaming of crushes, finding causes that inspire, and eagerly awaiting the all-important driver's license. The other good news is that for the most part your daughter's concerns are less about pop cultural trends and more about the great universals, the same concerns you yourself and generations before you experienced during adolescence. Be assured you can relate to your daughter without ever once checking out an MTV special or appreciating the merits of a pierced navel. You are not as "clueless" as your daughter insists. Although teen slang may have changed, girls still express the very same worries, fears, and hopes they always have.

UNIVERSAL THEMES

Whether they are speaking to a therapist, writing to a magazine, or seeking help from a camp counselor, girls are desperate for ways to solve age-old problems. They feel ignored ("My mother always pays more attention to my little sister"), mistreated ("My teacher was mean to me in front of the whole class"), and abandoned ("My so-called best friend just dumped me"). They worry that they're not as attractive ("The guy I like doesn't even know I exist"), smart ("I have to work harder than all of my friends"), or cool ("My friends want me to smoke, but I'm scared") as they would like.

Informally surveyed about what most "ticks them off," teen girls had this to say:

"People lying."
  (Erin, seventeen)

"Friends that talk behind your back."
  (Dana, thirteen)

"My parents not trusting me."
  (Lynette, fifteen)

"Not sticking up for myself."
  (Marjorie, fourteen)

"That all everybody cares about is looks."
  (Claire, sixteen)

"People who pick on other people who aren't cool."
  (Danielle, fifteen)

"My friend being mean to me for no reason."
  (Asha, thirteen)

"Guys that only notice your boobs."
  (Nancy, sixteen)

"Having a zit and somebody making fun of it."
  (Ainsley, twelve)

As you can see, feeling teased, judged, singled out, lacking in some way—these are the issues that still trouble teens like your daughter and that no doubt will trouble your daughter's daughter. The typical teen girl is struggling to feel self-confident and to reassure herself of her worthiness, at a time when increased academic and social demands—as well as rapid physical and emotional changes—seem to be fighting her every step of the way. Thirteen-year-old Rachel, as you will see below, exemplifies these common challenges. Although she is what most would describe as a typical, well-adjusted girl from a "good family," she described her life as far more tumultuous than settled, her emotions far more disconcerting than pleasant.

RACHEL

Rachel is a cherubic-looking, freckled girl who, like her mother, Bess (whose pain and self-doubt you read about in the last chapter), has dark, curly hair and bright eyes. Her first comment—"I know, I look just like my mother, ugh!" along with its accompanying grimace—set the record straight at once, communicating her growing desire to be seen as her own person. Rachel's appearance as well seemed to say, "I'm not my mother's little girl anymore." Counterbalancing her petite size, dimpled cheeks, and ponytail, which made her look even younger than her years, Rachel wore the teen uniform of the day: several friendship bracelets around her neck and wrists, dangly earrings, and a pair of beat-up Converse sneakers. As if to underscore her point, she also wore a thick swath of sky blue eye shadow on each lid—a feature that seemed, relative to the rest of her look, incongruous and forced.

Rachel came across as a delightful, animated, and engageable eighth grader, who claimed she had no idea why her mother brought her to therapy since she was not having any problems. Nevertheless, she appeared to enjoy the chance to talk. Most of all, she was anxious to share her opinions of her mother. "I know she's trying to be a good mother," Rachel conceded, "but she's going overboard. I can't do anything without her butting in and wanting to know every little thing about me." Rachel was confused about why her mother was so "overprotective": "It's not like I'm doing anything wrong or anything. But she still thinks I'm a baby. She has to let me grow up." Asked what she would like to do differently, Rachel talked about a desire to be allowed more freedom, "like go places with my friends, into town or the mall. I don't want my mother checking up on me every five minutes."

Although she stated that her mother was her biggest problem,

Rachel admitted that she had "a lot going on" at school. Calling her junior high a "weird" place, she described what she saw taking place among her friends. "Some of my friends are really changing, and not for the better," she added. "I don't know what's getting into them. My mother doesn't know this, of course, because she'd freak, but a few weeks ago, when we were at the mall, two of my friends started to take stuff from a store. I didn't know what to do, so I practically ran out of the store and waited for them outside." Rachel then described how confused she felt about these friends. Were they still her good friends? What would they try next?

The biggest change for her so far was that she was starting to like boys. "It makes the school day more fun when I have a cute guy in my class," she said. "I like this one kid, Scott. He's really hot, and a lot of girls like him, but he's too short for them. I'm perfect, though, since I'm, like, *really* short. It's just that I was talking to him and his friends the other day, and they acted like jerks. They're so immature." Rachel articulated as well that she was unsure how much she was comfortable doing with a boy. One of her close friends from elementary school, who had started "going out" with a boy, had recently made Rachel uncomfortable. "Sheila and Kenny were standing there on the steps going up to school, where everyone could see, French-kissing. It was so gross!"

As for her studies, Rachel was ambivalent. Although she claimed to want to go to a good college, in the next breath she said school seemed "stupid, a waste of time." It wasn't that the work was so hard, she said, but that "some of my friends hardly do any work, and they get better grades than I do. It's so unfair. I get sick of doing so much homework and studying for tests, especially when my grades aren't that great. And I'm not even in the advanced classes." Despite being only halfway through junior high, Rachel was already worried about going to the high school for her sophomore year. "It's scary there. I heard the seniors and juniors push you into the lockers and steal your stuff."

Rachel most enjoyed herself, she said, when playing soccer. She had done well at her tryouts and recently made a travel team that she liked, "except that some girls from another school act like they're so cool, and they're really cliquey." Asked about other activities, she said, "I used to be a Girl Scout because my mother was the troop leader, but I never liked it. Well, maybe when I was little, but I started to hate it, so I quit. My mother was mad about it, though. That's what I mean about her wanting to make all my decisions for me."

Despite her apparent confusion—for example, wanting more freedom to go to the mall and simultaneously feeling uncomfortable doing so—Rachel presented herself as sure of her needs and desires. Similarly, she claimed to know what she wanted from school in spite of expressing confusion about how much school mattered and whose values were whose. Yet asked if she wanted to talk further about what was going on in her life, Rachel immediately said, "No, I don't think there's anything wrong with me."

Although Rachel indeed had "a lot going on" in school, she surely had more going on in herself. Reading between the lines of her story, one caught glimpses of her struggles to deal with the multitude of developmental tasks thrown at her—all at once, it seemed—while maintaining a sense of herself as "okay."

Teens' developmental tasks

Here is a brief description of the adolescent challenges teens like Rachel and your daughter contend with, as well as what they typically have to say about them.

Physical Maturation

The physical metamorphosis that accompanies your daughter's puberty is driven by raging hormones that provoke her emotions, fuel her sexual urges, and intensify impulses of all kinds. The mood swings of adolescence are nothing short of infamous. Girls often feel battered by intense, mercurial feelings that occasionally seem overwhelming. Once they figure out what a particular feeling is, and perhaps understand where it has come from, it's gone, only to be replaced by another troublesome sensation they can't put their finger on. Eva, thirteen, spoke for many girls when she said, "It's so annoying. One minute I'm so happy, like if I got a good grade on a test or something, and the next minute I'm crying or I'll just get totally bummed out for no reason."

Prior to girls' gaining mature self-control, hormonal surges also provoke them to act on their impulses. The resources teenagers could previously count on to help them hold their tempers or tolerate frustration may temporarily abandon them. The daughter who, as a preschooler, would never raise a finger to anyone may, as a preadolescent, find herself smacking her brother on the head before she realizes what she's doing. Similarly, the daughter who got an A+ for her articulate arguments during a social studies debate may be the very one to "lose it" during a controversial discussion at the family dinner table, screaming and cursing at anyone whose views have offended her.

After these incidents, perhaps, girls can recognize the inappropriateness of their behavior and feel terribly embarrassed. They can also come up with all sorts of justifications or explanations: "I was overtired," "I was stressed," or "I just needed to eat." In short, they know what they did wasn't great, but they just couldn't help themselves. Their voices or limbs seem to have minds of their own. When hormones surge and bodies feel out of control, girls sometimes engage in sexual behaviors against their better judgment, a disconcerting predicament for those who had previously decided these actions were wrong.

Perhaps worst of all, girls can feel that their own bodies are suddenly out of control. Breasts may begin to poke out of slinky tank tops or make old, cozy sweaters too tight. Favorite jeans may become snug at the hips or leave gaps above the ankles. Waistlines may taper, thicken, and taper again—all unpredictably. Tamara, thirteen, put it this way: "I'm scared to look in the mirror these days. Yesterday I had this giant zit on my nose and my hair was so greasy it stuck to my face." And just when they least need more trouble, early teens often get orthodontic appliances, such as retainers and braces on their teeth, which make them lisp and further inhibit their smiles. Is it any wonder they're self-conscious?

As their bodies change, girls frantically compare themselves with others. First, they check to see how close their bodies are to whatever ideal they have formed in their minds. The questioning goes, "Are my breasts big enough?" or "Are my breasts too big?"; "Am I tall enough?" or "Am I too tall?" Too slim or too fat. Too lanky or too curvy. The checklist is endless. Some girls become so preoccupied with one aspect of their appearance that it becomes obsessive. Cindee, sixteen, said, "I hate my teeth. They're shaped so weird, and they're all yellow. Whenever I meet people, the first thing I look at is their teeth. Everybody's teeth are nicer than mine." Cindee admitted that she fantasizes about getting her teeth capped.

Second, girls reassure themselves of their normality by comparing themselves with their peers. Is your daughter reaching milestones on par with her friends, or conversely, is she earlier or later? When it comes to physical maturation, girls never, ever want to be the first or the last. Today there are girls who get their periods in third or fourth grade, well before the health education filmstrips about menstruation. Exquisitely self-conscious, they hide their budding breasts beneath oversize sweatshirts and minipads in zipped pockets of backpacks. Admitted Pat, ten, "I've made up tons of excuses not to go swimming or to sleepovers because my friends always make fun of me. The boys are even meaner; they snap my bra strap." At the other extreme, older girls still "stuff" bras and lie to their friends about having periods they desperately long for.

If these normal variations aren't uncomfortable enough, heaven forbid girls should have to deal with more distressing problems that set them apart from their peers. Girls who struggle with severe acne, obesity, or medical conditions (e.g., needing to check blood sugar, avoiding specific foods, wearing a back brace) suffer far more self-consciousness. Those who have such disabilities as impairments of vision or hearing or mobility often grow up feeling different, even alienated from their peers. Melinda, seventeen, spoke of what it was like being legally blind in a mainstream school: "I don't think I'm all that different, but I guess other people do. Maybe it's these horrible thick glasses I have to wear that've scared off kids at my school. They treat me like I'm a freak."

Coping with surging hormones, rapidly transforming bodies, and troublesome impulses would be quite enough for the average teenage girl. When you add the identity issues, social challenges, and achievement tasks described below, most girls feel they have more than they can handle. The enormousness of these psychological issues takes its toll. Teenage girls often become emotionally self-absorbed. Their "selfishness" is legendary.

Listen to fifteen-year-old Sofia, a teen described as "perfectly lovely," after being told her mother will be laid up for six weeks with a back operation: "How can she do this to me? Of all the times to go and think of herself! I have to find a dress and shoes for my semiformal. Nobody else can take me shopping." Told she seemed to be thinking only of herself, Sofia was indignant. "Of course I care about my mom," she insisted. "I don't want her to go through all that." It was just that Sofia's desperation to reassure herself, to believe that she would find something that would look good on her body so she could attend the dance, was the overriding crisis to her. Your daughter as well brings to her relationship with you all the worries, irritations, and frustrations that accompany these physical and emotional changes.

Finding Her Identity

One of your daughter's chief developmental tasks is to form a stable sense of who she is and where she fits into the world. As previously discussed, one way she is likely to be accomplishing this important task is by differentiating herself from you. To define herself as a separate individual, she is attempting to figure out her own strengths, weaknesses, hopes, and values. En route to this destination she is stopping off at numerous places to try various roles, behaviors, clothing, and language. Experimentation permits your daughter insight into what constitutes her "self." In the course of her adolescence, therefore, she may ally herself with a whole host of fads, causes, trends, and styles.

Such confusion about who she truly is and who she wants to become is disturbing to a teenage girl. To counteract these unsettling feelings, many girls pledge membership for a time in a group with its own, clearly defined character (e.g., the jocks, the freaks, the nerds). To be known as one of this clique, whatever it is, gives girls a sense of belonging, a sense of who they are. Meaghan, sixteen, who felt like an outsider in her new school, found solace in hanging out with a group of girls with similar sentiments. "We don't fit in anywhere," she explained. "We're not smart enough to be brains or athletic enough to be popular. We don't take drugs either. So I guess we're kind of the weird ones." In a way girls actually lose a sense of their individuality to gain the comforting identity of the group.

This is why girls frequently stereotype their peers. There are exquisitely thin lines, often invisible to mothers, separating who is "awesome" from who is "lame." It may boil down to the width of the legs on a particular pair of pants. Whether jeans are straight, flare, or bell-bottom may convey to your daughter's peer group all that needs to be said about a person. Much to your chagrin, your daughter may not hesitate to label other girls (e.g., "She used to be cool, but now she's a loser" or "What a geek; I'd never be friends with her!"), sentencing them to social oblivion. Insecure about herself, she may be intolerant of differences in others.

One of the best ways girls can reassure themselves of their attractiveness of course is to look identical to their peers. Your daughter's insistence on wearing the same number of earrings, color of fleece vest, or brand of black boots as her friends may be baffling to you unless you understand this motivation. While you're encouraging your daughter both to wear what looks good on her and to find her own style, she is fighting you tooth and nail to wear whatever uniform her crowd is currently sporting—regardless of how unappealing it is or how poorly it suits her. In fact, contrary to whatever sound reasons you offer, she must possess these prized items. Never mind if they sit unused a few weeks later, after the craze has passed.

It makes sense that when girls are so uncertain about themselves, they are highly vulnerable to the family's expectations and perceptions of them. Despite your daughter's protests to the contrary, she is extraordinarily sensitive to perceived criticism and rejection—especially from you. Aimee, fourteen, told of her mother's recently hurting her feelings: "Out of nowhere my mom says that my friend Kelly is a great gymnast. Like I'm not? What was her point, besides making me feel bad that I'm not as good as Kelly?"

Ironically, just as your daughter is criticizing you for any and all faults, what she craves for herself is plenty of reassurance and unlimited support. Even if she is consistently and relentlessly disparaging about your wardrobe, for example, she still wants your approval of the outfit she selected for a special occasion. Janelle, fifteen, asked her mother for an "honest opinion" of how a certain pair of shoes went with a particular dress. When her mother, appreciating the invitation to be of help, pointed out that the heels made the shoes too casual for the dress, Janelle was infuriated. "What does she mean by 'clunky'?" Janelle demanded. "Doesn't she know that's the style? Why is she always acting like I have bad taste? My mother just wants me to wear those dumb Mary Janes, like I'm a baby!" Although girls want desperately to be viewed as distinct from their mothers, they often interpret their mothers' different opinions as tantamount to criticism.

Becoming Independent

Your daughter is or will soon be asserting her independence, assuring you in no uncertain terms that she no longer needs to rely on you to do thus and such. Remember when your precious little girl cherished her special private times with you? Well, that child may no longer have a spare moment in her day for you. By early adolescence she may make it painfully clear that she has enough friends to socialize with, thank you very much. More to the point, it's simply too "embarrassing" to be seen with you or other family members. You could well say or do something that will humiliate her in her friends' eyes, and that is far too great a risk.

She doesn't want to confide in you, tell you about her new crush, or sit in the same room with you. The smile she used to beam when you asked her to go to a movie has been replaced with a scowl of disgust. "What?" she asks. "With you?" All she seems to want from you these days are car rides, new jeans, and extra cash for her social outings. She longs for the day when she can move out and live on her own. Any help you try to "inflict" upon her is viewed as an attempt to treat her "like a baby," as criticism, or as an out-and-out invasion of her privacy.

Darlene, fifteen, expressed shock at her mother's actions: "Last week my mother brought home two tickets to a concert I've been dying to go to. I naturally assumed they were for a friend and me. So I got psyched and asked my mom what time she would drop us off to the concert, and she flipped out. She started screaming that the two of us were supposed to go together. I'm sorry, but she must be joking. It's not like I'd go to a concert with my mother!"

Some teen girls go to absurd extremes to reassure themselves of their autonomy. One fourteen-year-old related this story: "I met this new girl in my health class who was so cool. One night she called me and was telling me all about her problems with her mom, who'd been really mean about the phone bill. She's been calling all her old friends back home, and her mother flipped out. I told her my phone bill was out of control too, and I'd gotten into a huge fight with my mother. I don't know why I said that 'cause it wasn't true. The trouble is, my mother overheard me saying this, and she came up to me and asked, 'We got in a fight?' "

To emphasize her independence and leave no doubt about her self-sufficiency, your own daughter may sometimes villainize you. It's not out of spite, but more to push you away and allow her to feel as if she were on her own. When she yells or slams, she may cease to feel childish and dependent, if only for a minute. Ironically, just as she is demonstrating how grown up she is, your daughter most resembles a two-year-old throwing a tantrum.

But don't be fooled when she tells you, "Mind your own business," or, "Leave me alone." The simple truth is that your daughter desperately needs to know you are there for her. In fact, the greater her desire to rely on you, the more she will mask her dependency with declarations to the contrary. Teenage girls are masters of disguise, turning feelings such as love into their polar opposites.

This is yet another way adolescence parallels the toddler years. Remember when your preschooler began toddling away at breakneck speed, giggling with delight, only to turn around to make sure you were still there? If you were no longer visible to her, it is likely her bravado evaporated instantly. She probably dissolved into despair. Teenage girls do the same thing, only it looks a whole lot different.

After hearing the majority of girls complain about not having enough freedom, there is almost nothing as heartbreaking as seeing girls actually wish for their mothers' involvement. Kate, seventeen, who was brought for therapy because of recurrent bouts of depression and self-injurious behavior, described being on her own for weeks at a time while her mother traveled on business. "It's fine with me," she protested. "I bum lunches off my friends, but it's just that I need money for my field hockey equipment. I don't know what to do about that." What she did, not for the hockey equipment but to demand that her mother pay attention to her needs, was the adolescent equivalent of a toddler meltdown: She failed her classes, tattooed her arms with safety pins, and had sex with more than a few boys.

Abby, fifteen, who was able to find a healthier solution, said, "I've been pretty much on my own since my father left. My mom lets me do as I please. I don't give her trouble or anything. She works really hard and has a tough commute. I completely understand. It's just that I'd like her to ask how my day went once in a while. I'd like her to do the normal mom stuff, like check my report cards." Regardless of how girls demonstrate their need, they desperately want their mothers to set limits to prove the depth of their love and concern.

Research bears out this phenomenon. According to a 1997 Roper Youth Report, the majority of today's adolescents cite parents as their number one chosen influence—over friends, teachers, television, and advertising—on issues such as drinking, decision making, and long-term planning. This report indicated that parents are gaining more rather than less influence in areas involving personal values and responsibility. Teen girls are looking to mothers for practical and emotional guidance.

Similarly, one of the key initial findings of the just-released results of the federally funded National Longitudinal Study of Adolescent Health, the largest, most comprehensive study of American teenagers, is that teenagers who feel strong connections with their parents are most likely to avoid risk-taking behavior, such as substance abuse, violence, and early sexual activity. These findings corroborate the multitude of girls who say that they need their mothers to listen to them and that they want to respect their mothers' opinions and beliefs.

So never mind that your teenager tells you she'd just as soon spend time with Cruella De Ville than you. Ignore the eye rolls or stares at her shoelaces when you give her feedback. Regardless of her begging you to keep such input to yourself, understand that she is taking in the information you're offering. Even when they don't agree with their mothers, girls can usually quote word for word what Mom said. If you can try to remember this when your daughter screams, "I don't care what you think!" or "You don't know what you're talking about!" you'll be two steps ahead of the game.

Achieving in School

Another major task of your daughter's adolescence is establishing herself as a student. Her ability to achieve academically is a critical source of self-esteem. For this reason, the complexity and demands of the school environment should not be overlooked. As your daughter makes the transitions to junior high or middle school and then again to high school, she faces a number of significant stresses.

Each time she enters a new school, your daughter is confronted with an unfamiliar building in which it is more difficult for her to navigate. One of girls' biggest fears is getting lost in the new building. Each new school has stricter rules, as well as graver consequences for misbehaving. Irene, twelve, said the worst thing about starting middle school was "finding out that if I forgot my homework, I had to come in early the next morning for detention. That never happened before." There are generally more students in each successive school, many of whom are unknown to your daughter because they came from different lower schools. Each time your daughter is a member of the youngest grade in her new school, she likely fears the prospect of being ridiculed or worse by older students.

For many reasons, girls who fared well in elementary school may begin to struggle in the upper grades, and those who do often feel ashamed. Assignments are longer and more complex, and they require greater organizational skills. As their teachers mark them more severely, girls may fail quizzes or tests for the very first time. They are also introduced to final exams, which hold increasing importance as they progress through high school. The stress and pressure of increasing competition in the upper grades are a frequent complaint of teenage girls.

Next, consider her teachers. Seven hours a day, five days a week (more or less a full-time workweek), your daughter faces some eight or nine different teachers—not to mention numerous school administrators—who observe her, instruct her, test her, correct her, grade her, and occasionally even punish her. These teachers don't have nearly as much time as the lower-grade teachers to get to know her. Whatever reputation she previously established is lost, and she has to start anew. Plus, it is harder for her to get to know her teachers. Every forty-two minutes or so during the school day your daughter enters a whole new world in which various teachers impose their own personalities, teaching styles, policies, expectations, levels of tolerance, idiosyncrasies, and bad days, all of which, like it or not, your daughter is forced to adjust to by the sound of each bell.

She no doubt likes and admires some teachers, dislikes and distrusts others. She probably has her preferences: a quiet, soft-spoken teacher or a dynamic, entertaining one; a serious, scholarly type or a stand-up comic. Chances are, there will be something hugely "annoying" about many of her teachers. Maybe it's the way one teacher taps his pencil on the desk, the way another smirks after distributing a quiz, or the way still another's hair flips up at the end. The teacher might be too demanding, too disorganized, too boring, too obscure. In truth, these failures might be overlooked were it not for the term paper responsible for canceling weekend plans.

More serious conflicts with teachers can also emerge. Girls may be furious when teachers give them "unfair" grades, outraged by being marked tardy when they were "definitely on time," and demoralized by being placed in an "inferior" group in the class. On occasion they are humiliated by a teacher's ill-timed or frankly inappropriate comment, punished because of something the class did or didn't do, or singled out in some way that makes them feel uncomfortable. When you add to this whole scenario hormones, ultrasensitive egos, and shaky impulse control, it's amazing and gratifying when a teenage girl can respect, learn from, and develop the occasional special relationship with her instructor.

Not getting along with a teacher often has serious academic consequences; specifically, girls are likely to perform worse in class. Asked why they're not doing well in math or English, for example, many girls will say, "Oh, I hate my teacher," as if that explained perfectly their underachievement. Despite her criticism or outright condemnation of teachers, however, and even if she blames them for her failures, your daughter knows these formidable adults hold power; their opinions will affect her chances to take certain classes, be accepted to college, seek further training, and get jobs.

So keep in mind these very real pressures your daughter may be facing each and every school day, even when you ask what happened and she tells you, "Nothing."

Establishing Peer Relationships

Not only is social success part of adolescent development, but it is probably central to your daughter's happiness. Friends are often everything to a teenage girl. By middle school she is looking to her peer group for the acceptance that will confirm her worthiness. She is probably preoccupied with making as many new friendships as possible. Increasingly your daughter will prefer to spend time with these friends, whose company she will probably value far more than your own. As difficult as this is for mothers, it is the norm.

Still, despite their importance, your daughter's friendships are probably far from smooth. She may well experience other girls as enigmatic, elusive, or unreliable. Some, no two ways about it, will be downright cruel. On any given day your daughter may be slighted, teased, or ostracized by girls she has considered her closest friends. She will find out someone has started a vicious rumor about her or backstabbed her. At some point some of these friends may even "gang up" and exclude her. A recent study by Nicki Crick, Ph.D., of the University of Minnesota, and Maureen Bigbee, of Ramsey Elementary School in Anoka, Minnesota, confirms that this phenomenon begins early. More than 10 percent of preadolescent girls (as opposed to less than 4 percent of boys) were victims of relational aggression, defined as rumormongering, manipulation, or emotional threats, such as withdrawal. These girls suffered lingering harm, including simmering anger that made them prone to outbursts, lack of social confidence, and poor future relationships.

Alliances among older teen girls are notoriously unstable. Friendships are constantly shifting as girls seek out others with whom they share like thoughts and interests. The best friend your daughter had yesterday, or since she was six, may suddenly get "annoyed" about something and reject her. Just keeping track of all that's going on takes enormous energy too. Debbie, fourteen, said, "I thought it would be better once we got to high school, but it's worse. I don't know who my real friends are anymore. I was supposed to go to the movies with my group last weekend, but these two girls blew the rest of us off at the last minute. I heard they went to a big party. Maybe we weren't invited, or maybe they thought we wouldn't want to go. I don't know."

Although insecurity about friends causes her considerable heartache, your daughter will be the first to defend them from any and all perceived suspicion or hostility on your part. If you dare question something a friend said or did, your daughter may react strongly, vehemently defending her or him. In fact, she may go to any length to justify or explain her friend's behavior, even if it makes little sense. Henny, fifteen, said, "I don't know why my mother and stepfather are all bent out of shape about Tom. So what if he wanted me to get another ride home from the pizza place? It doesn't mean he's a jerk. He just had to go somewhere else."

So tremendous is her desire to feel strongly connected to her peers that your daughter may appear to be estranged from her family. You may well feel that she is choosing her friends over family—and she is. Still, not only is this normal, but it is also in your daughter's best interest. She has neither disconnected from you nor ceased to love you. She just needs to convince herself that she is socially acceptable to her peers and capable of functioning apart from you.

When teens have troubling or unsatisfying homelives, however, the need for friends is intensified. These girls, it seems, cling desperately to whatever friends they can for the sense of belonging they crave. As a result, girls who lack comfortable relationships with parents are especially vulnerable to the negative influences of peers groups. For example, Kyle, the fifteen-year-old girl described below, was desperate to be with her friends at all times. In fact, she seemed frantic to do whatever was necessary to ensure that they continued to accept and include her.

KYLE

As her mother, Audra, described her in the previous chapter, Kyle was an angry, outspoken teen, who was only too eager to tell her side of the story about their relationship. However, her mother did not convey the internal confusion reflected in Kyle's appearance: conservative corduroy jeans and classic sweater juxtaposed with hiking boots, partially shaved head, and nose ring. Fueled by her fury, Kyle spoke quickly, almost breathlessly, as she described her mother. "She's my problem," Kyle stated emphatically. "Everything would be just fine in my life if it weren't for my mother. She's so screwed up. I mean, really, really crazy."

Kyle was most concerned with what she perceived as her mother's inaccurate portrayal of her. "I know she must've said I'm bad, that I'm hanging out with losers and stuff, but it's not true. My friends are really nice, cool people—unlike my mother. They help me a lot. They don't criticize me and tear me down, like she does. They don't scream and curse at me either." Asked when she thought the problems between her and her mother had started, Kyle blamed her parents' separation. "Before that, my mother was okay," she said. "But now she's all stressed out. And she keeps saying all these lies about my father. She's trying to make me hate him. She's so selfish. All she thinks about is her problems, but I have my own problems to think about."

School was apparently another source of frustration for Kyle, and another point of contention between her and her mother. Diagnosed with mild learning disabilities in younger grades, Kyle had received extra help for many years. But in tenth grade she decided she preferred to get along on her own. "I know my mom thinks my grades are horrible now, but they're not really," she said. "I just went down in one or two subjects. I always have trouble in math. And my history teacher said he gave me a D because I didn't make up a test, but I did. So I don't know why my mother is going ballistic."

Asked about her friends, Kyle admitted that a few were using drugs, but "I don't think that makes them bad people. My mother is prejudiced against my friends, but she's a hypocrite. She and her friends from work go out drinking on Friday nights, and I know she takes prescription pills. Those are drugs too." Kyle reluctantly added that she had tried drinking beer and smoking marijuana a few times. "I'm not the drug addict my mother accuses me of being." Fear of inciting her mother further, she said, made her avoid telling the details about going out with friends. "If she wouldn't get crazy on me, I would tell her the truth about where I'm going or what I'm doing. But why should I tell her I'm with a guy if she's just going to think I'm a slut?"

Coming full circle, Kyle expressed hurt and disappointment that her mother did not trust her. "I wish she could see that I'm not like my older brother, who really had big problems. I help my mom around the house, and I have two baby-sitting jobs after school. I love kids, and the families I work for like me," she said, her voice suddenly sounding terribly young and plaintive. Although clearly infuriated at her mother and only too eager to blame her for all her own troubles, Kyle made apparent her wish for her mother's support and approval. Despite her rage and outward protests, she wanted to get along with her mother as much as Audra wanted to get along with her.

With her parents focused so much on their own troubles, Kyle was lacking an anchor to keep her fast in the storm of adolescence. She appeared to go along with the current, without either a clear destination or a sense of direction. Though highly likable and not without her strengths, she was a worrisome teenager. In many ways she seemed unprepared to protect herself from some of the very real dangers girls face today.

THE SOCIETY GIRLS LIVE IN

In addition to the age-old aspects of adolescence, this culture is placing an extra set or two of worries on your daughter's plate. According to Kids Count, a project of the Annie E. Casey Foundation that tracks the status of children in the United States, in the five years from 1985 to 1992 there was a 6 percent increase in the violent death rate for teens fifteen to nineteen, a 44 percent rise in births to unmarried teens, and a 58 percent rise in juvenile violent crime arrests. It should come as no surprise that girls find themselves confused and overwhelmed with all the difficult situations thrust at them.

Said Jamie, fourteen: "It's hard enough getting used to high school, but I'm even more scared when I hear about kids carrying knives and stuff." Suellen, also fourteen, said, "My teacher keeps telling me I'm going to be a 'hot babe' by the time I go to college. He's even stared at my chest. It makes me really uncomfortable, but I don't know what to do." Vanessa, fifteen, said, "A couple of my friends have gotten pregnant. One had an abortion, but the other's keeping it. They're both really messed up, though."

Although some girls confess to being afraid of their schools, neighborhoods, or certain individuals, the majority appear unfazed. In fact, they subscribe to an unshakable adolescent conviction of their own immortality. Their thinking is that it's other girls who will get pregnant, raped, harmed by drugs, or killed by drunk drivers. These terrible things simply can't happen to them. Teens' careless, brazen, or risk-taking behaviors often reflect denial of their own vulnerability and even mortality. Because they don't acknowledge the dangers, they fail to take precautions. Some girls even flaunt an "I can take care of myself" attitude.

Not only are some teenage girls blasé about modern dangers, but they contend that something must be wrong with their mothers for being so fearful. More to the point, their mothers' rules and limits are designed simply to keep girls from having their freedom. The truth in these sentiments is that you probably are afraid for your daughter, even if she isn't afraid for herself. Consequently, your daughter may be correct that you give her a narrower berth than you were given. For example, Margo, fifteen, complained, "I know my mother was dating when she was my age. She used to meet guys on dates all the time. But if I suggested I was going to meet some guy, she'd go nuts!" Similarly, Elena, fourteen, said, "My mom used to ride the train into the city by herself way before she could drive. She would meet friends to shop and go to shows and stuff. But am I allowed to do those things? No!"

Your daughter doesn't appreciate that when you were growing up, school administrators didn't have to think about students' bringing loaded weapons to class. Even if you are shocked, she accepts the fact that some of her contemporaries contact strangers to arrange "dates" to lose their virginity. She expects that some of her friends will plan rendezvous with men they "meet" on the Internet. When you were your daughter's age, you couldn't imagine a world where Good Samaritans were warned not to help people unless they were wearing protective gloves. Until she or a friend personally experiences these modern dangers, she takes them for granted and wants to know why her overprotective mother is making such a big deal.

STDs and AIDS

When you were growing up, the big fears were unwanted pregnancy and venereal disease. Today girls are warned in health classes from the earliest grades to beware of more prevalent and deadly dangers. They are told that one bad sexual choice, even a broken condom, can mean a lifetime of infertility or the difference between life and death. But these are, for many teenagers, just words. Girls are the first to admit these warnings often go unheeded. When they are asked if they have protected sex, many say yes. But when asked the all-important follow-up question "All the time?," they look sheepish as they shake their heads. A 1997 survey by Who's Who Among American High School

Students found that only half of honor students who are sexually active use condoms and few of those see HIV and AIDS as a threat. Gina, eighteen, described the norm: "My friends don't usually bother with condoms."

Meredith, seventeen, learned of the potential consequences the hard way. "Last year I decided to go on the pill. My boyfriend brought me to the clinic and stuff, which was cool, but then they called me in and told me one of those tests came back bad. I have this disease now. I can't believe it." It is in retrospect that many young women become concerned about their reproductive health. Helena, a nineteen-year-old college sophomore, found out last year that a long-term boyfriend had given her genital warts. "I feel completely disgusting now. It's ruined my social life. Now that I'm finally in college, how can I date anyone? The thought of having to tell some hot guy that I have this disease is beyond humiliating." Although the average teenage girl has learned the facts, she just doesn't believe they apply to her.

Date Rape

Now that date rape has its name, it is more commonly and openly discussed today. Teen girls see articles in their favorite magazines and watch television programs that inform them of the truly frightening statistics about how many girls have been victims of date rape by the time they get to college. But when they think of the boys in their crowd or of a specific boyfriend if they have one, they cannot imagine their friends capable of such behavior. A seventeen-year-old who recently sought therapy after having been assaulted by a male drinking companion said, "How could I think anything like that could happen? I mean, his parents and little brother were home."

So when mothers express concern about date rape, girls are almost always distressed and even indignant about it. Kendall, sixteen, told how she felt when her mother attempted to speak to her after seeing an upsetting talk show on this very topic. "I thought, 'Oh, no, here comes another lecture.' Why does my mother have to panic anyway? I already know this stuff. I was, like, 'Yeah, yeah, see you later.' "

Like Kendall, girls are bored by hearing information about sexual topics they think they already know and are embarrassed to be discussing with their mothers. Many also feel patronized by their mother's concerns. As Eliza, seventeen, put it, "When my mom warns me not to be alone with a guy, it's like she's suspicious of him or something.

Doesn't she trust me to pick my friends? Does she think I'm so stupid I can't make good choices?" Girls are indeed placed in somewhat of a bind. On the one had, they are encouraged to feel comfortable with boys, to enjoy healthy friendships and wonderful relationships, and on the other hand, they are cautioned to beware what can happen behind the closed doors at high school parties and in dorm rooms. As pointed out above, teens' automatic defense of friends quickly overshadows any glimmer of apprehension they may have had.

Sexual Harassment

While sexual harassment is hardly new, it is certainly more apparent today than ever before. Harassment stories splatter headlines in newspapers and nightly news programs across the country. It is almost impossible for teens to avoid hearing about the latest political or military sexual harassment scandal. This may be the one problem girls will admit is not some "outside" issue that doesn't relate to them. Many are struggling with harassment in the hallways of their own schools; they report feeling humiliated when boys make provocative comments about their bodies or engage in name-calling of a sexual nature. Surprisingly, however, it is no small minority of girls who report they have been grabbed and pinched by boys as they walked through hallways.

Fran, thirteen, said, "Guys act like they're joking around and squeeze our boobs or grab our butts in the hall, but it's not funny. I get really mad, but what am I supposed to do?" Amanda, fourteen, said she was too shocked to react in these situations. "Besides," she added, "what good will it do? Even if I wasn't too scared to say something, are they really going to stop? My best friend told this guy to keep his hands to himself, and he called her a priss and told her to lighten up. Like we're supposed to think it's a joke." Although girls may share these stories with friends, few are comfortable confiding in adults. They don't want to "make a big deal" about such incidents, which they find embarrassing and unnerving. They would rather ignore sexual harassment than risk someone's not believing them or dismissing their concerns.

Alcohol and Drugs

Every year in school your daughter is taught anew about the dangers of drugs and alcohol. There may not be a teenager alive who hasn't been advised, "Just say no." Yet illegal drugs have never been more readily available or more easily obtained. According to a study by *Time* magazine in 1996, 68 percent of teens can buy marijuana within a day, 62 percent have friends who use marijuana, and 58 percent have been solicited to buy marijuana. The 1997 *Who's Who Among American High School Students* poll previously mentioned found that half of honor students drink, and 10 percent have driven cars while drunk. Your daughter is probably not surprised by finding drugs floating around elementary and middle schools and would refute the notion that experimentation is just for "city" or "troubled" kids. She is accustomed to seeing peers and possibly friends arrive for school "high" or "buzzed." She not only accepts that her peers drink and use drugs but knows which ones have used precisely which drugs.

This does not mean, however, that your daughter wants to discuss this information with you. In fact, she'd rather avoid it. You may be worried sick about this topic, but it is likely your daughter is not. "Ever since October my mom and I have been fighting nonstop," reported Margie, sixteen. "She read in the newspaper that this guy from my class got arrested for possession of marijuana. So now every time I'm invited to a party she freaks out that there's gonna be drugs. This is ridiculous. I know how to handle myself. I know what I'm doing."

Illicit drugs continue to be one avenue through which girls can experiment with new and different sensations, defy adults, and comply with their peer group. Many profess a desire to try smoking, drinking, or drugs "just once, to see what everyone is talking about." More often they use illegal substances at parties to alleviate anxiety and other uncomfortable feelings caused by social uneasiness. "I feel so much better after I have a beer," explained Priscilla, fourteen. "I can talk to anybody and not feel so stupid. It's so much easier." Seeing their friends drink and use drugs enables girls to reassure others and especially themselves that supposed dangers are exaggerated.

It should be said that there are scores of teenage girls who feel confident enough to take a firm and open stand against using substances. They state emphatically that they have no interest in smoking or drinking and feel not the slightest temptation to do so. Depending on their social skills, these girls have varying degrees of success in being part of a peer group. While some find contentment with a few soul mates who share their beliefs, others find ways to be accepted by the majority. Maya, fifteen, said, "I don't mind going to parties where my friends are drinking. They don't give me a hard time because I just hold a beer and pretend to take sips."

Unfortunately even girls who appear to have withstood the temptations of drinking, taking drugs, or having unprotected sex are not immune to difficulties. In fact, mothers who use the absence of these behaviors as proof of their daughters' well-being may be overlooking a crucial consideration: Rather than deal with their distress in these more visible ways, some girls work hard to keep their pain hidden. Instead of getting into conflicts with others, especially mothers, these girls take out their troubles on themselves, often developing self-injurious ways of coping. As you read Kirsten's story below, note how her reluctance to express genuine feelings, as well as her portrayal of the quintessential "good girl," helped conceal her struggles.

KIRSTEN

Tall and somewhat heavyset, her head bent forward as she walked, seventeen-year-old Kirsten did not give the same elegant impression as her mother, Elizabeth. Although she wore no makeup or jewelry except for a utilitarian watch, Kirsten was neatly dressed and well groomed, suggesting care in her appearance. Despite her request to see a therapist, she seemed ill at ease, looking aimlessly around the room. She sat passively in her chair, as if waiting for guidance or instruction in how to proceed. Her silence seemed as loud as a scream for help.

Slowly, in a whisper, she began to answer general questions about herself. She had a wonderful family, she said. Her parents were the greatest, especially her mom. Since her dad worked a lot and traveled, she was with her mother the most. She missed her sister since she had gone away to school, and unlike many of her friends, Kirsten believed her childhood had been relatively happy and carefree. She hadn't had to deal with divorce, her parents weren't alcoholic, and they were fortunate to be able to afford nice vacations. Kirsten thus outlined her life, as if following a checklist.

Asked about her relationship with her mother, Kirsten replied, "It's fine. We don't fight at all. She's a really good mother." As she spoke, the inflection in her voice suggested there would be a "but." A few moments later she added, "I don't know what to think. Sometimes I don't think I'm like the rest of my family."

Kirsten related that for many years she had not felt close to her mother. There was an easiness between her sister and her mother, she said, that wasn't there between her mother and her. "I can't really be me," she said finally. As she spoke, it became clearer that what both she and Elizabeth had described as closeness was really an absence of arguing. They remained committed to a tacit agreement to avoid unpleasantness at all costs.

One of the things Kirsten felt she could not share with her mother was a recent incident involving her friends that had caused her great pain. "I had been friends with this group all my life practically," she said. "We went to dance classes and youth group together. Plus, our parents are friends. One day I went to my lunch table, though, and there was no seat for me. I stood there waiting for someone to move over, but everybody acted like they didn't see me. My friends just stopped talking to me. I told my mother I had cramps so I wouldn't have to go to school." Kirsten believed her friends were tired of her being "a goody-goody who doesn't drink or have sex. I guess I'm not cool enough for them anymore."

At first she lost a few pounds because she was too upset to eat. Then she liked the way she felt when her stomach was empty and her jeans were looser. She had always felt she was overweight. "Once before, my friend and I made ourselves throw up and I thought it was stupid, but all of a sudden it started making me feel better. When I get home from school, I go in the bathroom, and then I don't feel as tense." After a while Kirsten felt more and more pressure to vomit.

This scared her. She had learned about eating disorders in school and didn't want to have one. Above all, she didn't want to worry her mother. In fact, she said, "my mom caught me the other night and got really upset. The last thing I want to do is see her really tense look. Then she gets quiet and kind of stays in her room for a few days." Clearly Kirsten was working hard to avoid causing her mother any distress. She was a high achiever in school, she participated in the activities her mother felt were important, and she skirted potentially controversial issues. "Why bother bringing up subjects that I know we'll disagree about?" she reasoned. Kirsten was trying to live up to an ideal that was very much her mother's standard for success.

Kirsten was so focused on being *good* that she had little freedom to explore anything that threatened this image. Notably she did not express any negative feelings whatsoever. If she delved into any dissatisfaction lurking beneath the surface, she would not be good— at least, not good enough. Instead, she found a way to release frustration without consciously becoming aware of her troublesome emotions.

In many ways Kirsten personified the "good girl" who astutely picks up on subtle messages about what is expected of her and attempts to live up to them. There were clearly defined standards in her family that went back for generations. In addition, she was a product of her community and the larger society, both of which perpetuated the ideals she aspired to and, at the same time, gave her mixed messages about what was expected of her and other young women today.

SOCIETY'S MESSAGES TO GIRLS

Your daughter too is susceptible to these at best confusing messages about what should be her most important priorities and which values are truly worthwhile. At their worst, society's messages are ultimately destructive, undermining your daughter's ability to speak up about injustices, to stand up for herself, and to protect herself. As you help your daughter make her way through the social challenges described above, keep in mind the following influences.

The Media

At the same time she is told to beware of sexual harassment, the possibility of date rape, and more lethal health risks, your daughter is being bombarded by the media with images conveying the importance of being physically attractive, desirable to boys, and sexually active. Think of the advertising by the fashion and cosmetics industries alone! Whether on television or in magazines, daughters continue to be confronted with ever-thinner models whose body shapes can be imitated by only 5 to 10 percent of teenage girls. Models her own age are portrayed in frankly sexual or suggestive ways. Your daughter is told, sometimes overtly, sometimes subliminally, to equate happiness with physical attractiveness and sexuality.

During the last week of December 1997 the following sample of articles were featured on the covers of national teen magazines: "The Smart Sex Report," "Great Looks—What Every Girl Needs to Know," "How to Be Safe, Not Sorry," "Quiz: Can You Keep Off Unwanted Pounds?," and "How to Snag Any Guy in the Zodiac." Is it any wonder girls are confused? How can they reconcile the seemingly opposing objectives of being sexually appealing and sexually safe?

Rage Goes Mainstream

AT LAST, SOME EMOTIONAL ROLE MODELS ARE SEEN AND HEARD! On the media front, which undoubtedly is among the most significant outside influences on your daughter, there is some good news to share. Film, music, and TV are slowly taking a turn for the better. No longer are all teen girls bubble gum–snapping slaves to fashion or desperate victims of slash-'em-up horror movies. In fact, young female superstars increasingly are expressing such negative feelings as frustration and outrage. These women, perceived as larger than life by adolescents like your daughter, are demonstrating that it is cool to be competent and assertive. They are thereby giving girls permission to express their own strong feelings.

Take Hollywood. Over the last few years movies have introduced to us intelligent and competent female teen characters who are strikingly ticked off. In *The Craft*, which came out in 1996, four teen girls who are social outcasts channel their anger into supernatural forces to seek revenge against schoolmates who ostracized them. *Scream*, released in 1997—and rereleased in 1998 because of popular demand—is about a bright and beautiful high school girl who takes revenge on the popular classmates who murdered her mother. The low-budget horror movie, issued without much promotion, went on to make more than one hundred million dollars. The movies *Matilda* and *Harriet the Spy* are about preadolescent girls with strong convictions and intact emotional ranges.

Television programs and talk shows are inundated with adolescent girls explaining why they feel mistreated and misunderstood. *Party of Five*, at one time rated the number one TV drama among youth, consistently and realistically shows teenage girls expressing frustration and anger. Adolescents particularly admire thirteen-year-old Claudia Salinger, who voices her feelings and isn't afraid to "tell it like it is."

In the last few years a change in pop music has been visible (or audible) as well. The lyrics of angry women rockers, such as Alanis Morissette, Tori Amos, and Fiona Apple, articulate the common fears, hostilities, and injustices that young women encounter. Instead of worrying over the mocking, sarcastic lyrics teen girls are quoting, it's time to be thankful that a forum exists that shows girls how valid it is to express their anger and frustrations. Just as Janis Joplin stirred up young women's feelings in the sixties, so we need to respect the efforts of women today who are promoting the same self-expression (whether the actual music speaks to you or not).

The fact that teen girls have feelings of anger, confusion, and disappointment is hardly news. That the media are reflecting these feelings certainly is. For better or worse, famous celebrities influence the way teens look, talk, and think. Although the media are still filled with images of teenagers whose top concerns are nail polish, hairstyles, mascara, and miniskirts, this is no longer the only type of model your daughter is seeing. The more teen girls see and hear female celebrities expressing feelings—no matter how "unpleasant" and "unladylike"—the more comfortable and confident they will be in doing the same. That is something to applaud.

Adults in Her World

Prevailing notions of how girls ought to behave have not, in many sectors of society, progressed beyond the old saying that girls are "sugar and spice and everything nice." Your daughter is no doubt getting many of the same messages you have about the undesirability of women's expressing strong negative emotions and being assertive. Her interactions with adults outside the home have undoubtedly reinforced expectations that she will "be good," "act ladylike," and not "be a nuisance" to anyone.

From her earliest days on the playground, for example, your daughter has been taught to play nicely and avoid hurting other children's feelings. Too bad if girls prefer to play with just one particular friend; they're taught it is wrong to tell someone, "You can't play." Rather than exclude anyone, girls believe they must invite every girl in class to birthday parties, even if one of them has been rejecting. If your daughter attempted to complain—much less to express her dissatisfaction loudly—it is likely she was hushed or given looks of exasperation.

Similarly, while boys have been encouraged to play rough, beat the other team, and "kill" their opponents, your daughter probably was told, "Girls don't do that," and admonished to "Calm down." Girls who have learned that their duty is to soothe others and avoid making waves will have a hard time voicing their angry feelings, much less standing up for themselves. While boys who do so are considered "strong" and "effective," girls are "aggressive" or "pushy."

Because girls are taught to put themselves in other people's shoes, they are sometimes unclear about the nature—and legitimacy—of their own feelings. For example, when her best friend canceled plans at the last minute and invited someone else in her place, Ivy, fifteen, rationalized, "She must have had her reasons. Maybe she felt bad about not inviting Carla and figured I'd understand." Asked about her own feelings, Ivy replied, "Well, I'm not sure because I don't know why she did it." Like many girls, Ivy concentrated on her friend's feelings and needs to the exclusion of her own.

Your own daughter, used to making relationships her number one priority, may well be putting herself second. More important, taught to keep peace and to soothe others, she may be loath to take a firm stand against injustice or mistreatment. Above all, she may shrink from assertively protecting herself when her actions may threaten the feminine image portrayed as sacrosanct by the media.

Her Peers

If there is one thing your daughter knows, it is that expressing strong feelings is tantamount to social suicide. This is not a message that needs to be spelled out for her; the clues are everywhere: subtle looks, condescending tones, avoidance. Lanie, fifteen, described what many adolescents are thinking: "If I say to my friends that something made me mad—or God forbid if I told them they made me mad—they'd roll their eyes and tell me to chill. So I try not to get ticked off. It's not worth the hassle." Similarly, Imelle, thirteen, got upset when a friend lied to her. "When I told her how I felt, she just ignored me, so then I yelled at her. She told me I was totally nuts and I'd lose all my friends if I kept it up."

The fear of being called a bitch may motivate your daughter to hide her anger at a friend, even to let it fester, rather than to confront the person and risk being shunned by the clique. There is a good chance she would prefer to stifle her rage, endure injustices, and seethe silently than to lose a single friendship. Your daughter knows that telling a friend she is in the wrong might make her feel good for the moment, but it is not worth being excluded from Saturday night's party.

If losing girlfriends isn't bad enough, the fear of alienating the opposite sex is often worse. For many teenage girls, boys' reactions may be even more significant than those of their closest friends. Your daughter, who may long for reassurance of her attractiveness, is probably apprehensive about confronting anyone if it means boys will label her pejoratively. When well-meaning mothers tell daughters that it doesn't matter what boys think of her, they instantly lose credibility. If girls believe that expressing genuine feelings risks losing boys' regard (or being labeled "ugly"), they surely inhibit their reactions.

Jill, seventeen, said, "I really liked this guy in the popular crowd, and we went out for a few months. Then he cheated on me with a girl at this party, and when I told him how mad I was, he kept telling me to 'just deal with it.' He ignored everything I said and told all his friends that I got crazy on him. Now they think I'm the big jerk." If she had it to do over again, Jill added, "I would have just broken up with him and never gotten into why."

Unfortunately what Jill will remember about this event is not that she assertively and directly told her boyfriend what she thought of his behavior. It is the fact that none of the "popular" guys looked at her again, much less asked her out. Social banishment, one of the harshest possibilities imaginable to a teen, hardly inspires a girl to continue expressing her true feelings.

For obvious reasons, going against the crowd is also difficult for teenage girls. Speaking up to individuals is hard enough, but risking the entire group's rejection is too awful to imagine. Hailey, thirteen, went out trick-or-treating with some new friends from middle school. When several began to vandalize mailboxes, Hailey said, "I didn't know what to do. I thought if we got caught and I got in trouble, my mother would never let me out of the house again. So I said I didn't think that was such a great idea. One of my friends looked right at me and said, 'What a loser!' I should've kept my mouth shut and hoped for the best."

Such sentiments make girls loath to acknowledge genuine, negative feelings. Instead, they deny valid anger, explain away or excuse injustices, and fail to learn much-needed skills. Of course, as you probably know, many are perfectly capable of taking out their frustrations on their mothers. However, the occasional inappropriate venting of feelings does not constitute healthy conflict resolution. As you consider the myriad challenges, mixed messages, and truly formidable tasks your daughter faces during her adolescence, only some of which are described above, you may be better able to appreciate the genuine distress underlying her inappropriate or exasperating behavior. This empathy will be a tremendous asset as you work on your relationship.

Chapter Four

Family and Cultural Influences

You and your daughter do not exist in a vacuum. Just as you have reflected upon each of your contributions to the relationship, the determinants of your mothering style, and the challenges of your daughter's world, so you must explore how your family and community influence the mother-daughter connection. Your relationship with your daughter is both part and product of the entire family—its values, traditions, expectations, and idiosyncrasies. Before you can focus specifically on your teenager and you, it is imperative that you explore how these larger issues—neither mother nor daughter, but the shared context in which you both live—shape the bond you develop with each other.

WHAT IS YOUR FAMILY LIKE?

Typically, what first prompts women to think about the nature of the family they are creating is their oldest child's transition from toddlerhood to early childhood. As kindergartners begin to visit classmates, who for the first time are not the children of their parents' closest friends, they gradually become aware of differences among families. They start to make comparisons between these new playmates' families and their own: "My parents yell louder than the Powells," "Wow, we're noisier and messier than the Morrisons," or "I wish my family played games together after dinner like Susan's family." These perceptions and their inherent questions encourage mothers to step back and view their families through their children's eyes, to become more conscious of their families' developing character, and to define for themselves what exactly differentiates them from others.

When daughters reach adolescence, this process often recurs, forcing mothers to reevaluate and revisit these earlier questions. As the issues confronting teenage girls change and become increasingly complex, you will probably find yourself needing to rethink some of your earlier beliefs. When your daughter gets strong messages about what is ideal from advertising, the media, and diverse friends, she is likely to demand periodically that you change to conform to her wishes. According to your daughter, "everybody" but her is allowed to sample a certain style, privilege, or experience. As the mother of a teenager you are also probably confronted more with others' ideas and values that make you question your own.

It is therefore crucial that you take the time to reconsider your family and especially to come to terms once again, if necessary, with the kind of family you are. Except perhaps for extreme abusiveness or permissiveness, there are few rights and wrongs. What is critical is that you are comfortable with the life your family has fashioned together and that you recognize its influence on your relationship with your daughter. You might think about how your daughter's family experiences compare with those of your own childhood. You might reflect on where your current expectations about families came from. Most important, you may want to define what changes, if any, you will want to make for your daughter. The following questions may guide you in the process.

HOW MUCH FAMILY TOGETHERNESS IS THERE?

There are of course wide variations in the degree to which families are close. For some, the fabric of family life is tightly woven, with parents and children spending much or nearly all free time together. For others, family members lead separate lives, sometimes interacting only around schedules or the occasional rushed breakfast. When you think about this issue, what do you wish for and expect in your family?

Thinking back to your family of origin, did you spend your childhood years mostly in the company of parents and siblings or, conversely, spend considerable time away from home? Some women report that as adolescents they sought a haven with the families of their dearest friends, preferring these "homes away from home" to being with their own families. If this was true for you, how might this experience influence your ideas about your own daughter?

To explore the concept of togetherness, it may be useful to reflect on how the dinner meal is handled in both your present family and your family of origin. Each of innumerable possible scenarios offers different opportunities for closeness and communication. At one end of the continuum is the traditional family dinner, which takes place at an established hour. All family members are expected to be present and discuss their days, current events, and other topics of interest. At the other end of the continuum there are those who grow up in homes in which there is no particular routine for dinner; children are expected to pitch in or fend for themselves. Many adolescents fix sandwiches and eat either in their rooms or in front of the television. Each of these families sends different messages to teenage girls.

At this point, before you begin to address the mother–daughter relationship specifically, it is helpful to be clear on your family's expectations about this issue. What degree of closeness makes you most comfortable? How might you be communicating these ideas to your daughter?

HOW MUCH GENUINE INTERACTION TAKES PLACE?

Consider not only how much actual time family members spend with one another but also the degree to which they get to know one another as people. Do your family members discuss their innermost thoughts? Do they demonstrate an interest in one another's lives? Mothers are less frequently conscious of this aspect of family life, which nevertheless has a powerful impact on the mother–daughter relationship. Your childhood experiences, personality, and values will determine your expectations. As you reflect on this issue, you may want to determine the degree of intimacy versus distance you would prefer for your daughter and yourself.

TO WHAT EXTENT ARE EMOTIONS DIRECTLY EXPRESSED?

Enormous variations exist among families in their comfort with feelings. In some homes, emotions are virtually taboo. In others, family members are taught to withhold the expression of negative feelings, such as sadness, disappointment, and especially anger. In fact, there may be no vocabulary available for anxious, upset, irritable, and infuriated feelings. In yet other homes, intense feelings are palpable and perhaps acted out but never openly discussed. It is probably the rare family that is sophisticated about the potential influence of the most subtle and unconscious of feelings.

Have you been raised in a family of "underground" emotions? If so, you may be one of many women who have worked hard during adulthood to achieve greater understanding of and competency with their emotional lives. Reflect on whether your comfort with emotions matches that of your family of origin. Most important, what expectations do you have for the expression of feelings within the mother-daughter relationship?

HOW IS AFFECTION EXPRESSED?

Again, there are enormous differences in the frequency and extent of affection shown between family members. To what extent, and in what form, is affection expressed? Is your family comfortable verbalizing that you care for and love one another? Are you physically demonstrative, such as by kissing, hugging, and touching? Perhaps you show your affection through actions rather than words. As you think about your background and personality, you may consider your comfort level with verbal and physical affection and, as a result, the expectations and desires you have for your daughter.

WHAT STYLE OF PARENTING DO YOU PREFER?

It is certainly true that one's parenting style is greatly influenced by how one has been parented. If you were raised by relatively authoritarian parents and unconsciously adopted this approach, you might expect your daughter to be quiet and obedient. If you adhere to the principle that "Children are to be seen and not heard," you might tacitly discourage, or even overtly forbid, your daughter to speak her mind or enter into debates. In fact, your family may censure or punish girls who speak up or "talk back." In contrast, if you adopt a more democratic parenting style, you might automatically encourage opinions that differ from your own and welcome discussion of controversial topics. In a more laissez-faire family, daughters might not be condemned for dissension, but there may be fewer opportunities to argue and therefore to resolve conflicts.

It is important to be aware of your family's unique biases in this area. What did you learn as a child, and what messages is your daughter getting now, about the right to disagree and to speak one's mind?

HOW IS CONFLICT HANDLED IN YOUR FAMILY?

Nowhere are variations in families more apparent than in their management of conflict. For some families, conflict simply doesn't exist. The mere thought makes people so anxious that they go out of their way to ignore friction, avoid arguments, and dodge potentially troublesome issues. Conversely, in other families life is a series of small skirmishes, endless squabbles, and continuous clashes with family members. It is not that families converse about the rules for handling conflict. Unlike other topics, in fact, such as "appropriate clothing," "good school performance," and "religious instruction," which are often freely and repeatedly discussed at the kitchen table, families rarely talk about how conflict is going to be managed. Despite the fact that these rules are unwritten, however, somehow children always pick up on the crucial cues.

FAMILIES' MESSAGES ABOUT CONFLICT

As you prepare to address and resolve conflict more effectively with your daughter, it behooves you to think about the influences of your family. Can you relate to any of the women below who speak of the destructive messages they learned from their own childhood experiences and were at risk for passing along to their daughters?

"Avoid Conflict at All Costs"

Georgina, a forty-five-year-old mother of two teenage girls, described growing up in a family that demonstrated in numerous ways the importance of avoiding conflict. "My parents never argued or openly disagreed," she said. "There was never any anger. It wasn't that everything was so terrific. It was just that we never talked about any problems; they were subtle and unexplained." Georgina believed that she unwittingly took her cues about conflict from her own mother, who "didn't show her feelings at all, ever. I equated her keeping feelings to herself with being strong, a good thing." One particular childhood incident stood out for Georgina as underscoring the need to keep conflict at bay. "My sister was swearing at my father, he screamed at her to shut up, and that's not something you said in my family. I was scared to death, especially when they started grappling hand to hand. My father hurt his hand. That was the first and last time anything like that ever happened. After that anger just disappeared." As an adult Georgina realized she was "frightened of anyone's expressing strong feelings. I've become afraid of starting something terrible." Her investment in avoiding conflict was so deeply ingrained that Georgina had to work hard to learn to tolerate and manage even minor clashes between her daughters and herself.

"You're Responsible for Preventing Conflict"

Gillian, thirty-six, recalled what it was like being the eldest of four teenagers growing up in a home divided by divorce. "Every afternoon I was expected to take care of my siblings, the kids, as I called them. It was my job to keep them out of my mother's hair. I rushed home from high school to make sure they didn't mess up the house. If there was one crumb on the counter, we all got it, especially my youngest sister, and then I'd feel terrible." So strong was the message to take care of her siblings that Gillian rarely attempted to address her own needs. She remembered once scolding her brother for misbehavior. "My mother was horrified when he started to cry. She was aghast about how I could have upset him. Never mind that he was torturing me." Gillian thus learned that voicing complaints wasn't tolerated. If expressing her feelings made anyone uncomfortable or hurt, it wasn't okay. Because she was given the role of caretaker and peacemaker in her family, responsible for protecting siblings, she became used to stifling her resentment. When her own daughter entered preadolescence, Gillian began to realize that unless she deliberately rethought her approach to relationships, her childhood role would "come back to haunt my daughter and me."

"Don't Expect Conflicts to Get Resolved"

In her late forties, Marie described growing up in a noisy, chaotic family in which adults expressed feelings not only openly but boister-ously. "It was the norm for us to be loud, yell at each other, and even argue heatedly at times. My father was especially cantankerous, screaming at my mother to get him this or that. Holidays were always the worst. My mother slaved away cooking, and as soon as the relatives arrived, my father kept shouting orders. She'd get angry and scream back, but he'd keep doing it. Nothing ever changed, and it went on and on like that for years."

Marie reported having a revelation the first time she spent a holiday with her future in-laws. "I saw so clearly, maybe for the first time, how people could handle things differently. I had gone there for Thanks-giving. They were a large group, pretty noisy like us, with a lot of little cousins running around. But when there was a disagreement about something, it was discussed quietly. I forget what it was exactly that Leo's parents were debating, but whatever it was, they talked about it civilly and reached some kind of conclusion. Then it was done, a far cry from the screaming matches between my parents."

Because Marie experienced that conflicts did not get resolved in her family, she grew up believing it was not worthwhile to address injustices. She unconsciously developed a pattern of ignoring negative feelings and making excuses for those who hurt her. But Marie was determined to teach her daughter something different. She said, "I want us to be honest with each other, to know that we can work out the things that matter to us."

"Conflict Isn't for Girls"

Women who grew up in families that upheld distinctly different standards for males and females recall vividly how their treatment differed from that of their brothers. Amanda, forty-eight, came from a family of six, three girls and three boys. "It still amazes me how sexist my parents were," she said. "My brothers were encouraged to be macho. They wrestled, they fought, they beat up on each other, and it was okay. I even remember one of my brothers punching a hole in his bedroom door, and my father saying something like 'Oh, he's just letting off steam.' But if one of my sisters or I pushed each other, forget it. We'd get this stern look. Once I threw my books on the floor and stomped off to my room. My mother had a fit, lecturing me about proper behavior. Nobody came right out and said this, of course, but we girls weren't allowed to be upset or make trouble. Heaven forbid we raised our voices!" It wasn't until Amanda's fourteen-year-old daughter accused her of being sexist, of allowing her brother but not her "to sass," that she recognized her unconscious acceptance and perpetuation of this gender inequality in her own family. Remembering how angry and resentful she had been as a teen, Amanda decided things needed to be different for her daughter.

"Conflict Is Destructive"

Sometimes conflicts are allowed to get out of control, even to devastating proportions. Karla, forty-four, came from such a family. "You couldn't miss controversy in my family; you practically needed protective gear to survive," she said. "From the outside I think we looked like the typical family. We lived in a nice house, went on great vacations, even went to church sometimes. But then there was the part nobody ever saw: the perpetual fighting, incredible blowups, scary stuff. When I was fourteen, and my parents finally got a divorce, I remember being kind of relieved because I could finally get some sleep. I was so sick of waking up to screaming and the sounds of things being thrown against walls. One time it was my mother. My father always had a wicked temper, but when he drank, you'd worry about huge brawls. The evenings were the worst, waiting to see what would happen." Karla recognized that her deep-seated fear of conflict stemmed from these early experiences. "I could count the seconds between my mother saying something and my father's rage. It was like thunder after lightning." Karla, like many girls who were raised in such families, tended to avoid conflict any way she could, including using substances to dull pain and withdrawing from others.

Other girls end up perpetuating the pattern of intense conflict they learned through early experiences with their families. In the same way that abuse breeds abuse, there is also a tendency to repeat explosive, uncontrolled ways of handling conflict. This includes verbal aggression, which can be emotionally devastating. Glenna, forty, the mother of a preadolescent daughter, is terrified she will repeat the pattern she learned in her own home. "My mother's words were much worse than her slap," Glenna said. "I hated hearing how worthless I was, how I would never amount to anything. Whenever we had an argument, I felt like a complete failure."

The most extreme, frightening expressions of family conflict— domestic violence, spousal battering, physical and sexual abuse—leave their indelible mark on women and in turn shape their responses to their own daughters. The obvious message is: Avoid conflict; it is disastrous. Thus, although anger and hostility are perfectly normal emotions, as common as joy or surprise, mothers often dread these powerful negative feelings. But if you forbid the constructive expression of such emotions in your daughter or yourself, you are limiting the potential for individual growth and for deepening and enriching your relationship with her.

EXAMINING THE CULTURE

Society often reinforces for women these powerful, familial messages to avoid conflict. To this day, in fact, women are frequently discouraged from acknowledging strong, negative feelings. In her book *The Dance of Anger,* Harriet Lerner writes that women are "the nurturers, the soothers, the peacemakers, and the steadiers of rocked boats. It is our job to please, protect, and placate the world."

In the workplace, schools, and neighborhoods, many members of society condemn women and girls who assert themselves, express dissatisfaction with the status quo, and, perhaps most of all, disagree with their male counterparts. Those who dare to express strong feelings or to stick up for their rights are often labeled "bitches," "shrews," "arrogant," and "crazy." Snide remarks about women's femininity and gender follow their efforts to assert themselves and right wrongs. Consider whether you have received the following messages.

"You're Not a Team Player!"

Women who work outside the home frequently report severe repercussions from their efforts to speak out about injusticies. Joan, forty-nine, a middle-level executive with a manufacturing company, sought therapy after getting her first negative personnel review. "I was told that I'm not diplomatic enough. That means I have a big mouth and say it like it is. That apparently makes people decidedly uncomfortable. Too bad! A few months ago, when I finally addressed an issue that had been brewing between my colleague and me, my boss told me to work it out as if I were a child. I felt like he wasn't taking me seriously. If I'd been a man, I think he'd view me as someone who was active and decisive. Instead, I'm told I'm not a team player."

Such anecdotes are not uncommon among healthy, highly successful women in the workplace. Has this been your experience? What lessons about your rights and effectiveness in handling conflict are you passing along to your daughter?

"You're Pushy!"

Life's most mundane experiences often reinforce these same messages. When Yolanda, thirty-three, took her preadolescent daughter to her first of a series of swim lessons, she was told by the clerk that the class had been overfilled. "I was pretty upset," she admitted, "but I thought I handled it well. At first I asked if there had been a mistake since we had never received a call informing us. But the young woman acted huffy, as if I were bothering her. There was my daughter, changed into her suit and all excited to have her first lesson, and I'm told there's nothing they can do. When I asked to speak to the administrator, the lady sighed as if I had asked the unthinkable and rolled her eyes to the other woman behind the desk." Clearly Yolanda picked up this more subtle message that she was being pushy. If she wanted to avoid being viewed as a nuisance or worse, she had to keep quiet, take her daughter, and leave—which, as she later regretted, is exactly what she did. Are you passing along such sentiments to your daughter?

"You're Hysterical!"

Such messages can come from other women and, perhaps most injuriously, even from friends. Tina, thirty-eight, who lives in a small rural community, found out accidentally that three of her friends were having a get-together to which she and her husband were the only couple of the group not invited. "I was pretty hurt, but I decided not to just smolder about it. I'd be an adult and tell the friend whose house everyone was going to how I felt. Instead of being contrite, though, she acted like I was the one who had the problem. She said they had assumed we were busy and even asked why I was 'overreacting' and being 'so emotional.' I was shocked." If you have had these sorts of run-ins with friends, how could these incidents affect your decisions to broach conflict with your daughter?

LOOKING FOR ROLE MODELS

As a result of these experiences within their own families and the larger community, mothers are often hard pressed to imagine a woman's handling conflict directly and successfully. In fact, ask a mother who comes to mind when she thinks about expressing dissatisfaction, much less outrage, and invariably she pictures someone ranting like a lunatic. Carol, forty-one, describes "my aunt Bertie, the premier example of what not to do. She had a huge chip on her shoulder, and nothing ever seemed to be to her liking. Aunt Bertie'd make these scenes in public that would humiliate me, even as a child. I dreaded going anywhere with her, and if we ate out, I used to pray the food would be okay. I can still hear her shrieking at waiters."

> *. . . it may be more important that women learn that they can stay connected in the presence of anger rather than learn to automatically vent their personal frustration on others*

without any attention to the impact of these feelings on others
(what some would call a male model of anger discharge).
—Judith Jordan

Although career women, female sports coaches, school administrators, and politicians are increasingly visible, it is still the rare woman
who can name another female who taught her how to handle conflict
well. Yet when women think of men taking a stand, equally undesirable images often come to mind (e.g., a gruff, intimidating, or authori-
tative man). Without positive role models, female or male, women
have difficulty overcoming the discouraging messages of their families
and society.

As a result, mothers are apt to inhibit the expression of strong
feelings, including aggression, even when it is in their best interest
to do otherwise. Perhaps more worrisome, women are then unable to
provide effective role models for their daughters. Anna, forty-three,
reported the following incident, which speaks to this truth:

On day one of a course in self-defense, a New York City karate
sensei stood in front of a roomful of mothers and daughters and asked
them to rise.

"Okay," he said. "Now pretend you're being attacked. Let's hear
the noise you'd make."

Silence filled the room.

"You're being attacked," he repeated. "Get angry!"

Again you could hear a pin drop. The instructor was far from surprised. Class after class, year after year, he had come to expect women
to be unable to mobilize their outrage, to be essentially paralyzed, even
when faced with protecting themselves from danger.

BETWEEN YOU AND YOUR DAUGHTER

Given the sometimes overwhelming prospect of managing conflict
with others, is it any wonder that mothers and teenage daughters come
to dread the inevitable struggles in their own relationship? You too
may feel uneasy about your ability to manage strong, negative feelings
that arise in your mothering. Fears of ruining your relationship, alienating your daughter, or being labeled disparagingly can immobilize you
when faced with the need to channel legitimate anger and resolve your
differences.

The situation is hardly different for your daughter. Because of powerful messages from the media, their peers, and culture in general, which were previously discussed, teenage girls typically develop neither a conviction of their right to address wrongs nor the expertise to do so effectively. Even if you have intended to raise your daughter to recognize her feelings and be confident enough to express them, you have been competing against these formidable opponents.

As a result, many teens are ill prepared to handle conflict with anyone, including their mothers. While you have your own set of reasons for dreading conflict with your daughter, she is probably apprehensive for different reasons. Instead of—or perhaps in addition to—fears of estrangement, your daughter dreads possible punishment, ridicule, or dismissal of her feelings. When girls imagine expressing strong negative emotions to their mothers, this is what they say most commonly comes to mind:

> "I'll be grounded for two weeks."
> (Andrea, twelve)

> "My mom'll tell me I'm getting all hysterical again."
> (Gail, fifteen)

> "If I say something, she'll just ignore me and I'll feel stupid."
> (Ava, sixteen)

> "If I tell her, she'll take it out on me."
> (Minna, sixteen)

> "She's not going to listen anyway. She has to be in charge."
> (Wendy, seventeen)

But if your daughter is so afraid of conflict, you may be wondering why it is that you two seem to be clashing by the hour. More to the point, why does your daughter readily use you as a scapegoat for her wrath?

Deep down your daughter knows that your love, unlike that of her peers, is unconditional and everlasting. Yes, you will be upset and disappointed when she misbehaves. She knows she will suffer the consequences of throwing tantrums, insulting you, and causing scenes. But she also realizes she can test the boundaries of expressing herself without diminishing the love you feel for her. You will not expel her from the family, cajole others to gang up on her, or, worst of all, abandon her. By taking out her feelings on you, therefore, your daughter has the chance to express herself without becoming a pariah.

Still, the occasional venting of frustration hardly makes your daughter skilled in handling her emotions. Like most adolescents, she probably has a lot to learn. And you are the ideal person to teach her. After reflecting on the messages you got from your mother, your family, and society, you may now be clearer on what you would like to emulate and what you wish to change in mothering your teenager. You have an opportunity to provide your daughter with a positive, effective role model for managing conflict.

As you become increasingly comfortable identifying and managing your own emotions, as well as handling conflict within the mother-daughter relationship, your daughter will learn by example. With your help, she will be better able to identify and express strong, even negative emotions constructively. Without a doubt she will benefit from your reminding her that her feelings are not shameful or destructive but can be channeled constructively. Both you and she will learn to communicate more effectively so that the two of you can resolve whatever conflicts arise in the course of your everyday life. The next part of this book will give you the tools to make this happen.

Part 2

Bridging the Mother-Daughter Gap

Chapter Five

Building on Your Strengths

As several mothers have quipped, daughters really should come with instruction manuals. The baby girl who had simple needs for love, food, sleep, and a dry diaper has evolved into a teenager who may be begging you for a respite from high school, a coed sleepover, permission to drink alcohol at home, or tickets to a controversial rock group. Somehow you have found yourself managing such daily routines as homework, sports, activities, chores, and so forth, as well as making decisions, providing discipline, and untangling dilemmas. Add to this the management of all too common adolescent crises, such as social emergencies and last-minute dire needs, and combine all the above with your daughter's sullen moods, provocative comments, and heated arguments. This of course doesn't begin to include the multitude of other work, household, and child-rearing responsibilities you have. It is obvious why many mothers often feel as if they were constantly putting out brush fires. It is even easier to appreciate how mothers can lose sight of the bigger issues, their ultimate goals and objectives in raising their daughters.

This chapter is meant to help you strengthen and reinforce the supportive foundation of your relationship, which will require some careful consideration. If you were constructing a house, for example, you would draw up detailed plans, changing and revamping them, as necessary, to guide you in this process. Although mothers often muse about what kinds of daughters they want to raise and the sorts of relationships they desire, few think deliberately about the practical course of reaching these goals.

The first step is to assess both your present relationship and how it differs from your ideal one. What is good about your relationship with your daughter? What strengths do you have that you would like to build upon? Conversely, what aspects would you like to change? As you identify answers to these questions, it becomes easier to develop a general approach to interacting with your daughter. Then, when you find yourself in the throes of conflict, if you have blueprints for a healthy relationship firmly in hand, it will be easier to feel grounded in your mothering.

YOUR PRESENT RELATIONSHIP

Undoubtedly every mother–daughter relationship has its own unique character. The quality of each of these relationships can, and usually does, vary at any time. Right now you may be experiencing merely an occasional "sass" or display of "attitude," a certain undesirable tone of voice perhaps, but little disharmony. Next week it may be a whole different story. You may be at your wit's end, uncertain about how to tolerate a single tension-filled hour in the company of your daughter. Or constant screaming, yelling, and nastiness may fill your days. You may be finding it impossible to avoid the turmoil of demoralizing fights that leave you continually exhausted and discouraged. Some of your daughters may be experiencing serious difficulties, such as substance abuse, eating disorders, or emotional problems. The family may be getting outpatient treatment or even have had a family member hospitalized.

Regardless of the seriousness of your family's difficulties or problems in the mother–daughter relationship, the concepts and strategies in this book can be of help. You will be able to make changes in the way you interact with your daughter so that you both communicate, express feelings, and resolve differences more effectively. Of course, you will tailor your efforts according to the nature of your present relationship. If animosity and mistrust prevail, it would be unrealistic to expect an immediate or miraculous turnaround. You will keep your goals modest and take one step at a time. But before you focus on making changes, it is often useful to get perspective by looking back at the history of your relationship.

Fortunately your teenage daughter did not just arrive on your doorstep, accompanied by all her adolescent moods, demands, and challenges. You have raised her for at least a decade or so, during which time you planted the seeds for the kind of girl you wanted to grow. In the past you two have surely gone through ups and downs. Your daughter no doubt did her share of naughty things; you probably made your fair share of mistakes. She may have thrown tantrums; you may have lost your temper. You have each been frustrated, felt enamored with each other, and had your respective terrific and terrible days.

Over the years, and throughout all this, you have come to appreciate the uniqueness of your relationship. This is a special, cherished, utterly irreplaceable connection. You've watched each other's faces light up as you have surprised and delighted each other. You've shared carefree moments, spontaneous pleasures, and jokes that nobody else understood. You've known just what to say or do to make each other feel better. At certain moments these precious memories can be lost amid the worry, heartache, and frustration of even one awful day. Unless you are careful, the strengths in your relationship with your daughter can become buried under the inevitable frustrations, worries, and disappointments. It is crucial that you continue to focus on what is good about your relationship. Keeping the positives in the foreground will enable you to nurture and use them in strengthening your connection with your daughter. As a start, ask yourself the following questions:

⇒ *Do you enjoy spending time with her and, if so, under what conditions? Are you two more comfortable at home or away from home? In the company of friends, siblings, or other adults or, instead, when it is just the two of you?*

⇒ *Do you like the same activities, such as playing games, watching favorite television shows, walking or running, going to the movies, crossword puzzles, or skiing? To what degree are you cultivating these common interests?*

⇒ *Do you share the same viewpoints or passions, such as the plight of migrant workers, the need for world peace, the safety of endangered species, or the importance of Title IX? Do you spend time together discussing or volunteering your efforts in these causes?*

⇒ *Do you and your daughter rely on each other's respective talents and various areas of expertise, such as in creative, analytical, or practical realms? Do you take advantage of such opportunities for mutual benefit?*

⇒ *Do you have ways of demonstrating your love for each other, despite your conflicts, for example, by giving each other a quick hug, writing a sweet note, doing a favor, or offering to make a special treat?*

⇒*Do you enjoy shared rituals such as cocoa at bedtime, shopping for holiday meals, or pilgrimages to the bookstore?*

⇒*Can you discuss books, movies, television shows, plays, or magazine articles together?*

⇒*Are you both committed to the mother-daughter relationship? Do you sense that your daughter prefers the peaceful times, the interludes when you two are on an even keel?*

⇒*How comfortable are the two of you in speaking about your disagreements and handling conflicts with each other?*

Some of these questions may inspire you to recall or even to discover pockets of strength that were created over the years of your relationship with your daughter. Appreciating these assets will help you and your daughter maintain them.

It is also helpful to examine dynamics in your relationship that may be less than desirable. Unless you assess this purposely and directly, you may overlook the possibility of correcting unproductive or even counterproductive ways of relating to your daughter as you work toward greater closeness. Although there are no hard-and-fast rules, a few maternal behaviors seem to be shoo-ins for alienating teenage girls. You might ask yourself the following questions.

MOTHER'S MOS

DO YOU COMPETE WITH YOUR DAUGHTER?

Although it is perfectly common for women to be envious of their daughters' youthful looks, vitality, and opportunities, it is quite another matter to act on these feelings. When mothers do inadvertently act out competitive impulses, daughters (as well as their relationships) frequently suffer. Mona, a forty-nine-year-old mother of teenage twin girls, recalled resentfully her own mother's blatant competition with her as she was growing up: "My friends had finally convinced me to get this two-piece bathing suit. I was bashful and unsure of myself, so they really had to encourage me. The next weekend, when I went to the beach as usual with my whole family and these close friends, there was my mother, wearing the same bathing suit as I was—only two sizes smaller. I am so conscious of never doing that to my daughter." If you hear yourself comparing your appearance with your daughter's, or if you criticize her looks, you might consider if competitive feelings have gotten out of hand.

Similarly, you may have strong feelings about your daughter's growing abilities and talents. Marcy, forty-three, said this about coming to terms with feelings about her sixteen-year-old's creativity: "I'm mostly happy for Tina and feel tremendous pride in her accomplishments, but there is this small part of me which I can't deny that feels envious. Although I'm a reasonably good artist, I see that already Tina's surpassed me. She's going to be able to do things I could never do. I'm learning to accept that more graciously."

In your effort to raise your daughter to be the best she can be, you may well be giving her opportunities you never had. Is this causing any resentment on your part? Do you sometimes feel you are giving her too much? Or are you comfortable with encouraging her to develop to her fullest potential?

ARE YOU TRYING TO BE HER BEST FRIEND?

It is understandable and desirable to want to sustain your connection to your daughter through her adolescence. But it is often a temptation for mothers to go overboard to make this happen. Many mothers attempt to become best friends with their teenagers. They may listen in on phone calls, offer help more appropriate coming from a friend, or, when their daughters' friends visit, act like one of the gang. A flagrant example of this occurred when the mother of a seventh grader walked up to where her daughter was standing with friends, put an arm around each of them, and yelled, "Buddy hug!" The teens were visibly appalled and embarrassed for this mother.

These mothers/friends frequently expect daughters to confide in them about the social intrigues of their junior or senior high school experiences. Worse yet, they may encourage these behaviors by confiding in their daughters about adult issues and then expecting the teens to reciprocate.

There is nothing wrong with staying close during adolescence. The problem is, it can be difficult to be a friend and a parent simultaneously. It is probably impossible to do both well. At times, in fact, acting as a parent makes you annoying, disappointing, even hateful. In your daughter's best interest, you have to say things she clearly does not want to hear. You must prevent her from doing things she desperately wants to do. Acting as a responsible mother hardly makes you a candidate for popularity. But be clear on which role is your priority, because teens can and will challenge this notion, almost on a daily basis.

ARE YOU TRYING TO BE TOO COOL?

Although teen girls are frequently preoccupied with achieving the elusive and transitory state of coolness, mothers quite simply should not be, particularly when they are trying merely to impress daughters. Despite her unsolicited and repeated "helpful" suggestions about how you can improve your looks, your daughter doesn't actually want you to be the coolest mom on the block.

One of the most obvious ways mothers try to join their daughters is by sharing their interest in trendy styles. But when mothers *wear* things more appropriate for their daughters' age groups, teens are understandably and thoroughly humiliated. Claire, age sixteen, described such an experience: "My mother tries to be too young. She looks like a jerk. One time she came to pick me up at school with about ten earrings in one ear. I thought I'd die." This is a reaction you can count on. Better to place your energy in finding other ways to connect with your daughter.

ARE YOU ACTING HOSTILE?

When mothers characteristically react to their daughters' emotional outbursts with anger—especially of the knee-jerk, explosive variety—they are raising the emotional temperature of the situation. Surely the mother-daughter relationship is intense enough. Not only do teens find it hard to listen in such conditions, but they tend to respond in kind. The result is often escalating expressions of aggression. Again, it is not that mothers cannot or should not be angry. They can and they should. But their expression of strong feelings must be controlled, thoughtful, and constructive. You are in fact modeling this for your daughter.

There is another common cause of women's hostility. When mothers are inexperienced with or afraid of conflicts, they are apt to restrain strong, negative feelings. Guilt and self-doubt further undermine their effectiveness in dealing with daughters. Mary Lou, fifty-four, said, "Before I learned how to handle my feelings, I used to hate it when my daughter got my goat. I couldn't stand the position she put me in, and I'd get doubly mad at her for making me feel that way. It sure helped when I got over that." When women avoid conflict, it is not a small possibility that unaddressed hostility will emerge uncontrollably—for example, in explosive rages or more subtle sarcasm, criticism, or punitiveness. Of course, these tactics, however understandable, are ineffective in dealing with teenage girls.

ARE YOU PRIMED FOR BATTLE?

Some mothers roll up their sleeves, don imaginary boxing gloves, and arm themselves for a decade of combat. Unfortunately a self-fulfilling prophecy operates here: Mothers often get what they expect. The characteristics that seem to predispose mothers to this approach are perfectionism and rigidity. When mothers are unable to tolerate and overlook minor issues, or when they demand daughters be flawless, they are guaranteed disappointment in themselves as well as in their teens.

With this mind-set, it is hardly a surprise that conflicts abound. Fourteen-year-old Colleen often boarded the school bus in tears. To help her daughter focus and perform her best in school, Colleen's mother forbade makeup and jewelry and made her pull back her thick, bushy hair tightly in a ponytail. No clips, headbands, or barrettes were permitted. Colleen resented conforming to her mother's precise specifications for her appearance. She felt horribly misunderstood and "babied," as well as angry that she was prohibited from experimenting as her classmates could.

This was a case of winning the battle but losing the war. Colleen couldn't wait to defy her mother in any way she could. She anticipated with glee every minor victory over her parent's control, regardless of whether it also deprived her of some opportunity or accomplishment.

Waging constant warfare not only is counterproductive but takes its toll on everyone.

ARE YOU WITHDRAWING?

Some mothers anticipate that at the onset of adolescence an enormous schism will develop between them and their daughters. Apprehensive, these mothers may withdraw before the trouble even begins. Eager to avoid arguments, mothers tiptoe around their daughters. They act pleasant but keep their interactions casual and superficial. Daughters, often interpreting mothers' emotional disengagement as proof of how "awful" they really are, feel rejected and abandoned. It becomes another kind of self-fulfilling prophecy.

"I used to think we got along great," said Johnna, a forty-seven-year-old mother. "But I realized I was actually being careful not to upset my seventeen-year-old. When she was already upset, I didn't want to make her more upset. When she was in an okay mood, I figured it was foolish to get her upset. At least now that we're being real with each other, we're more connected."

For some women, the desire to avoid conflict means failure to set limits. Mothers may surrender instead to their daughters' every demand, becoming permissive or, in some cases, even neglectful. Girls then redouble their efforts to test limits, often behaving outrageously or perhaps even self-destructively. They are practically begging mothers to take action, compelling them to regain control. The more daughters engage and provoke, the more mothers withdraw. One seventeen-year-old who was brought to therapy because of increasing drug use, school failure, and irresponsible sexual behavior said, "I wondered when my mother would ever, finally, do something." This mother was not uncaring or indifferent. She was simply frightened—of conflict, of anger, of alienating her daughter.

ARE YOU TAKING EVERYTHING PERSONALLY?

As discussed in Chapter 2, relationships with adolescent daughters are often veritable hotbeds of self-doubt for mothers. It is crucial to keep in perspective what is and what is not an issue between the two of you. When mothers are so intent upon thoroughly understanding each inter-action and gesture, their investment in their daughters' behavior may be too intense. Similarly, if mothers' own emotions match their daughters' mood for mood, they will wear themselves out. In such cases the mother may in fact be taking personally what ought to be neutral.

For example, while fourteen-year-old Calley was working on some social and academic problems in therapy, her mother called in a panic for an emergency session. Agitated and angry, the mother described escalating battles and worried that they would never survive the weekend together. Yet one statement was all that was needed to help this mother feel more hopeful: "What Calley is going through right now has very little to do with you." Looking slightly shaken, the mother sat back as the therapist continued: "She's having a bit of a rough time adjusting to the high school. Between the academic pressures, field hockey, concerns about fitting in, and discovering who her true friends are, she's got several issues she needs to work on. She just needs some time." "Oh!" Calley's mother said, with an audible sigh. "You mean, I can just be supportive?"

When you discard the notion that you are the cause of your daughter's difficulties, you may be relieved of the burden of fixing them. You can then become more objective and therefore free to offer your daughter much-needed sympathy, support, and encouragement.

Red Flags for Further Help

Perhaps you are worried about the possibility that your daughter may be "in trouble," emotionally, socially, or academically. You are not sure whether her behavior is "normal" for adolescents and if you should get her professional help. Alternatively, your daughter may have asked you if she could speak to a therapist. You may not know whether her problems are all that serious. Some mothers even feel upset, disappointed, or embarrassed by the thought of getting outside help. In your family or culture there may be a stigma against seeing a mental health professional. All these issues may leave you wondering what it is you should do.

If you have any of these concerns, it seems wise to follow through and address them to find out if they are valid and get peace of mind. Seeing someone who is professionally trained does not mean you have failed as a mother. On the contrary, you should congratulate yourself for your astuteness and responsiveness to your daughter's needs. No matter how devoted and caring you are, you are not trained to evaluate whether your daughter needs additional help. Even if you happen to have expertise in diagnosing adolescent difficulties, you still should seek an objective, outside point of view, just as you would consult with a professional regarding your daughter's medical or dental needs.

If your daughter is manifesting any of the following behaviors or symptoms, obtaining a consultation with qualified mental health and/or medical professionals will help you determine whether treatment is indicated.

- Sudden, dramatic change in personality, behavior, or friendship group

- Depressed or irritable mood nearly every day for two weeks

- A 5 percent gain or loss in body weight in one month

- Insomnia or hypersomnia

- Fatigue or loss of energy

- Feelings of worthlessness or excessive and inappropriate guilt
- Recurrent thoughts of death or morbid preoccupations
- Suicidal ideation, plan, or attempt
- Self-mutilation (e.g., cutting, carving, burning, etc.)
- Preoccupation with food, bingeing, or purging (vomiting) after eating
- Deterioration in school performance
- Making "final" arrangements, giving away prized possessions
- Running away from home
- Engaging in risk-taking behaviors
- Withdrawal from family and friends

Where to Go for Help

Many mothers, especially those who have never seen a mental health professional, can be perplexed about how to go about finding someone competent to help them. The various titles and fields—counselor, therapist, psychotherapist, psychologist, family therapist, psychiatrist—further complicate and confuse the situation. What is usually more important than specific profession, however, is whether the individual is well trained and specializes in assessing and treating adolescents.

As a first step, you might ask for referrals from a knowledgeable physician, trusted school guidance counselor, or friend whose opinions you value. Word-of-mouth referrals are usually best. It is wise to avoid getting a name from the Yellow Pages. Calling national or state associations will help verify that individuals have the appropriate credentials for their profession (specified levels of training and experience are required for licensure or certification). But determining that a therapist is on the roster of a professional organization or insurance plan will tell you nothing about the person's ability to work closely and effectively with your particular daughter and family.

Beyond offering basic competence, you must feel that a potential therapist shares your view of goals, will be available when you have need for consultation, and has the capacity to connect with your daughter. The two must be sufficiently matched to form a trusting relationship that will be the basis of their therapeutic work. To decide which therapist your daughter will "click" with, you may want to meet first with several individuals. Feel free to ask questions about the therapist's training, orientation, and style. Raise any concerns you have about treatment. Then trust your instincts. Even if the person you interview has impeccable credentials, if your gut feeling isn't good, keep looking. Conversely, if you walk away feeling positive about the person and your conversation, chances are your daughter will too. Depending on your daughter's maturity and insightfulness, you may want her to have a say in choosing her therapist. Certainly, if she meets with the one you have chosen once or twice and says she just can't speak to that individual, you'll want to consider a change. But once therapy is under way and your daughter is facing up to difficult issues, she may raise the issue of incompatibility with her therapist as a way of avoiding the discomfort of therapeutic work. Unless there are compelling reasons to the contrary, that's when you will probably need to support her continuing with the therapist.

Many times mothers have questions about how much contact they will have with their daughters' therapists. This is an important issue to raise during the initial consultation. Although different therapists have different styles, it is crucial that your daughter know that what she discusses will remain confidential between them—unless the therapist deems there is danger to herself or to others. You should find out from the outset how the therapist views and facilitates input from parents. But you want to feel assured that if something important arises, there is a mechanism in place through which you can communicate with your daughter's therapist.

If you believe your daughter needs professional help but she resists your suggestion, you have several choices. You can consult with someone who can hear your concerns, judge their seriousness, and give you appropriate advice on how to handle your daughter's resistance to treatment. You can decide instead that you will seek help for yourself to enable you to cope better with the stresses and demands of parenting your daughter. Or you can insist that your daughter meet with one or two qualified individuals to obtain their professional recommendations, just as you would if your daughter needed to see a medical specialist. It may assure you to know that after the fact many girls are grateful to their parents for giving them the opportunity to learn more about themselves and make important changes in their lives.

YOUR DAUGHTER'S CONTRIBUTIONS

At the same time that you examine your part in the relationship, you must focus and build on your daughter's contributions. She does, after all, make up the other half of the mother–daughter connection. You cannot accept all the responsibility for making and sustaining changes. Not only are you concerned about raising your daughter with certain qualities, values, and competencies, but these same issues have an enormous impact on her relationship with you. This means that your ability to build the mother–daughter relationship will, by definition, be influenced by her strengths and limitations at every stage of her development.

Of course, you do not expect to sculpt her life perfectly. No mother, however fervent her wishes or outstanding her skills, has complete control over how her daughter evolves. There are numerous other influences, such as her genetic endowment (temperament, intelligence, talents), birth order, and life events. There are also the substantial effects of family dynamics, which you examined above, and other relationships in your daughter's life. You probably also need to remind yourself that the worrisome behavior or habit your daughter displays today will be gone next week. Nevertheless, assessing and coming to terms with your daughter's salient characteristics are crucial at this stage of examining your relationship.

For one, the qualities you endeavor to instill in her will shape your responses. Whether you would like her to comply with the status quo or to be an independent thinker will determine, for example, whether you will stress her need to obey over her right to challenge. Whether you want your daughter to believe that pleasing others takes precedence over pleasing herself will have an impact on your reactions to her setting priorities. Whether you like your daughter to be feisty or submissive, outspoken or reserved, a follower or an initiator will govern which of her behaviors you punish, tolerate, condone, or encourage.

Despite your best intentions, you must acknowledge that the mother-daughter relationship will probably never reach your ideal, especially during the teen years. At least some of your hopes may go unrealized. If your daughter tends to be a highly private person, for example, she will probably not volunteer to tell you her innermost fantasies or the intimate details of her social life. If you encourage self-disclosure, you may be frustrated by her difficulty accessing her emotions. Depending on your preferences, you may perceive your daughter as either too clingy or too aloof.

How can you handle these potential sources of friction? Being aware is half the battle. The other half is acceptance. At some point you realize that all you can do is help clarify and enrich your daughter's strengths, while helping her improve or compensate for her weaknesses. Through this process you will make the most of your relationship.

BLUEPRINT FOR A STRONG FOUNDATION

As you know, determining what you desire from the mother-daughter relationship is a highly personal process. No two mothers will identify identical sets of assets, values, and goals. Yet there are some general guidelines to be shared, which may help you build upon your strengths, bolstering the foundation of the mother-daughter relationship. These principles seem necessary (though not sufficient) to make possible a close, trusting, and enduring connection to your daughter:

Listen and Learn

Perhaps the single most powerful skill in your repertoire of mothering strategies is to listen to your daughter. This is still the most effective way to learn about her thoughts, feelings, and experiences. For this reason, it is wise to make every effort to become an expert listener. Please note, however, that you are advised to *listen* rather than to *ask*. There is an enormous difference. Most adolescent girls loathe answering questions. In fact, they are instantly annoyed by such "probing" or intrusive questions as "How was your day?" and "What happened with your friend?" You may have noticed your daughter's secret determination to reply to your questions with the least number of syllables possible: "uh huh," "yup," "mmm," "nah," or "fine." She may also have honed the fine art of merely shaking her head imperceptibly or, better still, mumbling unintelligibly. All these responses result in your learning almost or absolutely nil.

Of course, you must ask the essential questions. But do everything in your power to stifle unnecessary queries, which will stop the flow of information like a tourniquet. Also, when you do decide to ask questions, you may want to use these ten strategies to help you learn as much as possible about your daughter:

- Avoid asking yes or no questions, which halt conversation.

- Ask for ideas and opinions rather than facts.

- Listen attentively by looking at your daughter (but not staring).

- Allow her to finish speaking without interruption.

- Feel free just to listen rather than to offer your immediate opinion.

- Pay attention whenever she is speaking, not just when she is upset.

- Don't act as if you already knew what your daughter was going to say.

- Be respectful rather than condescending of her ideas.

- When she clams up, tell her you'll be happy to talk to her another time.

- Remember the difference between asking and interrogating.

You may be one of the lucky few whose daughters are delighted to fill them in on the things that pique their curiosity or elicit their concern. If so, count your blessings, but it is still wise to become an astute listener. When your daughter is speaking to you, her siblings, her father, or her friends, listen carefully. Is she saying different things to different people, or is there consistency? What is she not saying? Can you read between the lines?

You can also keep informed about your daughter and her experiences by staying in tune with what is going on in your community. One of the best sources of information is usually other mothers. Casually chatting during a softball or soccer game, on line at the cleaners, or at the board meeting of an organization can provide invaluable discoveries. For example, when Bess found out that some of Rachel's classmates had been caught shoplifting, she was able to guess why her daughter had suddenly stopped pressuring her to go to the mall. Although Bess chose not to share this information directly with her daughter, she did raise the general issue of shoplifting as well as what options Rachel might have if she found herself in such a situation with friends.

Similarly, staying aware of current happenings in the school and town is important, especially when you are no longer in your daughter's information loop. You would want to know, for example, why the local high school recently instituted a Breathalyzer test requirement before each student enters a dance. What events led up to this change? What actions or precautions might you want to take to address this issue with your daughter?

Becoming an expert on your daughter—her unique needs, desires, concerns, attitudes, and thought processes—will help you build a solid relationship with her. Knowledge is always a valuable investment.

Keep Your Roles Distinct

Since someone has to be the parent, it might as well be you. This simple concept is often overlooked. Although you may be close to your teenager, you are not her contemporary. When she matures into adulthood, you might well become her best friend. But during adolescence she desperately needs a mother, and you are the person who fills that role. She has plenty of peers with whom she can establish friendships. You as her mother have to do what her friends cannot: Set and uphold firm, clear guidelines; be her ballast as she bobs and struggles through adolescence.

When Kyle was in eighth grade, she had difficulties in science class because of failing grades and clashes with her teacher. Desperate to be close to her daughter, Audra listened to Kyle's complaints, agreed with the "unfairness" of the teacher, and went immediately up to school to protest her daughter's grade on her latest project. Taking on the role of a sympathetic friend prevented Audra from stepping back and encouraging Kyle to take responsibility for her own role in these difficulties and helping her find viable solutions. For example, perhaps Kyle needed her mother to suggest improving her study skills, preparing more thoroughly for class, or better organizing her notes. Above all, she needed her mother's objective, adult perspective.

Just as you should not attempt to be your daughter's contemporary, so you should not expect her to be yours. Your daughter cannot be an adult, and she will not benefit from being treated as your peer. There is an unfortunate trend in this society for children to grow up faster than ever before. They are often given adult responsibilities, privileges, and problems before they can handle them. However intelligent and mature your daughter is for her age, and however enjoyable her company, she should not be your confidante. There are many ways in which this typically happens. Maybe you are dating and want advice. Perhaps you share your frustrations about your daughter's siblings or desperately need to divulge a family secret. Mona, sixteen, described telling her mother how it felt: "Every night my mom used to ask me if I wanted to watch TV with her, which was fine with me because I'm not supposed to on school nights. But then she'd start complaining about my dad and how he's a workaholic and she's lonely. I started feeling really uncomfortable. It took me a few weeks, but I finally told her, and she stopped doing it."

Your daughter should take advantage of her only opportunity to be a teenager. It is therefore important to reinforce the boundary between parents and children, a basic limit your daughter needs for both her own development and a healthy relationship with you.

Acknowledge and Work Through Feelings

First, consider your feelings. Whatever they are, it is important not to ignore or suppress them. By now you realize this includes even unpleasant feelings, such as frustration, confusion, and anger. Not only is repressing feelings unhealthy for you, but it sends the wrong message to your daughter. If you do not seem to have feelings, it makes you appear inhuman, uncaring, or, worse yet, perfect. Research psychologists recently demonstrated that when parents encourage emotional expression and talk about their own feelings, children are better able to cope and to empathize; in other words, they are more socially competent. Conversely, when parents discourage the expression of negative emotions, children have more social problems.

Your teenage daughter is astute enough to know you have feelings, so unless you express them, she has to wonder or guess what they are. You thereby place on her the burden of understanding you. At times you may choose not to act on your feelings or to share them with your daughter unless it is appropriate or useful to do so. But your feelings are indispensable tools. They alert you to the need to do something, to get further information, to make corrections.

Within their relationships with daughters, one of the most difficult emotions for women to express (other than anger perhaps) is regret. The words "I'm sorry" often seem hard to say. Mothers often feel compelled to show their daughters only their surest, most capable sides. But you do not have to be perfect. In fact, trying to appear so is futile; your daughter will see through any guises and cease to respect you for using them. In addition, the ability to apologize can be invaluable to your relationship with your daughter.

Marjorie, mother to fifteen-year-old Adina, related this pivotal incident: "We had had words one day, Adina and I, and each of us had gone off in our respective corners. I couldn't stand not speaking, so I knocked on her door and asked if we could forget our argument. She was still belligerent, though, and condescendingly told me that it would be nice if I could apologize, just that once. Those words kind of hit me over the head; it's exactly how I used to feel. My mother's refusal ever to be wrong drove me crazy. So I told her I was sorry, because I really was, and her whole attitude changed. She calmed down, and the argument really felt over." Whether you feel apologetic, worried, regretful, sad, or upset, it is crucial that you model the expression of these legitimate emotions for your daughter.

Second, your daughter needs your help to acknowledge and work through her own emotions. The act of your empathizing with what she is feeling, essentially appreciating and sharing in her emotions, helps her define her experience. This is useful because teen girls are sometimes unsure of what they are feeling. Your daughter may be far better at acting on her feelings than identifying them. For example, she may avoid certain situations or actions because of unacknowledged anxiety.

Or she could be screaming at the top of her lungs, threatening to move out, clenching her fists, and giving you a look that would freeze Niagara Falls, but ask her why she is so angry, and she claims, "I'm not mad, I just hate you!"

When you can tolerate your daughter's ability to get angry and take a stand, you are teaching her priceless lessons. You are tacitly permitting her to experience this fundamental human endowment. The capacity to have and to express feelings enriches one's life. You are not condoning her method of expressing pain (e.g., kicking table legs, leaving dirty dishes for you, calling you a witch) but are helping her discover the depth of her feelings. You are validating her ability to trust her own perceptions, to be genuine, to set her own standards, and to ask assertively for what she wants—in essence, supporting your daughter in becoming a healthy young woman.

Choose Your Battles Carefully

Unless you want to wear yourself out from unrelenting daily battles with your daughter, be selective in what you choose to fight about. Have a good reason to confront her. This principle is so important that an entire chapter is devoted to helping you develop criteria for making the most difficult, far from clear-cut decisions.

As a basic principle, it is worth describing what can happen when mothers are extreme in one direction or the other—that is, fighting too many or too few battles. It is common sense that if you point out every gum wrapper left untrashed, mention every stolen minute past her bedtime, or remind her of every homework deadline, your daughter will regard you as a nag and dismiss your concerns. Tension and chaos will preside in your home, and you will lose effectiveness for the big battles that are truly worth fighting.

Worse yet, teens often feel intimidated and helpless when they perceive their mothers as unnecessarily harping or overly critical. In response, girls tend to rebel, either overtly or by passively failing to comply. Conflicts thereby increase. This very situation was created between Colleen and her mother, the one who made every hair ribbon and barrette the impetus for a power struggle. Colleen not only had little respect for her mother's judgment but was hell-bent on opposing her mother's every wish.

At the other extreme, when mothers are desperate to avoid the risk of unpleasantness, they often fail to set whatever limits might cause conflict. Jessica, thirteen, was growing up with a mother whose philosophy of encouraging trust and openness discouraged her from setting guidelines. Because of her mother's faith in her, Jessica was free to make her own decisions, to go wherever and with whom she wanted. The trouble was, Jessica was often overwhelmed by the choices she faced. Without rules, she had trouble setting her own limits and developing internal self-control strategies. When she got into trouble, she resented her mother's after-the-fact efforts to correct her.

The ideal seems to be avoiding extremes, deliberately and prudently deciding what constraints are important—and sticking firmly to them. In short, choose your battles carefully. Chapter 7 will help you with the more difficult middle ground, when it is a challenge to decide what issues are truly worth battling over.

Negotiate, Negotiate, Negotiate

Since your daughter is no longer a young child, she probably does not accept without question your parental values and rules. She has a developmentally based need to question why you take certain positions and make specific decisions. This is not the same as questioning your authority. It does not necessarily mean she is being disrespectful. As she develops greater capacity for abstract thinking, your daughter is increasingly capable of making connections between ideas. She is trying to understand the principles underlying your actions.

Reesa, forty-four, described her realization of the different parenting skills needed for adolescents: "It took a whole lot of battles, and talking to other mothers, for me to get what my daughter was saying. She kept accusing me of treating her like her six-year-old sister. I was used to strict parents. What they said went; it was the law. I didn't expect my daughter to argue with me, so it seemed rude, and I resented it. I've come to understand what it means for her to challenge my decisions; it's a different process."

When you listen to your daughter's arguments (not necessarily agreeing with them), you are encouraging her to reason. When you negotiate with her, you are building her problem-solving skills. You are teaching her to use her resources to get what she wants. It is not that you will automatically capitulate to her demands; rather, you are giving her the opportunity to get her needs met if she can convince you that they also meet your standards. There is, like any negotiation, give-and-take. You are showing your daughter you are committed to this process.

That having been said, there are also times mothers should not negotiate. When the difference is clear in your own mind, your daughter will sense that too. For example, when Brianna, fifteen, asked if she could go to a concert on a school night, her mother said no, but she was feeling ambivalent. "I didn't want to set a precedent by letting her go, but I was also thinking of how well she was doing in school, and I wanted to reward that," Helena said. "It was as if Brianna had a sixth sense about that and began an all-out campaign to convince me. She was relentless." Yet Helena described an incident some weeks later that had a different outcome. "Brianna had been recuperating from acute Lyme disease for several days when she asked to sleep at a friend's house. This time when I said no, I was emphatic. Brianna must've known I really meant it because she didn't give me a hard time." When daughters' requests or intentions are inappropriate, outrageous, or dangerous, they need to hear, "Sorry, there will be no discussion about this," or "It's nonnegotiable."

Be Flexible

If nothing else, adolescence is a time of rapid change. Consequently, there are few absolutes. Strategies that worked like a charm yesterday to coax your daughter into doing dreaded chores or open up about her problems may fail miserably today—and may backfire tomorrow. This is one of the aspects of girls' adolescence that challenge mothers most. Just when you're getting in a groove, everything seems to change again.

Keeping an open mind to the possibility of change—in your daughter and in yourself—is the best tactic. Many mothers of teenage girls confess that when they look back, they feel sheepish about how harshly they used to judge other mothers of adolescents. For example, while her own elementary school-age girl was all dressed up for religious services or family occasions, Sarah, fifty-one, would look askance at jeans- and sneaker-clad teens and wonder, "What can their mothers be thinking?" Now, when her own teen daughter is fighting religious attendance tooth and nail, Sarah is humbled: "Who cares what she's wearing? If she shows up, I'll be happy."

"Never say never" is a good philosophy. You will never know

when your daughter will engage in some behavior or present a problem that previously you would never have imagined remotely possible. Similarly, today you might swear you would "never in a million years" grant her request to do something; tomorrow, given the available options, it might seem the wisest, most workable compromise. Being flexible allows you to reevaluate your daughter's wishes continuously in the context of her ever-changing abilities and developing maturity.

There is a fine line, however, between being flexible and caving in. If you genuinely change your mind because you have rethought an issue and made a better decision, that's being flexible. If you rescind a decision because you cannot tolerate your daughter's relentless badgering, threatening, or whining, that's caving in.

Differentiate Your Experience from Hers

When you empathize with your daughter, the focus should be on what *she* is feeling, not on what *you* may be feeling. To keep your experiences distinct, it is important to know your own sensitivities. Be aware of what typically riles you up. That way you can figure out if your daughter's experiences are problematic for her or for you. Take one situation common to the adolescent girl: making plans with friends. The two mothers below found themselves interpreting their daughters' experiences according to their own sensitivities.

Janet, forty-five, described herself as an extremely organized person who needs to make plans far in advance. "It drives me crazy when people can't make up their minds or when they decide things last minute. That caused big problems between my daughter and me in her early teen years. Her best friend would call on Saturday afternoon to ask her to do something Saturday night. I'd get upset, thinking this girl wasn't treating my daughter well, you know, using her to get together last minute if nothing better came up or if something else fell through. My daughter would get furious and tell me I didn't understand, that was just how kids were. It *was* hard for me to understand that my daughter just didn't have the same problem with this as I did."

Olivia, the thirty-eight-year-old mother of twelve-year-old Claudia, offered another example of the importance of keeping distinct her experiences from her daughter's. "My Achilles' heel happens to be feeling let down by people. So it drives me nuts when people make commitments or promises and then don't follow through. About two weeks before a big school dance my daughter told me she got invited to sleep at a friend's home afterward. The night before, she casually mentioned to me that her friend forgot she had invited her and had to cancel. She forgot? How does someone forget? So then my daughter was stuck with no plans." How did Olivia respond? "Well, I wanted to tell my daughter that this liar was not welcome in our home anymore, I was that livid. But I could see Claudia didn't feel mistreated and wasn't the least upset. So I kept quiet and waited to see what she would do."

Olivia's strategy was excellent. If she had expressed her fury to her daughter, she would most likely have shut off Claudia's ability to discover what she herself was feeling. When you have a strong reaction to something your daughter experienced—at school, at home, or with friends—it is always wise to determine whether you are truly empathizing with your daughter or simply responding to your own sensitivity.

Maintain (or Develop) a Sense of Humor

This principle is no doubt self-explanatory. If you have never been one to see the humor in trying situations, it's time to develop this ability—quickly! A sense of humor is one of the most valuable survival skills any mother can have. When all else fails (e.g., the middle school principal calls to report that your daughter has just teetered into school on stiletto heels), find the morsel of humor in the situation and enjoy a good laugh. You will feel better. Moreover, when your daughter is able to laugh along with you—even at herself—you will know you are making true progress.

Contrast these two "I had the worst day" stories, both contributed by Yvonne's daughter. "When my daughter was turning thirteen, she came home once saying she'd had the worst day. So I asked her what happened. She got furious. 'What? You don't believe me?' she snarled. I said to myself, 'Huh? What am I missing?' Then, about a year later, we had a similar discussion with a very different outcome. Greta had come home from school all upset again, shrieking that she'd had the worst day possible. When I asked her what had happened, she said that they had run out of her favorite yogurt at lunch, she had gotten a paper cut, and when she went to throw out her wrapper, her gum had fallen in the garbage! I almost cracked up because it struck me as ludicrous, so I just looked at her while I composed my expression. To my surprise, after a moment or two Greta looked at me and burst out laughing.

Actually we both did. What could have been another long evening of sulking and nastiness turned into a delightful time together."

Make up your mind to find the humor in your daughter's mundane "tragedies," inconsistencies, and ironies—even when she cannot. Laughter can truly be the best medicine for living with a teenage girl.

Empower Your Daughter

For your daughter to *feel* capable and competent, she must *be* capable and competent. Now more than ever, girls need self-esteem based on who they are and what they can do rather than what they look like. Encourage her to learn, to build her skills, and to demonstrate her efficacy. Allow her as much responsibility as you think she is capable of taking on. As she matures and develops, relinquish control over areas in which you are no longer needed. When she doesn't need help, don't offer it.

Treat your daughter as a valuable member of the family. Expect her participation in the family and her contribution to household chores. When a very troubled adolescent is sent to a residential treatment facility, one of the most beneficial components is inclusion of the teen in the therapeutic community. For example, after a year at a therapeutic boarding school, Leah, sixteen, found that "it made me feel needed when kids in my new 'family' relied on me, and when they appreciated what I did, I felt really great." All girls benefit from feeling their contributions are valued.

Encourage your daughter to add her ideas too. Solicit her opinions about current events, her positions on political issues, and her input on decisions affecting the family. (It does not mean that you will allow her to make adult decisions, just that you value her thoughts.) Ask her for her expertise in areas of interest, her help in researching a topic on the Internet, or any other talent she offers. Remember too to make sure she knows you appreciate her efforts.

Another aspect of validating your daughter's worthiness is helping her acknowledge and use the range of her emotional reactions. It is especially important to empower teenage girls when they are distressed about injustices. Instead of being uncomfortable and immobilized, your daughter needs to learn that strong feelings, such as anger, are not only natural human reactions but powerful tools that resolve conflicts, help relationships grow, and facilitate necessary change. As her ability to handle conflicts with you improves, she will be more effective in addressing perceived mistreatment and settling disputes within relationships. But when she is outraged by wrongs she discovers in the larger community, she is particularly likely to need your support to channel her feelings constructively.

Annette, forty-three, told of this sort of experience a few years back when her local government voted down a proposed teen center. "My daughter and her friends wanted a safe place in town to Rollerblade and skateboard. The merchants had opposed the center because of safety issues on sidewalks. These kids were really upset about the vote and didn't know what else to do other than fume. So a few of us parents got together and helped them come up with a plan. Just taking action made them feel better, especially when they were successful in getting support from different kinds of places. I think they'll never forget their role in making the teen center a reality."

Every time you empower your daughter to speak up, to take on responsibility, and to channel her feelings into action, it is an investment in her future—and in yours. She will be not only a capable, confident individual but one whom you will admire and whose company you will enjoy.

Think Positively About Conflict

Remember, conflict is not the enemy. Instead of viewing conflict as the wedge cleaving you from your daughter, you should see it as the glue holding you two together. Alexandra G. Kaplan and Rona Klein, contributors to *Women's Growth in Connection,* state, "Conflict is a necessary part of relationships, essential for the changes that must be made so that the relationship and each person in it can change and grow." You may still be skeptical about just how conflict can benefit you and your daughter. If so, consider these three key functions:

- **CLEARING THE AIR.** In the course of living with anyone—a daughter, spouse, or roommate—there are bound to be disagreements ("You did so leave the milk out!"), misunderstandings ("I thought *you* were going to walk the dog!"), and irritations ("I hate it when you hum while eating cereal"). Between mothers and daughters, these possibilities barely scratch the surface. But in the hopes of keeping peace, or avoiding war, mothers often stifle their feelings and struggle to contain mounting resentment. Similarly, girls attempt the path of least resistance, sometimes resorting to sneaking around, "creative" explanations, even lying to avoid ugly clashes with mothers.

When you and your daughter can say what is on your minds, when you can get off your chests all the accumulated grievances, slights, and hurts, you will actually find more peace of mind. You can comfort each other, apologize, and move on.

• **MAKING CHANGES.** Unless you and your daughter express your dissatisfactions and articulate your desires, how can you two work out your differences? Conflict is a terrific impetus for change. Your daughter, who is in a constant state of flux during adolescence, needs to test whether you can change in response to her needs. She needs to address whether you will allow her to shave her legs, give her privacy when she has friends over, or let her see R-rated movies. Similarly, by voicing your concerns, you may spur your daughter into developing desired attitudes, adopting appropriate goals and behaviors, and maintaining family values.

Conflict provides opportunities for collaboration and compromise that in turn build respect and closeness. Hannah, a fifty-four-year-old mother to eighteen-year-old Ariel, related an anecdote that turned around their relationship: "When Ariel was in her mid-teens, things were awful between us. On one occasion it was something little that set me off, I can't remember what, but suddenly all this stuff was spewing from my mouth: how angry Ariel had made me, how she was pushing me away, and how confused I was. Ariel lost no time in coming back at me with all kinds of accusations: how I didn't give her the benefit of any doubt, how miserable I was making her, on and on. What really struck me, though, was 'You're always judging me!' At first I was defensive. But then I decided I was very quick to react, very quick to give my opinions. Maybe that was why she was avoiding conversations and avoiding me. After that I tried hard not to do that, and I think it made a big difference in how we got along."

• **STAYING CLOSE.** The ability to engage in conflict with your daughter enables you to stay close to her. The experience of expressing strong feelings, listening to each other, and working through disagreements actually deepens your relationship. You have shared something very real, increased your trust, and demonstrated your commitment to each other. In contrast, when mothers and daughters are unable to express how they feel to each other, their relationship will unquestionably be limited. Perhaps conversations will remain guarded and superficial or become scarce. Instead of intense feelings, there are little or no feelings, a sense of disconnection. In this way the absence of conflict results in the absence of growth; relationships stagnate.

• • •

Decide, instead, that every conflict between you and your daughter will be an opportunity to get closer. Every clash, argument, and struggle mean that you are actively engaging with each other. What you have to do is learn the best ways to manage these situations. There is actually nothing magical about conflict resolution. It involves specific skills that can be learned as easily as bike riding, sign language, and grocery shopping. By becoming an expert yourself, you will be able to instill your daughter with emotional competence, an aspect of her education far more vital than music appreciation, computer literacy, or goaltending.

Chapter Six

Recognizing Your Styles

Without benefit of either society's sanctions or positive role models, many women and girls develop ineffective styles for managing negative emotions. Instead of acknowledging your feelings and using them to assert yourself, ask directly for what you'd like, or resolve conflicts, for example, perhaps you routinely seethe or smolder in silence, snipe when your daughter least expects it, withdraw, or make her feel guilty.

Some of these emotional styles are actually worse than unproductive; they are damaging to you, your daughter, and the relationship itself. Why? As seen in the examples below, when feelings remain unacknowledged, when they are inhibited from direct expression, they often fester or crop up unannounced. Some are unintentionally acted out in a variety of destructive ways. Whenever you think (after the fact, of course), "Why did I do that?" or "Where did *that* comment come from?" your psyche is tipping you off to a powerful but thus far unexplored emotion.

When such feelings drive behavior, women and girls feel an understandable lack of self-control, an absence of competence. It is as if their tongues or limbs had lives of their own. In some cases, in fact, women report that observing themselves saying and doing certain undesirable things (sometimes over and over) makes them feel sheepish, foolish, even ashamed.

Despite all this, mothers and daughters often fall back on undesirable emotional styles, for several reasons: They may not recognize what they are doing, they may be unsure of the alternatives, or they may be more comfortable doing what is familiar, successful, or not. "That's just me" and "I've always done that" are frequent explanations.

It's all fine and good to admit to one's faults, but it is hoped you won't leave it at that. The drawbacks of repeating old, unconstructive behaviors make a compelling argument for change. One, you perpetuate the shame and frustration that result when interactions are repeatedly disappointing or upsetting. Each time you see yourself engaging in such behavior, your self-regard is eroded further. Two, you teach your daughter by example to use these unproductive methods of dealing with conflict. Three, you fail to provide your daughter a positive role model for responsible expressions of feelings. Not only will she be ill prepared to handle struggles she is having with you, but she will have similar difficulties in other important relationships in her life. Four, being unable to channel emotions constructively impacts on relationships enormously. You may react in ways that are at odds with your goals for raising your daughter. Unwittingly you can create hurt and resentment that in turn provoke her inappropriate or retaliatory behavior.

For these reasons, taking control of your emotions, and helping your daughter take charge of hers, are key components of working on the mother-daughter relationship. If you are so inclined, you can definitely change your patterns. No, it won't happen overnight; it will take a concerted effort on your part. It also takes courage to look at your own self-defeating patterns (it will be far easier to pinpoint your daughter's). Recognizing your style is the first step in learning a better approach. Do you see either yourself or your daughter in any of the following descriptions?

LASHING OUT OR EXPLODING

Screaming and Yelling

Probably one of the most prevalent complaints by mothers and daughters alike is "too much screaming" in the relationship. It's not that an occasional raised voice is problematic. When used judiciously, a statement at just the right decibel level can effectively emphasize one's point. Moreover, in some families, as discussed in Chapter 4, yelling is simply the accepted mode of communication. Some mothers say, "I'm just a screamer." This style becomes an issue when either mother or daughter cannot tolerate the behavior in the other.

Even more important, when mothers and daughters compete for power by screaming louder and louder, or when discussions deteriorate into explosive, hurtful insults or shouted accusations, the damage lingers. In some families, mothers or daughters yell or scream as a sure-fire strategy to terminate the discussion. It's as if one or the other had said, "I've had enough." When this pattern predominates, for whatever reason and especially when rational discussion is prevented, it is unlikely that conflicts get resolved.

Throwing, Stomping, and Slamming

When your daughter is unable to verbalize her feelings, she may resort to slamming doors, pushing siblings, kicking or throwing objects, and stomping upstairs. While temporarily gratifying, these strategies not only distract from the verbal expression of angry feelings but usually exacerbate tensions between the two of you. Said Christine, twenty-five. "When I was growing up, I was known for losing it when I got mad. Throwing whatever I could get my hands on made me feel better for about a minute, but then I'd feel terrible about being so over the top, especially when my sisters called me crazy." Like Christine, your daughter does express some feelings when she explodes, but at the expense of her self-control and effectiveness. Worse yet, she fails to communicate clearly or accurately either the reason for her distress or her solution to the problem.

Mothers of course lose their tempers occasionally as well. You may confess to flinging silverware, slamming cabinets, or grabbing daughters before you can stop yourself. Everyone has her limit, including you. Berating yourself for these occasional outbursts is unnecessary. As long as these moments do not become the predominant pattern in your relationship, they are unlikely to be earth-shattering or scarring for your daughter. In fact, it doesn't harm teenagers to learn the limits of how far they can push their mothers. However, do not underestimate how scary it is for girls to see mothers throwing and slamming. Your daughter is looking for you to provide the self-control she finds precariously lacking in herself. For the record, hitting is one of few absolutes: It is always destructive, both to adolescents and to the mother-daughter relationship.

INDIRECT EXPRESSIONS

Avoiding direct communication with those who cause your distress can occur through your expressing your feelings indirectly or by taking them out on someone else entirely. The four types described below may ring a bell. Mothers and daughters often resort to these tempting methods, regardless of their ineffectiveness, because they are preferable to uncomfortably confronting those who actually upset them.

Passive-Aggressive Behavior

Although superficially acquiescent, girls unconsciously may resist your demands and frustrate your authority, all while maintaining their good intentions. In this way they are able to express hostility without taking any responsibility for it. Janie, twenty-one, admitted that there may have been a connection between her habit of "forgetting" to tell her mother important phone messages and being ticked off at her. "At the time I was indignant that my mother would accuse me of it," she confessed, "but it makes sense to me now. The thought of yelling at my mother was foreign to me. What else was I to do?" Other common passive-aggressive behaviors include forgetting to call you when she's late, procrastinating on chores, subtly attacking you to others, and sabotaging your best-laid plans. In addition, this concept may shed light on your daughter's previously inexplicable "accidents," such as ruining your clothes in the laundry, misplacing jewelry she borrowed from you . . . you get the picture.

The same holds true for mothers. If you find yourself "forgetting" to do errands for your daughter, being late to pick her up from activities, or falling short of your promises, she is probably picking up on some of your unstated feelings. It would then be confusing for her to reconcile what you say with what you do. When you disappoint her by doing any of the above, she is likely to react by accusing you angrily of being rude, irresponsible, childish—or any other adjective she has heard you use to describe her. Above all, your daughter is learning from you that confronting others directly is too scary, if not impossible, to contemplate.

The Guilt Trip

When your daughter does everything in her power to point out how utterly derelict you are in your mothering—everything, that is, but tell you straight out that you upset her—she is trying to make you feel guilty. You will catch her sniffle, sigh, sulk, and toss infinite "poor me" looks your way. The reason this strategy is used so commonly by teenage girls is that on occasion it works. Said Deena, fifteen: "Whenever my mom's really fed up or worn out, all I have to do is pout and she'll usually come around." But although your daughter, like Deena, is probably glad she gets to do what she wants, it is unlikely she feels good about her tactic. "Feel sorry for me" is the plea of a weak position. She has not stood up for herself and dealt with the situation directly, and she knows it.

Mothers have also been known to make their daughters feel guilty as a means of expressing their own hurt, frustration, and anger. Have you ever reluctantly agreed to do a favor for your daughter, such as to take her somewhere, and then complained of a headache, yawned loudly, or sighed continuously when she wasn't appreciative enough? If this is something you characteristically do, understand that your daughter will see your cries for sympathy as annoying and martyrlike. Worse, you are modeling a way for her to get attention through manipulating others. As a result, she may learn that women cannot or should not set limits. This is not your goal. In fact, there is one thing you surely want your adolescent daughter to know: When it is in her best interest to do so, she has your permission—no, your blessing—to say no.

The Silent Treatment

If, instead of sulking and pouting, your daughter sits in a room with you and pointedly avoids both eye contact and conversation, she is engaging in the silent treatment. Other signs are her answering only when specifically questioned or using as few syllables as humanly possible. "If I'm mad at Mom," said twelve-year-old Maya, "I'll answer everything she says with 'yup' and 'nope.' It drives her crazy, which makes me at least feel a little better." Yes, you understand your daughter's message when she uses this tactic, but her approach is passive and indirect. If she uses this technique outside your relationship, she will put herself at the whim of others. Basically, she will have to keep herself secluded until she gets some measure of what she wants, and that may very well never happen. This emotional style typically breeds feelings of ineffectiveness.

Mothers who use the silent treatment to express hostility are deliberately avoiding focusing attention on their daughters. This is different from consciously not speaking to your daughter when you are too upset to control yourself. Under this condition, it is appropriate to say, "Give me time to cool down." But if she sees you avoiding eye contact and mumbling monosyllabic answers to her, she is forced to guess your true feelings and to wonder what is preventing you from expressing them directly.

Sniping and Sarcasm

For some girls, being sarcastic and sniping at mothers are too thoroughly enjoyable to resist. You've gotten a taste of this when you have forbidden her from going somewhere and she has responded with dripping sarcasm, "Oh, no big deal. I'd much rather hang out with you thrilling people than go to a boring beach party with my best friends." Or out of "nowhere," when you least expect it, she launches a well-timed barb in your direction: "Oh, please, tell me you're not going out in *that!*"

These strategies accomplish two things: You get the message that she's upset, and she gets the satisfaction of hurting you. But making you guess the real reason for her hostility is passive and ineffective; if you never find out, you two may never get a chance to resolve the problem. More likely she will succeed only in making you angry and eliminating any inclination you might have had to grant her wish.

Sarcasm works the same for mothers. When you overhear your daughter yelling at her sibling for using her CD without permission—which reminds you of the missing sweater she "borrowed"—might you say, "Oh, and you're so good at asking before taking?" Similarly, if you've purposely kept quiet about your daughter's less than stellar science grade and she remarks that she's bored, do you say, "Well, you must have lots of extra time since you're not studying science"? What your daughter hears is your hostility, rather than the underlying message: "I'm concerned about your not studying enough for your exams." Instead of bringing up a valid issue in a way that encourages her to hear it, you are more apt to provoke retaliation, alienate her, or teach her that sarcasm is a legitimate means of making her point.

Making Jokes

In the guise of being funny, some girls make biting, even cruel remarks. Your daughter may, for example, casually mention how lazy, ugly, or mean you are and then say she was "just kidding" when you get upset. In such jokes there is usually a grain of seriousness, a core of underlying aggression you are responding to when you flinch. Unaware of her own hostility, however, your daughter only becomes more indignant when you feel hurt. Your "misinterpretation" of her humor is incomprehensible to her—not to mention "annoying." As Debbie, fourteen, put it, "My mom has no sense of humor sometimes. Like, the other day she was ticked off, and I told her that she looked like Elmo on *Sesame Street,* with her eyes all bugging out, and she just walked out of the room. She should lighten up. I was only kidding around!"

Perhaps once in a while you tease your daughter to vent frustrations. Maybe you "joke" that you too might be able to get twelve hours of beauty sleep per night if you had someone to clean up after you. Or you remark that with your daughter's current level of klutziness, you're anticipating a whole new set of dishware by summer. It is important to realize that with their shaky self-confidence, teasing especially confuses and upsets teenage girls—so much so that they will stay awake at nights pondering whether there was truth in the remarks. Even if your daughter is the reigning family jokester, realize that she will not appreciate a single chuckle at her expense.

MISPLACED EMOTIONS

Many times, when girls are upset, especially with themselves, they prefer to pin the blame on someone else. Of course, their favorite targets are their mothers. Your daughter could have totaled the car, failed an exam, gotten drunk, broken up with her boyfriend, or acted nasty to her friends, but whatever she did, you're liable. If you weren't so snoopy or rude or unfair, the incident never would have happened. In this way your daughter is able to deny responsibility for her behavior; it is easier, more pleasant, and far less threatening for her to blame you.

Another variation on this theme is your daughter's taking out her frustration or anger at you on herself. After you deny her the "coolest" new jeans at the mall or scold her about an infringement of rules, she sulks in her room and refuses to take phone calls. (Of course, she is really punishing herself; she desperately wants to make plans to go out with her friends.) Or upset by something you said or did, she decides not to study for an exam. Some girls take this tendency to a worrisome extreme by hurting themselves physically when upset: banging their heads against a wall, smoking, dieting, carving, burning, or cutting their bodies. In these behaviors is a wish to make their mothers suffer.

Sometimes your daughter may enlist someone else to express her feelings for her. When she says to her sister, "Don't you think Mom really skimped on our birthday presents this year?" she is attempting to get her sister upset. If she manages to succeed, perhaps her sister will express feelings for both of them. Unfortunately your daughter is practicing the finer points of manipulation rather than the skills of direct communication.

Mothers sometimes misplace feelings on their daughters as well. Can you detect a pattern of getting into arguments with your daughter whenever you have a fight with your husband, are exploited by a boss, or feel slighted by a friend? While it is true that teen girls frequently say and do irksome things, thereby offering plenty of rationalizations for your hostility, they detect your "unfair" attempts to blame them for your personal frustrations. Understandably they feel mistreated—and act accordingly. Over time your daughter will become resistant to considering your viewpoint, even when you are justifiably upset, because she will have lost trust in your responses to her.

Suppressed emotions

Under this heading comes an assortment of strategies, all of which avoid direct expression of feelings. When your daughter is upset about having to do something she abhors (e.g., visiting her grandparents, attending a religious service, watching her brother play sports), she might, for example, develop a twenty-four-minute virus or an acute migraine. These developments will potentially excuse her from her obligations without a confrontation. If you ask her directly whether her symptoms were caused by her not wanting to go, she insists that she just doesn't feel good and is wounded by your suspicion ("Nothing's wrong; why should I be upset?"). Conflict has been successfully avoided.

Unfortunately it will not always be obvious when your daughter is keeping her feelings inside. For example, it is impossible to know when she is fantasizing about "getting even" with someone who angered her or when she is quietly berating herself. When teenagers find powerful feelings intolerable, a few may express pent-up tension or rage through eating disorders, substance abuse, and self-mutilating or inappropriate sexual behavior, all of which, as discussed in the previous chapter, should prompt you to seek help.

Mothers suppress unpleasant emotions as well. Sometimes you may escape them by fantasizing about taking "early retirement" from motherhood, running away to a deserted beach, or trading in your daughter for a younger, sweeter model. Perhaps you have thought about switching daughters with another mother, since each of you finds the other's teenager far easier and more pleasant to get along with than your own.

While daydreams don't resolve conflict, they do allay tension and are not in themselves harmful. It is worrisome, however, when mothers strenuously suppress negative emotions in hopes of appearing perfect, in control, and problem-free. Are you thinking this could be you? Ask yourself if your definition of a superwoman requires you to be perpetually cheerful, eager to do for others, and tolerant of whatever comes your way. Even if you seem to have the perfect life—you love your job, have good friends, and are pleased with your appearance—you will succeed only in teaching your daughter that she too should aim to be perfect. Not only do girls learn to set impossibly high standards for themselves, but they learn that expressing negative feelings is a sign of personal weakness.

Quite possibly you have read through these ineffective communication styles thinking at least once, "That's me!" Perhaps this recognition made you feel embarrassed or guilty. This was hardly the purpose. These are nearly universal behaviors, which probably every mother and daughter can relate to at some point or another. The important thing is to be aware of what you are doing so that you can appreciate the effect of your actions on the mother–daughter relationship and then adopt more beneficial communication tools.

Chapter Seven

Choosing Your Battles

Lately it may seem your life with an adolescent daughter has become one big dodgeball game. Only the incoming rubber ball your daughter keeps hurling your way is an endless series of potential conflicts. Yesterday she came downstairs in a miniskirt that wouldn't cover a Barbie doll's derriere; today she refuses to attend the "idiotic" annual family get-together; next week she'll undoubtedly sneak in a long phone chat with her best friend while supposedly studying for her big final, postpone her chores yet again, or inform you that your new dress was really designed for someone younger and more petite.

Any one of these events, which can be wearing, frustrating, and more than a little wounding, can result in yet another blowup between the two of you. Depending on what the rest of your day has been like, and where your tolerance level is, you can feel yourself catapulted straight into that old familiar scenario: fists clenched as you bellow, "How dare you!," "Your behavior is not okay!," or the ever-popular "Do not come out of your room until I tell you to!" If you swallow your anger, instead, you very well may seethe until the proverbial smoke comes out of your ears.

These scenes can sometimes escalate into dramatic sulking and week-long silent treatments. If you and your daughter continue down this pathway, you believe your relationship will surely disintegrate, your sanity along with it.

LETTING THINGS SLIDE

So what are you supposed to do? Unresolved conflict not only is unconstructive but tends to churn inside you, making difficult situations unbearable. Still, must you address every minor irritation and relatively insignificant disappointment? If you don't, will the tension between you two build until it reaches irreversible or catastrophic proportions? Thank heavens, it is neither necessary nor advisable to touch on every little issue between you and your daughter.

There are many occasions when it will be in your best interest not to confront your daughter. Many mothers find this a tremendous relief, although in part it is because the word "confront" has become loaded with dangerous imagery for mothers: screaming matches, thrown objects, and out-of-control outbursts, to name just a few. It is important to clarify that confrontation simply means facing up to an issue, dealing with it head-on, rather than ignoring it or handling it indirectly. As you will see in the chapters ahead, confrontations can and should be well planned, thought through carefully, and executed confidently. In fact, by the end of this book you will have a chance to see—and, it is hoped, to experience firsthand—the many benefits you and your daughter will gain from confronting each other.

Even in the most positive sense of the word, there will be times when your best choice will be not to confront: to step back from a situation, assess it, and decide consciously to let it pass. Letting go of relatively inconsequential conflicts allows you to preserve both your and your daughter's stamina for matters that are truly important. Plus, as you refine your skills in the chapters ahead, you will be that much more successful when you can concentrate on the issues that matter most to you. Once you figure out how to evaluate just which struggles are worthwhile, you will have achieved an essential component of the art of conflict management: picking and choosing your battles wisely.

Although this skill can be useful for all mothers, it is particularly crucial for those whose relationships with daughters have become intensely conflictual. If you are loath to get into yet another go-around, yet are determined to do something, anything, to improve your connection, you might want to concentrate your efforts on this important principle. Essentially, rather than say more and further escalate discord, change your relationship by saying *less*. You are not giving up, withdrawing your attention, or reneging on your maternal responsibilities. You are doing something active to make positive changes.

While this may come as a relief for some, it creates problems for others. If you are not supposed to take on every single controversy, how do you know how to select the most appropriate ones? If you are going to confront your daughter sometimes and not other times, can you do so without sending mixed messages? If you choose to ignore something, are you letting her "get away with murder"? How can you be sure you are consistently picking the right battles?

You can't. No matter how hard you try, you will occasionally fumble and find yourself scolding your daughter for the pettiest of reasons: leaving her window open before a thunderstorm; forgetting to close the milk carton; watching too much TV on a summer afternoon. Other days you will do just the opposite: Instead of reacting directly to her verbal assaults or sarcastic launches, you will seek refuge in your room, unnerved by the ferocity of her comments.

Your goal cannot be perfection; it is helpful to accept from the outset that you will never be 100 percent correct in choosing your battles. But you can develop and maintain a framework for making choices that will minimize the time, energy, and emotional resources you waste on unnecessary struggles. In other words, you can minimize the stress on you, your daughter, and your relationship. As she begins creating more of a life for herself outside the home, it will become increasingly important for you to make the time you do share as rewarding as possible.

WHEN IT FEELS OVERWHELMING

Ginny, a mother of sixteen-year-old twins, was simply hoping for a little peace and quiet: "I am going to lose my mind if these skirmishes with my daughters don't start easing up. On any given day the three of us will fight about why they can't wear leather jackets, how much eye liner is acceptable, why they can't use the car, why they have to do the dishes. Some days I can't even remember my reasons anymore, and when they sense that, it's all over. They push me until they get exactly what they want. I'm constantly exhausted. I want to know how I can make things better so I won't feel this way for the next three years."

Tired and fed up with the demands their daughters keep making, mothers may be especially challenged by all the new situations and dicey decisions thrust before them. It is easy for mothers to forget that they don't have to respond to all of their children's demands. If you don't pinpoint which battles are worthwhile, you will find yourself involved in one big, ongoing dare: Bet you can't handle this one!

One mother complained: "Sometimes I wonder if my daughter asks for certain favors just to provoke me. Like last week she told me she wanted to start dating a guy who's old enough to be her father, who I'm not even convinced she likes. But she had this look on her face like 'What are you going to do about this one?' I had no idea, so I just said no to get it over with. This of course led straight into her attack that I don't trust her. What was I supposed to do?"

DECIDING WHETHER TO CONFRONT AN ISSUE

At first the challenge of choosing battles wisely can make every day feel like an uphill climb. You may find that even after weighing the facts carefully, you still aren't sure whether confronting your daughter on a specific issue is right or wrong. Unfortunately there are no magic formulas or absolutes to offer. Your priorities in raising your daughter—mainly what values you want to instill in her and what goals you hope to accomplish—will be your guide.

It will be worth your effort to think through this issue. Unless you establish a general approach, you are likely to feel overwhelmed by the endless challenges that arise in the course of raising your daughter through her adolescence. Developing guidelines also offers the advantage of consistency in decision making. Each time you are thrust into a situation, you won't feel the need to reinvent the wheel, so to speak.

Below are high-priority considerations when it comes to assessing whether or not to address an issue with your daughter. You may or may not agree with all of them. The goal is not to convince you to use these strategies or these particular values but rather to help you establish a framework with which you decide which issues *you* believe are truly worth taking on with your daughter.

Safety

Example 1: Your daughter is dropped off from a party not by her friend's parents, as agreed, but by an older brother who is known to have driven while drinking.

Example 2: You go into your daughter's bedroom to leave a note on her desk and find a pack of cigarettes dangling out of a drawer.

Example 3: After "meeting" a man on the Internet, she's planning a date with this virtual stranger in a nearby city.

- **CONFRONTATION VALUE**. Teenage girls need their parents to establish clear guidelines to ensure their well-being and safety. Your daughter may be testing the limits of what is acceptable in your household. As unpleasant as it may be to struggle over these incidents, and despite assurances that "I know what I'm doing" and protests that "you just don't trust me," she desperately needs you to be consistent and unwavering when it comes to her safety. Your approach in this area may have to be black or white; there is little room for compromise when the stakes are so high. The simplest, most straightforward message works best here: "No," "That's not acceptable," or "There's no negotiation on this."

Achievement

Example 1: Despite promises to "try harder" and get better grades, your daughter fails two midterm exams.
Example 2: Although she says she intends to go to college, she has yet to send for an application and has no plans to take the SAT.
Example 3: The brand-new flute you bought her is collecting dust on her closet floor; she has not practiced in two weeks.
- **CONFRONTATION VALUE**. If it is important to you that your daughter try her hardest to live up to her commitments, then you will make it your business to remind her of these values. She also may need you to help her structure specific daily study and practice times. She might need to hear periodically that you expect her to work hard, to set appropriate goals, and to finish what she starts. Your daughter will be likelier to comply if she has had a role in establishing standards (i.e., they are consistent with her own goals). It is also important to make sure everyone's expectations are realistic.

Autonomy

Example 1: Although a family trip is planned for next summer, your daughter wants instead to go live with a friend who moved away.
Example 2: She insists on taking the subway to a school function, even though you offer to chauffeur her and her friends.
Example 3: Despite your daughter's solid foundation of religious instruction, she decides she has had enough and skips classes.
- **CONFRONTATION VALUE**. Determining whether your objection is based on concerns about safety, feelings of rejection, or a need for

your daughter to think as you do should help you decide whether or not to make an issue out of each of these situations. If her plans or beliefs do not violate major values or pose a threat, you may have to live with them even if you disagree with them. But her normal developmental need to establish autonomy has to be balanced against family standards and what you can tolerate. Regardless of whether a compromise is feasible, however, it is important not to condemn your daughter's opinions when they are an outgrowth of her efforts to develop as an individual.

Character Development

Example 1: Having canceled long-standing plans with her cousins at the last minute when her friends invited her to a concert, your daughter insists, "They won't care."

Example 2: Walking by her room, you hear her tell a friend the very secret she just swore to her sister she would never divulge.

Example 3: Your daughter tells you proudly about her terrific grade on a science lab, which you believe she copied from a friend's notebook.

- **CONFRONTATION VALUE.** Teens are notorious for seeing themselves as the center of the universe. They may behave as if rules and standards of decency applied to others but not to them. You may choose to reinforce your belief that your daughter cannot do as she pleases without regard for other people's rights and feelings. Although she cannot make everyone happy and surely will have to disappoint people in her life, you do not want her to be cruel or insensitive. Similarly, if honesty is a given for you, then you need to react to the process by which she achieves success rather than merely to her ultimate accomplishments. For you, the means won't justify the end. Consistently telling her when her behavior is out of bounds gives her tools to do so for herself as she matures.

Being Taken Advantage Of

Example 1: You notice on the telephone bill that your daughter made five long-distance calls during the week she supposedly lost phone privileges.

Example 2: You spontaneously permitted her to invite several friends to sleep over, but they kept you up half the night giggling and playing loud music.

Example 3: You permitted your fifteen-year-old daughter a half glass of champagne on New Year's Eve but later found the empty bottle she and a friend finished.

- **CONFRONTATION VALUE.** When your daughter takes advantage of you or does something clearly against your stated wishes, you want to convey emphatically that she is risking the very trust that is central to your relationship. Although she asks for greater autonomy, her behavior actually encourages you to be suspicious and to check up on her. When mothers fail to express their feelings of being hurt, wronged, and mistreated by daughters, they feel exploited. For you to feel good about yourself and have a successful relationship, it is essential that you ask to be treated decently.

When She Needs You

Example 1: A note left casually on the kitchen counter alerts you to your daughter's best friend's drug problem.

Example 2: You find out through the grapevine that one of her friends is having unprotected sex or may be pregnant.

Example 3: You suspect that at least some members of your daughter's group are responsible for the recent vandalism in the neighborhood.

- **CONFRONTATION VALUE.** It is likely your daughter will be ambivalent about coming to you with these problems. Because she wants to be helpful and loyal to her friends, she may feel that telling you would be betraying them. Yet your daughter is no doubt overwhelmed by her inexperience with these serious matters. If you relate your information to her (matter-of-factly giving her the facts, without divulging your source) in the spirit of offering a sounding board, she may be relieved the secret is out so she can discuss it with you. If she refuses to speak to you, make sure (1) she is safe and (2) she knows your "door is always open" if she changes her mind. By initiating the conversation, she knows the topic is not off-limits.

WRONG REASONS TO CONFRONT

You Need to Prove Yourself Right

Yesterday my daughter, Ellie, asked me why I don't go to the movies, and I told her that I think old movies are much better than today's trash. She got offended and told me that she didn't think they were so bad, and we got into this heated argument about it. I could see she was get-ting more and more upset, but I just kept on trying to prove that the clas-sics were better. By the end of it I realized that winning my case had become way too important.

While many women acknowledge that the need to prove themselves "right" is hardly good cause for confrontation, it is easy to get swept away. Few like to be challenged, much less by their own children. When mothers engage in battles of who's right and who's wrong, per-spective is lost, unnecessary conflict is created, and trust and respect are diminished. Daughters are also taught that it is acceptable to battle for sport. To avoid this, it is best to think about the importance of pur-suing a particular course as the discussion begins.

You Are Threatened by Her Budding Independence

My daughter, Samantha, asked if she could have a birthday party last month, and I was delighted. I went out and bought this fabulous fon-due set, so the girls could enjoy a gourmet meal. When I showed it to Samantha, she looked at me like I was from Mars. She insisted they would order their own food: pizza and soda. I was thinking, What kind of meal is that for a special occasion? I don't know why I kept trying to tell her how much fun fondue would be. Now it seems silly, but it doesn't matter because she wouldn't even listen.

As your daughter develops her own opinions and tastes, it is crucial she have opportunities to experiment. This does not mean you need to allow her to pierce her nipples, hang out with the "druggie" crowd, or paint her bedroom black. You will have to determine what you can and cannot live with as you go along. But it is wise to permit her plenty of opportunities to express her uniqueness. She may want to play an instrument that grates on your nerves, be friends with a girl you find ditzy, preach about the latest political cause . . . and so on.

Because her choices are different from yours does not mean that she is insulting you or that she is ready to start her adult life without you. It simply means that she is beginning to figure out who she is and how she wants to represent herself to the world. Most of the "new tastes" she picks up will be short-term test runs anyway. Reminding yourself of these points can be helpful as you attempt to respond differently to your daughter.

Instead of feeling angry or threatened and giving her disdainful looks when you don't approve of her choices, for example, you might encourage her to discover her own likes and dislikes. Besides, if you try to force your own tastes on your daughter, she will probably cling more tenaciously to her red hair dye or love for rap. By your respecting her right to choose, your daughter will learn that your love is not contingent on her being exactly like you. By encouraging her to explore her various facets and move toward independence, you will foster her self-worth.

You Are Taking Out Other Frustrations on Her

Last week I found out my father might be really sick, and I was a wreck waiting to hear the results. One night my daughter, Jessie, came home with a friend, and I asked her to wash the dishes before doing anything else. She asked if she could do them after they had watched their favorite TV show, and I yelled, "I asked you to do them now. Respect that." My daughter looked mortified, and the next day she told me that I had humiliated her in front of her friend. She was right. There was no reason why the dishes had to be done at that second. I was just feeling out of control, and she was there.

This one is an easy trap to fall into. When you are feeling anxious, angry, hurt, or otherwise upset, you may not realize you are looking for someone—anyone—on whom you can vent these feelings. Enter your daughter, who has perhaps been somewhat frustrating to you lately, and you have the perfect target. Nearly every mother has made this mistake on occasion and felt the inevitable regret afterward. As you may imagine, however, continuously taking out your distress on your daughter forces her into doing one of two things: (1) accepting inappropriate responsibility for your burden, which is not a pattern you want her to establish, or (2) labeling you irrational and avoiding you at all costs. When you sense this dreaded scenario about to replay like a worn-out video, push the stop button. Do whatever you need to do to get control. If you need to be by yourself for a few minutes, it's okay to tell her that. Your daughter will respect your ability to ask for what you need and will learn, by example, that she herself can ask for time alone.

You Feel You Have to Show You're in Control

Even though it's summer, I think it's important to have rules that my daughters live by. I don't want them to take advantage of me either. So when I came home from work and realized that Gina had watched a two-hour movie instead of just a one-hour show, I felt I couldn't just ignore that. Then my other daughter came in twenty minutes past her curfew the other night. I wanted to put a stop to it, so I punished her too. Then I felt bad because the girls pointed out, and rightly so, I think, that these were pretty minor crimes in the grand scheme of things. They've been such good kids. I should've let these little things go.

There's a big difference between being in control and being controlling. When daughters follow the spirit of your rules, they're already demonstrating respect for your authority. It is unrealistic to think teenagers will conform perfectly to your expectations—nor should they. Mothers usually find that punishing for minor offenses is counterproductive. Especially if they believe mothers are being petty, girls may become resentful and rebellious. Again, keep in mind your ultimate goal: What are you trying to teach your daughter as a result of making an issue out of an incident? This may be a situation in which you decide to lose the battle to win the war.

THE CLASSIC BATTLE STARTERS

Some arguments between mothers and daughters have both "inevitable" and "explosive" written all over them. These include, but are in no way limited to, boys and dating, curfew, makeup, and driving privileges—sticky topics you probably fought over with your own mother. Although you may be weary of your daughter's relentless "pushing," it is usually best to keep an open mind and hear her out. Even if you know in advance the answer will be no, you might grant her the courtesy and respect of listening to her. Finding out why the issue is important to her will not only help you understand her but help her understand herself. Dialogue helps her reason out loud. She may even discover that the issue isn't as important as she originally thought. Either way, she learns to put her feelings into words, a prerequisite to engaging in effective discussion. These are the notorious issues, or battle starters, that mothers and daughters are almost guaranteed to lock horns over:

The State of Her Bedroom

When it comes to deciding which battles are worthy, it may seem that issues concerning your daughter's bedroom crop up most frequently. As one mother said, "You wouldn't think the state of one little room could cause so much damage in a relationship." That is because, to mothers, it is just that—a bedroom, a place to dress and sleep—but to daughters, it is the only place on earth to feel comfortable and revel in privacy. If you are picturing your daughter's paper- or clothing-strewn bedroom with exasperation, you know of what many mothers speak.

At the crux of most bedroom issues is a genuine question of ownership: Who's room is it? When she screams, "Get out of my room!" she doesn't seem to understand that you own that room, just as you own or rent the entire apartment or house. You may also feel that your daughter's room, like the rest of your home, reflects on your taste, cleanliness, and ability to maintain a household. If you need a compass to navigate your way to her closet, you are probably not all that happy about showing your house to friends and relatives. You feel your daughter should respect this room, and you, by keeping it relatively clean and neat. So what's the big deal?

The big deal is that in her heart of hearts, your daughter believes she is the owner of this room. Her bedroom is the one location she can call her own—a place to ponder, analyze her new curves in private, write in her journal, practice kissing on a pillow, examine her pimples, and talk to her friends in private. Furthermore, her room is a refuge. All day long your daughter is expected to prove herself to others, to teachers, coaches, parents, friends, and guys; in the sanctity of her bedroom, she does not have to answer or prove herself to anyone. She can be herself. So when you attack her bedroom, you are essentially attacking her personal domain.

Because your daughter treasures her bedroom, she finds nothing wrong with making it her own, however she sees fit. She sees no problem in painting her walls jet black ("I'm not depressed, I just think it looks cool!"); littering her floor with clothes ("I know exactly where everything is!"); playing cacophonous music ("If you don't like it, don't come in!"); hanging posters you find graphic and obscene ("You don't have to look at it. It's my room!"); refusing to make her bed

("Why should I? I'm just going to mess it up at night anyway!"). The potential for bedroom blowouts is enormous. When it comes to negotiating this arena, you may find yourself weaving through a veritable obstacle course.

That said, be assured it is possible to respect your daughter and her need for her space without relinquishing your values. Ultimately, because it is your home, you do have the right to establish what you can and cannot tolerate. It may be helpful to think through these common issues to decide which are truly important to you:

"HER ROOM IS A PIGSTY!"
"IT LOOKS LIKE IT WAS HIT BY A TORNADO!"

There are a few things you as a mother may find helpful to remember. One, your daughter's room (no matter how abominable) reflects her taste and style, not yours. Two, it is well within the range of normality for teens' rooms to look condemnable. Being a temporary slob does not make her a lesser person. Three, as discussed above, it is important that she feels comfortable in her own domain.

So what compromises can you offer? Perhaps you can handle a messy room if she will agree to keep her door shut. That way no one else has to see it. Maybe she can have all the clutter she wants, but no food is allowed; or dirty dishes have to go back to the kitchen. Perhaps the clothes you paid for must be hung up; nothing can be left out that might attract small creatures; or she must clean up whenever visitors will be taking a grand tour of the house. Choose the issues that are truly important to you, and explain them to her clearly. If need be, you two can agree upon and sign a written contract to avoid future claims of "I didn't know that was part of the deal."

"MY CHILD HAS NO TASTE!"

Another set of considerations comes in when you want to encourage your daughter to develop her own taste and aesthetic sense, even though you cannot believe how bad her taste is. For example, while one mother objects to "a ridiculous poster of some guy in a skimpy Speedo," another is aghast that her daughter sleeps on a bare mattress on her floor, and still another is horrified by "a penis-shaped candle that my child thinks is hilarious." Where do you draw the line between unseemly and intolerable?

Again, compromise, as well as your ability to play it cool without criticizing her taste, is key. Perhaps you allow her to decorate as she pleases—as long as there are no permanent markings that destroy the value of the room (i.e., holes in the wall, torn wallpaper, disassembled furniture). If there is something in the room that clearly infringes upon your family values, you can certainly tell her. "I feel very uncomfortable with that marijuana collage you have" works much better than "You have five seconds to get that out of my house!" Also, remember to save your veto power for a disturbing satanic poster, not for the papier-mâché giraffe you find merely distasteful. She can hear that while she is living in your house, it is important she respect the values of the family—even if she doesn't agree with all of them. When she goes off to college or finds her own place, she can decorate however she pleases.

Her Fashion Choices

Another issue that almost guarantees mother-daughter fireworks is appearance. How are you supposed to choose among the dozens of clothing battles being slung your way? What's more important to address: her new look of half shirts, beach ball-size earrings, and ripped jeans or the fact that she cannot see what's wrong with wearing her favorite T-shirt four days in a row? Maybe they're equally important; they certainly get under you skin similarly. You mourn the days when you could dress her in adorable clothes that you both loved. Now you feel there is little you can do to prevent her from wearing what she chooses. After all, you can't stop her from changing her clothes or makeup once she gets to school.

First, remembering what she is up against will help you empathize. As discussed, certain clothes are considered cool by her classmates, while others get her labeled "uncool," "nerdy," and "totally 'last year.' " Mothers can easily forget their own, sometimes painful experiences with this type of peer pressure. Moreover, friends do notice, comment, and criticize—now more than ever. Don't forget the dictates of MTV, current magazines, movies, and television about what is in and out. Whoever said, "Clothes don't make the man," had no idea what it is like to be a teenage girl, who is defined on a daily basis according to her wardrobe.

Whereas some girls hit upon a particular style that makes them feel confident and comfortable (and relatively clear of social rejection), others change fashions as often as they change moods. One day it's a classic, no-fail Gap outfit, while the next brings a seventies polyester dress. Who knows what the next in style will be? Moreover, while your approval used to matter when it came to your daughter's appearance, it is now the very reason to trash an outfit or look. Here are some of the issues you will likely face.

"I CAN'T BELIEVE SHE'S WEARING THAT!"

You are horrified to admit your daughter has no fashion sense whatsoever. You know she thinks the same of you, but your outfits don't elicit double takes in public. Why would she choose to make a spectacle of herself on purpose? you wonder. Isn't it your job to help her develop some taste? Said one mother: "My daughter is into the whole retro thing, and I can't believe the ugly polyester skirts she'll wear to a party." Another mother added, "I tell her that the baggy jeans and T-shirts she wears make her look androgynous, but she says she wants to look like that." Mothers constantly fret about what others "can possibly think of" their daughters—and them.

Although the thought may make you cringe, the best advice is this: If it is a matter of personal taste, let it go. Fortunately the topic is clothes, not plastic surgery. If her choices are temporary, experimental, and relatively harmless, if the worst result is a bizarre outfit, it is prudent to stay out of it.

But, you may ask, what about the piece of clothing she's been wearing every day for almost an entire week? Teen girls are often so relieved to find a piece of clothing that fits well and draws compliments that they wear it into the ground, driving some mothers wild. What to do when your daughter is on day four of wearing the same white turtleneck? Perhaps you might suggest the two of you go shopping to buy a few more just like it, or negotiate an amount of times per week that she can wear it (say, one or two). If she demands to know why you care so much, you can explain to her that it has to be cleaned. If she cares about her appearance, she needs to be concerned about personal hygiene as well.

"BUT SHE'LL FREEZE TO DEATH!"

Your daughter used to listen to you when you told her to wear mittens or zip up her snowsuit. These days she may go out in the dead of winter without a jacket. Although tempted to run after her with a sweater and scarf, you know she would refuse to wear them. Further, you would surely get a lecture on treating her like a baby. So why not let it go? Your daughter must learn to listen to her own body and meet its needs. If she gets cold while she's out, she'll shiver and find a way to keep warm rather than catch pneumonia. Not only will she survive, but she might even remember to bring a sweater next time. It seems far better to focus on more serious or irrevocable matters.

"SHE LOOKS LIKE A TRAMP!"

Questionable fashion sense is one thing; exposing cleavage or other body parts is another. At a time when teen girls are desperate to win approving glances from guys, many girls go for the easy approach: miniskirts, crop tops, tank tops, lacy see-through shirts, etc. This wardrobe transformation may be sudden. The mother of a fifteen-year-old girl complained: "When I sent my daughter to camp, she was wearing khaki shorts and a T-shirt. The day she returned home, she was wearing cutoff shorts and a halter top that barely covered her breasts. I nearly had a heart attack!" How do mothers react when their daughters come downstairs in inappropriate clothing? Many panic, scream, and threaten (e.g., "You have two seconds to go upstairs and put on something decent!"). This is a case in which mothers need to assert that their daughter dress more appropriately.

One strategy is to agree that she is right to be proud of her body, that it is fabulous, but that it is not okay for her to wear clothing you find sexually inappropriate, and you can define exactly what that means to you. Maybe it is that you don't want her cleavage, navel, or uppermost thighs exposed. Maybe you don't want her clomping around in shoes with x-inch heels. You may not approve of permanent piercing or sexually provocative tattoos. With each new fashion craze you'll set the standards. If she cries, tells you that she hates you, and says she's the only one in her grade whose mother feels this way, you can be understanding and acknowledge her frustration—but not be inclined to budge. If she is sneaking out of the house in inappropriate clothing, you will have to demonstrate that there will be natural consequences for her behavior. When you are in the throes of these situations, it is hard to believe that your daughter will ultimately respect you for setting limits and sticking to them.

Makeup, Accessories, and Piercing

If you looked in the closets of your daughter's classmates, you could probably mix and match the wardrobes of many of them. Teen girls are hyperconscious about how others dress, and they follow fashion trends as if they were law. You know this from every time your daughter assures you she doesn't have the "right" jeans, sweaters, boots, and sweatshirts. Girls are given the most leeway from peers in the area of their stylistic touches. A funky necklace, a wild nail polish color, or highlighted hair allows girls to separate themselves from the herd—without straying into ridicule and ostracism. Unfortunately what teens often consider small stylistic extras are construed by moms as horrifying and extreme.

"SHE LOOKS LIKE A CLOWN WITH THAT MAKEUP!"

It started with a little cover-up. You had to do something to quell your daughter's fit over her first pimple. Little by little, however, she introduced new cosmetics. The sheer lip gloss was fine, so you let that slide. But the black raccoon circles ringing her eyes? No way! The bright red lipstick that makes you gag? Forget it. As your daughter sees more and more girls from class experimenting with makeup, you can be sure the intrigue of "fixing" her own face is around the bend. Again, working with her and setting clear limits are the best course. Perhaps lip gloss is fine with you. Maybe you can live with pimple cover-up and light mascara. Try to find an item or two you can agree on, help her select the right products for her, and teach her to use them properly. You might assure her that she is beautiful as she is, without makeup. Even when she sighs and says, "Of course, you're going to say that; you're my mother," she will be relieved when you do say it. One note of warning, though: Never, ever suggest that your daughter should wear makeup because the suggestion will only make her feel unattractive.

"I DON'T CARE IF HER ACCESSORIES ARE TEMPORARY; THEY'RE STILL HIDEOUS!"

Most mothers would agree that there is a huge difference between permanent versus temporary accessories. When your daughter explains that she needs a streak of blond highlights in her hair, a temporary tattoo, or a toe ring, you might consider compromising. You may not approve of the look, but it helps to remind yourself it will undoubtedly be gone before you know it. If it makes you queasy to watch your daughter traipse off to school with dangly earrings or a temporary tattoo around her ankle, you might make a deal with her. Perhaps you will tolerate her wearing them only during weekends or after school. If she insists that she needs a permanent tattoo of a string of daisies around her ankle, you may well think twice. If you feel dead set against it, you can tell her she will have to wait until she's an adult and out of the house.

"I DON'T SEE WHY SHE NEEDS MORE HOLES IN HER BODY!"

Here's a battle that makes almost every mother recoil: body piercing. For the previous generation, the big negotiation used to be at what age girls were permitted that classic rite of passage ear piercing, in which they got little pearl or birthstone studs in their ears (that is, one per ear). Now the dilemma is about little rings encircling your daughter's eyebrow, nostril, belly, nipple, or elsewhere. When it comes to permanent or health-related alterations—a real tattoo or body piercing—even the most liberal mother may well put her foot down. Teens rarely have a concept of what it will mean to walk into a job interview some years down the road with a tattooed ankle. That is where your role as protective mother comes in. Though you temporarily "ruin" her life, if you are lucky, someday you will be thanked.

TEACHING YOUR DAUGHTER TO CHOOSE BATTLES

As discussed above, if your relationship is to improve maximally, your daughter must do her part as well. The first thing you might teach her is how to select which issues she addresses with you. Instead of constantly provoking you and accusing you of heaven knows what and telling you she thinks you are wrong about every little thing, creating an atmosphere of perpetual discord, she can learn to choose her battles carefully. The challenge is to help her find the right balance of standing up for herself without becoming contentious. When you teach your daughter how to choose her battles with you, she will also learn to do so outside your relationship.

Said the mother of one thirteen-year-old: "Sometimes my daughter seems to argue just for the sake of arguing. Like last week Julie came home and asked me if she could read a book that would be considered R rated. She knew I'd say no, and she was prepared with a whole dissertation on her civil rights and freedoms. I was too tired to get into a whole dialogue with her, though, so I just said, 'Do we really have to do this, Julie?' She could tell I wasn't taking the bait, I guess, because she just shrugged and walked away."

There are a thousand and one variations on this theme. Your daughter can choose to make an issue every time you annoy, disappoint, or anger her—or not. As you focus on selecting your own battles with her, you might explain that you too dislike the frequent fighting and want to make a joint effort to improve your relationship. She may benefit from hearing that you have decided to think things through more carefully instead of confronting her right away and that you hope she will do the same. Then you can help your daughter figure out her own set of guidelines for distinguishing which are worthwhile. If both of you make this effort to change your respective patterns, daily life will undoubtedly be smoother.

SETTING GUIDELINES

Below are some questions your daughter can ask herself when she is unsure whether getting into a battle with you is a good idea. She (and you too) will find these same criteria helpful later, when she practices expressing her dissatisfaction to others.

IS IT GOING TO MAKE THE SITUATION WORSE?
For example, taking out her disappointment on you to relieve herself of blame will inevitably come back to haunt her. Suppose you have told your daughter that she cannot go on a trip unless she brings her science grade up to a B. She agrees but ends up spending the majority of her study time on the phone. When she earns a resounding D on a test and lowers her grade further, she is furious that she will not be able to go on the trip.

Ideally your daughter should ask herself what will happen if she begs you to go. She needs to realize the situation will not change (it is to be hoped that you will not even consider wavering from the consequences). In fact, clashing with you about this issue will only demonstrate that she is not yet mature enough to take responsibility for her own actions. She will risk making you even angrier. It would be better for your daughter to concentrate on how to do things differently next time, as opposed to trying to change the rules of the game.

IS SHE TAKING SOMETHING OUT ON YOU THAT IS UNRELATED?

As discussed, teens tend to overreact to everyday situations in soap opera style. The friend who tells her that her hair looks "frizzy"; the guy who breaks up with her because she's "too nice"; the orthodontist who announces she needs braces: the list of potential explosives on any given day is mind-boggling. Heaven forbid you suggest she keep her problem in perspective. You are already her favorite scapegoat.

Alicia, mother of fifteen-year-old Marie, said: "My daughter came home from this party last Saturday night in a huff. I asked her what was wrong, and she said, 'This stupid haircut you told me would look good is disgusting. I look like a freak. How could you lie to me?' I just sat there with my mouth hanging open. But now I know enough to understand that wasn't the real issue. The next day I found out the scoop: The girl who drove Marie to the party got drunk and told everyone that Marie wasn't a virgin. I had no idea this was what was really bothering her."

It is unrealistic to hope your teen daughter will consistently be able to figure out and put into proper perspective what is upsetting her. In fact, good luck finding a teenager who can. But that doesn't mean you should bear the brunt of her feelings every time she becomes upset. You are not being "insensitive" or a bad mother if you assure your daughter that you will always be willing to listen and discuss what is on her mind but that you will not allow her to take out her problems on you.

IS THE ISSUE ALL THAT IMPORTANT?

Some things that you do and say will drive your daughter up a wall (e.g., "Why do you always have to tell me that you love me? It's so embarrassing!"). As hard as this is on mothers, it is equally draining for teens, who are consumed by the perception that every situation can make or break their lives.

Jamie, fourteen, said: "Last month I ended up screaming at my mom because she said I couldn't go camping for the weekend with these guys. When she said no, I told her I hated her for treating me like a baby. The weird thing was that I realized later I was a little nervous about the plan. But at the time it seemed like a good idea."

Try explaining to your daughter that it will be easier for you two to work out the big issues if she weeds out the unimportant ones. The best way for her to accomplish this is to stop and think carefully about each situation before acting—a valuable skill for her to have when dealing with anyone.

NEVER TOO LATE

Sometimes your daughter will ask herself the above questions and still be unable to decide whether or not she should confront you with an issue. She might worry that unless she expresses her feelings immediately, the opportunity will be lost. Fortunately that's not how it works when one chooses one's battles. You can assure your daughter that there is rarely a statute of limitations on when to work things out with you—or anyone. She should feel comfortable expressing her concerns anytime, be it two weeks, two months, or two years after the fact. Ideally she will learn to address problems promptly, before they grow and fester. But there is no such thing as "too late" when it comes to righting wrongs. Then, of course, you have to prove you mean what you say. When she tells you that a comment you made three weeks ago has been bothering her, you will have to refrain from dismissing it or asking why she waited so long to tell you. You might respond differently by dealing with it right away. Show her that she will be taken seriously regardless of when she gathers the nerve to discuss her feelings.

Said Margaret, sixteen: "My mom always told me that we could discuss anything, but when she started hanging out with me and my friends all the time, I didn't know how to tell her that she was really bugging me. So I didn't say anything for weeks, and the longer I waited, the worse I felt about doing it. Finally I realized I was starting to be kind of mean to her, and if I didn't say something soon, I was really going to blow it big time. So I told her. At first she seemed really embarrassed and upset, but then she started leaving us alone. It was good."

Your daughter will feel more confident expressing herself when she sees that you, like Margaret's mother, will take her seriously. Again, the goal is to have your daughter walk away feeling good about standing up for herself. By practicing these strategies on you, she will be able to confront others who might mistreat her in the future.

Rewarding her efforts

It won't always be easy for your daughter to decide whether a battle is worth taking on. Sometimes she will make mistakes, telling you off and then deeply regretting it or, conversely, remaining silent when she should have said something and perhaps exploding later over a minor issue. Most mothers experience a knee-jerk impulse to punish daughters in these situations. Instead, you might acknowledge her error while giving her permission to make some bad judgment calls. After all, how is she to learn? Daughters are nearly always comforted (whether or not they will admit it) by hearing examples of their mothers' mistakes ("Remember when I yelled at you for_____? I was wrong"). You will be demonstrating that this is a skill to be developed and improved. What better way to show each other how much you value your relationship?

Lastly you will want to reward your daughter with positive feedback when you recognize that she has thought through carefully whether to broach a topic with you. When you tell her that it probably wasn't an easy choice to make and that you are proud of the way she handled it, she will know you recognize her efforts. A little appreciation will go a long way in encouraging her to stop and think before she confronts you next time. She will also gain much-needed confidence to use these skills in her interactions with others.

Chapter Eight

Expressing Yourself Effectively

Once you have determined the most important topics to focus on with your daughter, happily discarding the need to focus on each and every issue that arises, you may feel more empowered and confident. The thought of confronting your daughter effectively surely seems more doable when you know you can concentrate your efforts where it counts. Whether you've decided to address her nasty treatment of her younger sibling, the decline of her schoolwork, or the trust between you, you're eager to resolve what has been troubling you.

However, a part of you is still apprehensive. Perhaps you've attempted to get your point across before, but despite your best intentions, your conversations spiraled into a deluge of tears, insults, or glares. If so, it would be hard for you to feel all that hopeful of success this time around. Yet you will probably plunge into this confrontation in spite of your trepidation because you know the issue must be tackled. The inevitable tension, hurt, or moratorium on speaking between you and your daughter will eventually blow over. So the question becomes, What can you do to ensure you will walk away from this discussion feeling good about yourself and the way you and your daughter handled the situation?

The skills described in this chapter can help you express yourself clearly and effectively. More important, they will guide you to communicate with your daughter in ways that will maximize your chances of being heard and understood. Some strategies may sound familiar to you—from classes, workshops, counseling, marital sessions—but will be applied to the mother-daughter relationship. Other suggestions may simply clarify or place a name on what you are already doing. Still others may make you think, "That might just make a difference," or, "I'll give it a try."

No strategy in itself will be a panacea for your relationship. Some may help; others will not. They are not offered with the idea that you should try to implement every single tool, but rather that you may find some particularly useful. It is expected that you will gravitate to the strategies that come more naturally to you, but try to keep in mind that all can be learned.

Regardless of what you learned in the past, as well as your present style of mothering, you can change the way you communicate with your daughter. Mothers often describe feeling stuck initially: "That's the way I am." But if you focus on practicing a single behavior, whether it's using "I" statements or the twenty-second rule below, you may find that you can indeed change the course of an interaction with your daughter. You will see that saying something different, or saying something differently, can make a world of difference. Just take one step at a time.

As you decide which approaches might work for you, remember that you are also modeling for your daughter ways in which she too might improve her own communication style. If she sees you making efforts to try new behaviors, she is likely to follow.

Responsible communication

As defined in the previous chapter, confronting your daughter simply means dealing with an issue head-on. Although teenagers dislike hearing that mothers are unhappy with them, you act on your convictions anyway, in essence telling your daughter, "I know you won't like this, but I have to say it because it is my job as your mother, and your job is to be accountable for your behavior." When you speak with your daughter, you will want to think carefully about not just the content of your message but also how you deliver it. The way you confront your daughter can be as important as, or more important than, what you say.

A major consideration is that you can separate your feelings about the situation from the message itself. That is, you can tell your daughter what is making you upset, frustrated, bothered, concerned, or angry without explicitly expressing these feelings. While your emotions are indispensable in alerting you to the need to take action, you don't necessarily have to express them. You can choose to do so only if this assists you in reaching your goal.

For example, when you're annoyed because you have to take your daughter to school after she has missed the bus for the third time, you'll want to say, "I'd like you to set your alarm earlier and get better organized so this doesn't happen again." In this situation it may be irrelevant or even distracting to express your irritation. You are merely communicating that you want your daughter to behave differently in the future. But when you find out she's been telling people something about you that was supposed to be private, saying to her, "It's not okay to betray confidences," may not be enough. If your goal is to help her realize how her actions affect others, you will want your daughter to know that her behavior hurt and angered you.

The art in communicating effectively is using your knowledge of yourself and your daughter, as well as your intuitive ability, to make these decisions with finesse. Although this aspect cannot be taught, it can certainly be learned. Once you practice the basic skills, you will develop an internal inventory of what works best. You will learn what approaches coincide with your particular strengths, how to read your daughter's idiosyncratic nonverbal behaviors and moods, and, therefore, the likelihood of a strategy's being successful at a any given time. (For example, you may find that when your daughter keeps her eyes glued to her doorknob, it's a good clue she will not be listening to you; hence, postpone discussion.) Remember that you are the expert on your daughter. Trust that no one is as capable or as motivated to learn to connect with her as you; trust in yourself.

Practicing these skills will help improve your relationship with your daughter by opening lines of communication (at least you're talking) and promoting positive changes. Confrontations promote collaboration, compromise, and creative solutions for your differences. At the same time, you will be modeling communication and conflict resolution strategies for your daughter that will be crucial for healthy relationships in her future. Here are ten strategies that have proved effective:

Step One: Check Your Emotional Temperature

The first step in confronting your daughter is by now a familiar one: deciding whether or not it is actually a wise idea. When you check your "emotional temperature," so to speak, you are assuring yourself both that your diagnosis of the situation is correct and that your emotional arousal is at an appropriate level. Because the feelings kindled in the course of raising a teenage daughter are extraordinarily complex and often multilayered, this preparatory step is often helpful in preventing unnecessary conflict. So before you confront your daughter, be sure to determine whether you are truly reacting to something she has done or to something else that would be unproductive or even inappropriate to address.

For example, when two fourteen-year-old friends announced their plan to stay out all night at a bonfire after the school dance, their mothers had divergent reactions. Lucille found the request "ludicrous. I even said, 'That's funny,' and my daughter went off to her room in a huff." Marianne, on the other hand, was outraged. Her response, she admitted later, was the result of an incident that had happened to her as a teenager. She had stayed out all night after a school event and had been "terrifyingly close" to being raped by a drunk high school senior. Fortunately friends had come to her rescue at the last minute, but the incident haunted her for years. Of course this memory triggered her to "go nuts" when her daughter asked if she could stay out after the dance.

As Marianne put it, "I was so livid that at first I handled it all wrong and we had a huge blowup. When I told my sister what happened, she said to me, 'Don't you think this is related to what happened to you?' All of a sudden I realized I wasn't even angry at my daughter. I was actually terrified that she would find herself in that same situation I had been in." Marianne's discovery enabled her to change her approach to her daughter and resolve the dilemma to everyone's satisfaction.

Anger is an ideal cover-up for anxiety. It is understandable that given the task of keeping daughters safe through adolescence, mothers panic as often as they do. But before you respond angrily, it is important to ask: What harm did your daughter actually do? Did she disappoint you? Mistreat you? Are you furious at her lack of judgment? Like Marianne, you may find your daughter's request made you anxious or put you in an uncomfortable position, but the key to responding appropriately and helpfully is to realize this was probably not her intent. Remembering your daughter's developmental tasks will help you understand the motivation underlying what would otherwise be perceived as absurd requests or inconsiderate demands. In such cases you may decide to handle issues differently or let them pass.

It is also wise to think twice about confronting your daughter when you are taking her behavior personally. Remember the sensitivities you became aware of earlier? Here is where you can apply that knowledge directly to interactions with your daughter. For a Spanish-speaking mother who values academic achievement, for example, a daughter who fails a Spanish class is likely to incite wrath. Or when a mother is also a schoolteacher, she may feel her daughter's underachievement reflects poorly on her. In these cases be clear about why you're confronting your daughter: because of her insufficient preparation or irresponsibility or because of the disappointment or embarrassment she is causing you?

If, after soul-searching, you give yourself the green light to go ahead and broach an issue, make sure your emotional temperature is just right. Determining this is highly individual; Ralph Waldo Emerson put it well when he said that we boil at different degrees. You want to reap the motivating and energizing benefits of emotions such as anger while avoiding the overstimulation that interferes with clearheadedness. That is, you don't want to be so enraged that you can't think straight. To communicate effectively with your daughter, you will need to stay focused and think sharply.

Step Two: If Necessary, Cool Down

Suppose you decide your emotions are in the red zone (i.e., danger alert: You're so fired up you could boil over at any second). As the American critic George Jean Nathan said, "No man can think clearly when his fists are clenched." Neither can the mother of a teenage girl. There are numerous strategies for reducing your arousal to a more manageable level.

- **GIVE IT TIME.** The "count to ten" adage is based on the principle that anger dissipates over time. If you feel too upset to confront your daughter judiciously, put it off, sleep on it or give yourself a cooling-off period. Unless the situation is urgent, waiting until you feel more in control will not jeopardize your goal; in fact, you will be more likely to achieve it.
- **DISTRACT YOURSELF.** Reading an interesting book or doing a task that requires concentration (e.g., reconciling your checkbook or focusing on an engrossing project) is often helpful. You cannot focus on nurturing your hostility at the same time as calculating your balance or preparing for a presentation.
- **SOOTHE YOURSELF.** Do something that historically and consistently

reduces your distress: Meditate, do a mindless chore, exercise, take a bath, call a friend.

- **EMPATHIZE.** Empathy works well. Imagining how your daughter must feel, putting yourself in her shoes, can help deflate your wrath.
- **USE HUMOR.** Think of whatever is funny about the situation. Or at least imagine how ridiculous or ironic it will seem ten years from now. At the very least, rent your favorite silly movie or call an amusing friend.

Step Three: Think Through Your Goal

Too many times mothers begin to confront their daughters about an issue without first being clear on exactly what they want to accomplish. Once you are face-to-face with your daughter, who may be staring at you impatiently with her hands on her hips, it will be difficult to think of your main idea, much less to express it articulately. Keeping her waiting not only will make her tune you out but will make her that much more irritated when you next approach her. Take time to determine what message you want to get across beforehand (e.g., "It was very hurtful when you made fun of me in front of your friends," "I need to know where you are at all times so I know you're safe," or "I'd prefer that you be truthful"). If you are having trouble figuring out what you are so disturbed about, try writing in your journal, talking to your husband or a friend, or simply allowing yourself more time.

Step Four: Choose a Good Time

Now that you are ready to approach your daughter, pick a moment when she will be most receptive to discussion. For starts, you might seek her out when she is relatively calm and not preoccupied with some other pressing issue. This does not mean waiting until your daughter is worry-free, a state that is inconsistent with adolescence. It just means that there are times when she will be more or less able to hear your concerns. Aren't there times when you typically want to be left alone? Think back to when your daughter was a toddler; remember the hours just before dinner, the "witching hours," when you could not cope with any additional stress? Your daughter has her own witching hours. Here are general factors to consider.

- **TIME OF DAY.** Your teen may well have a different sleep/wake cycle from yours. For instance, if she can barely keep her eyes open in the morning, postpone a serious conversation until after school. Of course, by evening, when your daughter may just be coming alive, you may be too exhausted to talk about anything more serious than the weather forecast. Or more rarely, your daughter may be most receptive first thing in the morning, before she experiences any frustration. With this in mind, it is in your best interest to get to know your daughter's patterns and take advantage of those times when she is most open to discussion.

- **DEGREE OF PRIVACY.** Teens' normally high level of self-consciousness and hypervigilance for potential embarrassment will take precedence over whatever message you are attempting to impart. It would be difficult to think of a single exception to the rule of never confronting your daughter in front of her friends, the ultimate humiliation. This also applies to bringing up issues in the presence of your friends, your relatives, or strangers. During adolescence, teens even become hypersensitive to their siblings' perceptions. Speaking to your daughter privately will prevent her from being distracted by thoughts of what others will think of her. It maximizes the chance of her hearing you.

- **LEVEL OF STRESS.** There is only so much anyone can handle at any given time. By definition, teens are overloaded. If you know that your daughter is anticipating an anxiety-provoking event (e.g., academic test, physical exam, new school, breakup with a boyfriend), you will probably want to adjust your timing accordingly. Give equal consideration to positive life events, whose stressful effects are frequently overlooked. When your daughter is planning for a team playoff, an exciting date, or a driver's test, she may be minimally able to respond to what you consider important.

Step Five: Talk to Her Directly

When confronting your daughter, be sure you deliver the message personally. Avoid the temptation to communicate secondhand by getting another family member to do your "dirty work." Some mothers maneuver the situation so that siblings will report bad news ("You're in big trouble! Mom says she's really mad at you"). Others have their husbands do the disciplining, even when the situation has nothing to do with them ("Your mother said you were rude to her").

Messages that arrive secondhand usually fall on deaf ears. Moreover, you will miss opportunities to model direct communication for your daughter, who probably could use the lesson. Teens are notorious for dealing with problems via tangled networks of friends, which usually create innumerable distortions and circulating rumors. You can set a different example for your daughter by telling her directly and precisely what is making you concerned and what you would like her to do about it.

There is a distinction, however, between confronting your daughter directly and doing it face-to-face. The former does not necessarily require the latter. Since your overriding goal is to make yourself heard, ask yourself what mode of communication would be best for your daughter. Here are the main advantages of each alternative:

- **FACE-TO-FACE.** It is intense and quick, and it offers the best opportunity to ensure she perceives your message accurately by immediately correcting any misinterpretation. This mode may be needed for girls who are relatively inattentive, distractible, or uncooperative.

- **WRITTEN.** Under less emotional conditions, you have the chance to consider carefully and even correct what you say. (Erasable pens, backspacing, and whiteout are invaluable.) You will more easily resist becoming flustered or sidetracked. Similarly, your daughter will have the chance to reread your message until she "gets it," to digest it slowly and to think before reacting. If your message embarrasses her, she can save face by reading it in private. Then she can choose whether to write back or to discuss the matter with you in person. You can get creative with how you send written messages: a note under the door, in the backpack, via E-mail, etc.

- **COMBINATION.** Although you write a note, you don't have to send it. You can use a letter as a kind of rehearsal, working out the kinks in your message until you get it just right. Then you can speak to your daughter in person. Or you can write a note simply saying you would like to speak to her when it is convenient. Then she has some control about when and where a discussion takes place.

- **TELEPHONE.** Since many teens conduct a good portion of their social lives via the wires, they feel most comfortable on the phone. When mothers call home, daughters may actually welcome hearing from them. Sometimes a quick telephone check-in can be a disarming, spontaneous prelude to a long and satisfying discussion.

Step Six: Boost Your Chance of Being Heard

When distraught, mothers can easily lose sight of courtesies that might be automatic under more tranquil circumstances. You may need to remind yourself of the following strategies to maximize the chance of your message's being heard.

- **KEEP IT BRIEF.** Instead of delivering long, agonizing "lectures," shoot for the twenty-second rule. The premise of this rule is that the window of opportunity when one speaks to teenage girls is generally about twenty seconds. If you can't say what you want within that time, you should rethink your message. Many mothers do not realize how scary confrontations can be for girls. When they are rolling their eyes, sighing, and looking around the room, they are struggling to protect themselves from what they fear will be devastating words. You communicate most effectively, therefore, when you're brief. Ask yourself: "If my daughter hears nothing else (because she won't anyway), what is the core message I would like her to receive?"

For example, fourteen-year-old Nell and her mother got into a battle about whether Nell would be permitted to leave high school grounds during the school day when she started her freshman year the following fall. Here are examples of statements that first break, then adhere to the twenty-second rule:

DAUGHTER: *Will you let me leave school to get a slice of pizza?*

NOT

MOTHER: *You are never going to do that. Do you hear me? That is absolutely off-limits, and will never, ever happen. The last thing I want you to do is be in the car with underage drivers. Some of these kids will have just had their licenses for two days, and you expect me to let you be at their mercy? What can you be thinking? The most important thing in the world to me is—*

DAUGHTER: *Mom, okay, okay! Stop! I get it!*

BUT

MOTHER: *I'm sure you can't wait for that much freedom, but I think not until you're a senior.*

OR

MOTHER: *I'd feel more comfortable with that idea if I knew the driver. Maybe when you get your license.*

It may be challenging to distill your reasons, rationales, beliefs, and general wisdom down to mere pearls, but it will be worth your effort. The benefits of the twenty-second rule are cumulative. Once you adhere consistently to it, your daughter will no longer be apprehensive about being overwhelmed by a long lecture; instead, anticipating you will be brief and to the point, she will be able to focus on your words.

- **MAINTAIN A POSITIVE TONE OF VOICE.** Keep your voice conversational, the tone pleasant and neutral. Avoid sarcasm, bitterness, whining, and outright hostility. Otherwise, teens will hear and respond to your tone rather than to your message. They are likely to become immediately defensive, interrupt you, or tune out what is too painful. As Dr. Samuel Johnson advised two centuries ago, "You raise your voice when you should reinforce your argument."

- **BE COURTEOUS.** Speak to your daughter as you would speak to a cherished friend. Otherwise, you will be courting resentment. You are also communicating your abiding love for her, which remains intact despite her possible errors and inadequacies. You thereby present a model of conflict that includes respect, which you hope she will emulate when she is angry with you. As an old Chinese proverb says, "Do not use a hatchet to remove a fly from your friend's forehead."

- **KEEP TO THE PRESENT.** Forget about what happened yesterday, last week, or when she was nine. Rehashing past crimes will only make her defensive and distract both of you from the current issue. Consider the following examples of desirable versus less successful responses:

> DAUGHTER: *Please let me go to this party! I'll do anything if you'll let me.*

> NOT

> MOTHER: *The last time I let you have your way, you took advantage of me.*

> OR

> MOTHER: *Look what happened when you went out with Derek!*

> BUT

> MOTHER: *What assurance can you give me that you'll live up to your end of the bargain?*

> OR

> MOTHER: *I need to know that you'll do as you say.*

When you rehash past mistakes, all you are accomplishing is making girls feel hopeless to change things for the better. They figure, "Why bother?" Sticking to the present empowers them.

• **USE "I" STATEMENTS.** Saying how you think and feel is a good way to get your message across without being accusatory or presumptuous. Girls have an easier time hearing "I" statements. Contrast these pairs of messages:

NOT

MOTHER: *You're making the whole family lose sleep.*

BUT

MOTHER: *I have a hard time sleeping when you're not in the house by curfew.*

NOT

MOTHER: *You can be really vicious.*

BUT

MOTHER: *It hurts me to hear you speaking to your grandfather that way.*

• **USE DIRECT, CLEAR STATEMENTS.** Keep it simple to avoid confusion. It is no fun to make your whole argument and then hear your daughter ask, "And your point was?" Aim for stating the essence of your message as uncomplicatedly as possible, without preamble or digression.

NOT

MOTHER: *You know, there's something I really want to talk about with you, and it reminds me of when I was your age and feeling kind of lost, not knowing what I was about. Your grandmother and I had our moments, and I still think about that time.*

BUT

MOTHER: *You know, I've been thinking that we haven't spent that much time together lately, and I'd like to. What would you say to treating ourselves to lunch Saturday?*

- **ASK FOR WHAT YOU WANT.** Putting a positive spin on your message is always wise. Rather than say what is wrong, give your daughter an idea of how to make it right. Contrast these pairs of statements:

NOT

MOTHER: *You're such a liar!*

BUT

MOTHER: *I would prefer you tell me the truth no matter how bad you think it is.*

NOT

MOTHER: *Why are you always so lazy and disrespectful when I ask you to do chores?*

BUT

MOTHER: *I'd appreciate it if you would unload the dishwasher now.*

- **BE SPECIFIC.** Vague or generic requests may sound polite, but they're less likely to bring about desired results:

NOT

MOTHER: *Please try to be neater.*

BUT

MOTHER: *I expect you to put your laundry in the hamper, not next to it, every morning before you leave for school.*

- **EMPATHIZE WITH HER.** When you must disappoint, scold, request, or confront, empathizing with how your daughter is feeling is like putting money in the bank. You are contributing to the reserves of good feeling between the two of you. This is possible even when your thirteen-year-old daughter makes a preposterous request:

DAUGHTER: *Chrissie's brother invited me to go to a party at his college next weekend.*

NOT

MOTHER: *You must be crazy. Do you think I would really let you do that?*

BUT

MOTHER: *I know it must sound really exciting, but I'm sorry, it's out of the question.*

Even if she is still angry and upset, she knows that you care, that you understand her feelings, and that you took her request seriously. She knows you did not respond out of anger, spite, or "hatred." While she still won't be happy, this approach takes the sting out of her disappointment.

- **ASK FOR HER HELP.** If you are stuck trying to think of a Solomon-like solution to a stubborn dilemma, enlist your daughter's input. Not only does she have a stake in this issue, but you communicate how much you value and respect her thinking. Try:

NOT

MOTHER: *Forget it. I can't think of any way to get you to your retreat this weekend.*

BUT

MOTHER: *Okay, I'm out of ideas. Let's put our heads together and come up with some creative solutions to the transportation problem so you can go to that youth group retreat.*

- **USE AN EXAMPLE.** When you and your daughter are truly stymied, the issue may be too close to home. To gain objectivity, think through the problem as if it were occurring to people you know. Try:

NOT

MOTHER: *I can't make you understand. Let's just forget it.*

BUT

MOTHER: *Suppose it was your friend Lisa who told you that her mother read her postcard. What would you say to Lisa that might make her see her mother's point of view? What do you think her mother should do?*

Step Seven: Be Aware of Your Body Language

You can say all the right things in the world, but if your body language conveys something else, your daughter is going to notice the discrepancy. You want your nonverbal cues to be warm and confident so they back up your words instead of defeating them. Again, your daughter is learning from your behavior. Here are some things to watch out for.

- **EYE CONTACT.** It is difficult to strike just the right balance between no eye contact, on the one hand, which feels evasive, cold, and even withdrawn, and glaring intently at your daughter, on the other hand. Be reassured, however, that if you don't master this delicate maneuver to her standards, she will give you helpful feedback on the order of "What are you staring at?"

- **POSITION OF ARMS.** Why is it that when scolding daughters, mothers usually have the odd habit of pointing at them? Although even young children probably do not need to be reminded their mothers are speaking to them, adolescents find this mannerism particularly intrusive and condescending. Crossing one's arms in front of the body is generally perceived as defensive and distancing. A relaxed, natural position, with arms at your sides, is probably best.

- **BODY POSITION.** It is usually courteous to place one's self at the same level as the person to whom we are speaking. It is no different when one confronts teenagers. Since they are likely to be lounging on their beds or lying on their bedroom floors, standing by the door and towering over them are likely to be perceived as threatening. To converse more comfortably for both of you, try sitting on the bed or floor (after asking if it's a good time for her, of course).

- **PHYSICAL CONTACT.** There is an enormous difference in how much touching both women and girls enjoy. Some teens hang on to their mothers like baby chimps, while others recoil from a mere brushing of the hand. If your daughter will tolerate it, why not pat or hold her hand, give her a backrub or scratch her back? Regardless of the actual words you use, your daughter would be hard pressed to conclude that you "hate" her while you are making such loving gestures.

Step Eight: Modify According to Your Daughter's Needs

Although you cannot control completely your daughter's reaction to what you say, these suggestions may at times help make her more receptive.

- **BEGIN BY GIVING YOUR DAUGHTER SOME SAY OVER WHEN AND WHERE A DISCUSSION WILL TAKE PLACE.** Let her choose the most convenient time and location (e.g., her room, the family room, etc.).

- **IF YOUR DAUGHTER LOVES A PROLONGED DEBATE, SET A REASONABLE TIME DEADLINE.** Agree to take a break. Conversely, if your daughter prefers to evade an impending confrontation (hoping you will forget), mention that you need to resolve the matter by a specified time.

- **IF YOU SENSE YOUR DAUGHTER IS FEELING INTIMIDATED, EASE UP.** Some girls benefit from being given the option of calling a time-out when they feel overwhelmed. Or she may do better speaking to only one parent at a time if she feels "ganged up on." If necessary, try a less intense method of communicating, such as notes, E-mail, telephone calls, etc.

- **MAKE A SPECIAL DATE TO DO SOMETHING FUN TOGETHER.** See a play, take a hike in a nearby park, or just pamper yourselves. You'll have to use your judgment here. Whereas some girls are so pleased and relaxed that they are more tolerant of brief discussions, others feel betrayed if mothers use this time to bring up controversial topics. Test the waters, or ask your daughter.

- **WHEN THE CONFRONTATION IS URGENT, INSIST THAT YOUR DAUGHTER LISTEN TO YOU.** The operative word here is "listen." You cannot make her speak. In fact, forcing her to do so is counterproductive. But you can talk to her, telling her (in twenty seconds or less) the essence of your concerns (for example, safety) and what you are requesting of her as a result.

Although she may be too busy rolling her eyes, tapping her foot, or shuffling her homework papers to reply, your daughter is probably listening carefully. She is registering your caring, your anxiety, and the thought processes underlying these feelings. Rest assured that regardless of her reaction—or lack thereof—your daughter has heard your message.

Step Nine: Keep an Argument from Becoming a Fight

The above preparations and strategies are designed to minimize your daughter's defensiveness and hostility, and maximize her receptiveness to hearing your message and resolving your conflict. Regardless of how perfectly you follow these suggestions, however, your daughter may still dislike what you are saying. To make you stop talking or to get you sidetracked, she may employ any number of tactics, such as interrupting ("But wait!"), nitpicking minor points ("I couldn't possibly have done that yesterday because I stayed after school!"), and going on the offensive ("You're the one who's been in a bad mood!"). Now what do you do? Here are some ideas that have been helpful to other mothers.

- **KNOW THE DIFFERENCE BETWEEN ARGUING AND FIGHTING.** There are several distinguishing characteristics: Arguing can be constructive; fighting is destructive. Arguing clears the air and allows you to go on; fighting fuels the flames of discord. By resolving conflicts, arguing makes relationships stronger; fighting serves mostly individual purposes of venting feelings or getting across one's own point of view. Arguments keep the central goal in focus; fighting is haphazard. In arguing, respect for the other is maintained; fighting ignores the perspective and feelings of the listener.
- **IGNORE AS MUCH AS POSSIBLE.** Don't get sidetracked by attempts to distract you from your essential points. In fact, keep your main point in focus and stick to it. For example, suppose you tell your daughter that she may not sleep at her friend's house when the friend's parents are away and the seventeen-year-old sister is in charge:

DAUGHTER: *You never trust me!*

NOT

MOTHER: *I do trust you. How can you say that? Didn't I let you go to basketball camp?*

BUT

MOTHER: *This is not about trust. I don't feel comfortable with you staying there when her parents aren't home.*

- **REPEAT YOUR BOTTOM LINE.** In emulation of the old "broken record," an effective strategy when confronting your daughter is to repeat your core message calmly and distinctly regardless of how provocatively she responds.

DAUGHTER: *You have no idea what it's like to be young!*

MOTHER: *Well, regardless, it is my job to keep you safe.*

DAUGHTER: *Everyone else's mother is so much cooler than you!*

MOTHER: *Perhaps, but it's my job to keep you safe.*

DAUGHTER: *You don't trust me!*

MOTHER: *I'll say it again. The bottom line is that it's simply my job to keep you safe.*

- **TAKE A BREAK.** If, after arguing a considerable amount of time, you and your daughter seem to be going in circles, suggest a brief cooling-off period. You each can catch your breath and clarify what is important to you. You will thereby interrupt an unproductive cycle and renew your discussion with a fresh outlook.
- **DRAW THE LINE.** It is neither necessary nor advisable to tolerate abusive behavior. If your daughter becomes rude, begins name-calling, or is otherwise inappropriate, you can always end the discussion. Refusing to collude in escalating the argument is crucial. If your daughter will not go to her room, as you request, it will be up to you to separate yourself. You might tell her you will not speak to her when she is being inappropriate and then walk away.
- **STAY IN CONTROL.** Drawing the line should go a long way in keeping a discussion from escalating into a fight. But no matter what, it is important to stay in control. Sometimes it takes all of a mother's willpower to refrain from lashing out, insulting, or retaliating. Above all, it is crucial to prevent an argument from becoming physical.

Step 10: Reward Your Efforts

When you put into practice any of these steps, you will feel good about yourself and the way you handled a situation with your daughter. As in learning all skills, there will be times you will use them with ease; other times you will be so frazzled, tired, or fed up you'll be unable to get yourself to do the "right" thing. It is good to anticipate and accept that this is likely to be the case. But now that you have some alternatives at your disposal, you are probably no longer feeling quite so stuck. And regardless of whether any one particular interaction goes well, you can feel good about the positive steps you are taking to improve your relationship with your daughter. You can take pride in becoming an even stronger role model for her. Take a deep breath, enjoy any moments of tranquillity, and revel in your accomplishments.

What to Avoid

If you really want to get your daughter to listen to you and resolve an issue, you might avoid the following behaviors, which mothers have found consistently undermine these goals.

• **ACCUSING HER.** Saying things like "You never do what I ask" or "You're the most self-centered person I know!" is not likely to elicit a positive response. In fact, what possible reaction can your daughter have other than to become defensive, withdraw, or retaliate?

• **CALLING HER NAMES.** Saying, "You're such a slob," or, "You look like a tramp in that sweater," is unlikely to encourage your daughter's cooperation or contrition. Can you imagine her saying, "Oh, I'm sorry, Mom. I'll try to correct this problem from now on"? Also, name-calling opens the door for your daughter to respond in kind, a good formula for escalating a conflict.

• **TELLING HER WHAT SHE'S THINKING OR FEELING.** Girls are especially resentful when mothers presume to know better than they what they are thinking and feeling even—in fact, especially!—if it is true. You will never know whether you're right if you tell your daughter rather than ask her. Saying, for example, "I know you're thinking how awful I am," or, "You must feel so betrayed by your friend," is a sure way to invite your daughter's wrath.

• **EXAGGERATING.** Even if you realize you are using poetic hyperbole, your daughter may not. In the heat of the moment she may take everything you say literally. So if you say, "This is the worst thing you've ever done," or, "I don't know how I can ever forgive you," she is liable to draw conclusions that you would wish she hadn't.

Auto Communication

Considering the amount of time mothers spend taxiing daughters to school, activities, and social occasions, these golden opportunities for communication should not be overlooked. Car rides (along with bus and train rides) offer chances for powerful, intimate exchanges. Being alone with your daughter is probably a rare and precious occasion. Privacy from other people and lack of interruption by doorbells (and, until recently, phone calls) guarantees undivided attention. There is also something disarming about driving longer distances. While mothers are intent on the road, eye contact is kept to a minimum, freeing girls up to say or ask things they might not otherwise. Perhaps as girls are lulled by motion into a more relaxed state, defenses soften and confidences are inspired.

The flip side, however, is the possibility for some of the most intense, volatile interactions. While mothers may relish having captive audiences, teens can feel uncomfortably trapped. It is therefore important to keep conversations pleasant and teenagers relaxed. When they have felt overwhelmingly "attacked" by long-winded lectures or relentlessly interrogated, girls have frantically tried to open doors to free themselves from moving cars. So use this time judiciously. Cultivate these car trips as special, one-on-one opportunities. Ask as few questions as you possibly can. Do your best listening, and encourage your daughter's confidences with short responses (e.g., "Oh?" "Really?" "Hmm"). Many mothers have been rewarded with unanticipated questions and unimagined information. Buckle your seat belt!

Chapter Nine

Handling Her Outbursts

One of the more comforting aspects of your work thus far—identifying your strengths and less desirable patterns, choosing your battles, and refining your communication skills—is that you've been in the driver's seat. With some reflection, determination, and practice, you've probably on occasion (though not always, of course) noted some indisputable improvements in your interactions with your daughter. Perhaps she actually listened to what you had to say without interrupting you, running off to her room, or coming back at you with an insulting remark. Probably this has allowed you to feel more in control, more effective. Your confidence in being better able to get your point across without causing a major blowup has likely reduced your anxiety about approaching your daughter on important issues.

But as all mothers know, it's not always possible to plan such "discussions." In fact, you may find yourself drawn into arguments when you least expect them. Your daughter may surprise you with an outburst, confronting you with a litany of complaints about what you allegedly did—or didn't do. When she tells you at peak decibel level, for example, that you're the meanest, most hypocritical or insensitive mother to walk the earth, you may find yourself dazed and shocked.

Even if you can admit that her accusations may be partially well founded, the manner in which she blasts them out in machine-gun succession inhibits you from getting a word in edgewise. Just when you think it can't get worse, she drops the bomb: "I *hate* you!" Hates you? Who does she think she is? Who raised this ungrateful child?

The most competent of mothers confesses to being overwhelmed and intimidated at times by her daughter's extreme expressions of hostility. Although you know you'll both survive such attacks, you would much prefer to sit peacefully in a room together, discussing your points of contention and treating each other with civility and decency. Of course.

Although you may understand her frustration, sadness, or pain, you undoubtedly resent it when your daughter unleashes her emotions at you explosively and unfairly. Who wouldn't? Similarly, despite your strong commitment to her developing expertise in acknowledging and expressing strong negative feelings, you'd be delighted if she would practice those skills on someone else for a change. Sure, you want her to trust in what she is feeling and be able to speak her mind. You don't want her either to withdraw from you or to ignore her own reactions. It's just that you'd prefer not to be the target of such outbursts. In fact, to avoid these incidents, you may feel you are walking on eggshells every time you see her.

Realistically, it is unlikely you will completely avoid becoming a target for your adolescent's wrath. Moreover, regardless of whether your daughter's hostility is legitimately directed toward you, how you respond has an enormous impact on her development: her tolerance for negative emotions, her capacity to express them, her sense of having an effect on others, and her ability to enter into and maintain close relationships. Remember that your relationship is a prototype for others in her future; as she confronts you, she learns most from observing what you say and what you do.

HOW TO RESPOND

Even if you accept that it is not only normal but healthy for your daughter to confront you on occasion, the explosive or otherwise inappropriate manner in which she does so can leave you reeling, unable to think clearly or to mount a constructive response. This is one situation you'll want to be prepared for when it arises. Mothers often describe all sorts of thoughts and feelings swirling through their minds when they are caught in their daughters' outbursts. You might have wondered what types of limits you should set and how to know when behavior is "normal" versus out of control. Others describe with dismay their own equally destructive knee-jerk responses in these situations. Are there strategies to help you manage your daughter's wrath better? Absolutely.

High on your list of priorities might be responses aimed at containing rather than inflaming her emotions. Your goal is not to defend yourself in hopes of proving she's wrong or to make her feel guilty for expressing her feelings. Your goal is to defuse the situation so that she can gain self-control, limit destructive behavior, and discuss the matter with you more effectively at a later time.

The first step is to recognize the event for what it is: a release of her tension. Even before you determine whether her outburst is about you or something else entirely, it is helpful to say to yourself, "No matter what she says, I will not respond immediately." You can choose to listen or not, but you don't have to answer her right away. This will allow you to achieve the emotional distance needed to think rationally and react appropriately. You might also be more inclined to see your daughter's viewpoint if you were not automatically taking her accusations personally. At the very least, buying time can stop you from responding impulsively and unproductively. As a start, consider avoiding these less than desirable responses, which only serve to escalate conflicts:

DAUGHTER: *You're the worst mother, and you're ruining my life!*

MOTHER: *What are you talking about? You've lost your mind!*

OR

MOTHER: *If you think you can talk to me like that, guess again. I'm not taking you to your friend's house!*

OR

MOTHER: *You have no right to yell at me. You're not going out on weekends for a month!*

Once you decide not to respond in a defensive or inflammatory manner, you have other choices. If you are so inclined, you can listen to your daughter vent (rant and rave). Some mothers are able to do this and even believe it is necessary for their daughters to get tensions and frustrations "out of their systems." They listen without interrupting, even if their daughters are unrelentingly accusatory or they have no idea what their daughters are talking about, in hopes that the girls will feel better. When their daughters are finished, mothers expect that a conversation will be possible.

This strategy is not for everyone. Some mothers believe their daughters' embarrassment and shame at their lack of control are not worth the release of tension. Research confirms other mothers' experiences that girls only get more worked up by "rehearsing" what made them angry in the first place. More important, perhaps, when mothers ignore or at least give the impression they are unaffected by their daughters' accusations or vindictiveness, some girls may get the message that mothers willingly serve as their whipping posts. Ask yourself if this is the role you want your daughter to play in her relationships. Would you want your future granddaughter to behave this way toward your daughter?

If you do feel comfortable letting her vent, set clear limits on what you are willing to tolerate. The first time she crosses a boundary of what you consider acceptable, break into her monologue (a simple "hey" or hand gesture conveying "stop" should do it). This will give her a cue that she needs to rein herself in. Letting your daughter behave abusively is in neither her best interest nor yours. Allowing yourself to be victimized only gives her the message that this is what women do. Plus, your seething resentment will seep out, interfering with your empathy, support, and overall ability to parent her effectively. If she goes too far, it is perfectly acceptable to tell your daughter what she needs to do differently to continue the discussion. Above all, resist getting embroiled in further conversation. If she persists, you can firmly and repeatedly restate your position. Consider these options:

DAUGHTER: *I had the worst day, and it's all your fault. You've always been mean, but now you're a bitch. I hate you!*

MOTHER: *I can see that you're upset, but I won't listen to you unless you find a more respectful way to talk to me.*

DAUGHTER: *Why? I'm just telling the truth. You're acting like a bitch.*

MOTHER: *I will not listen to you curse at me. If you want to discuss this, you'll have to stop attacking me.*

DAUGHTER: *You think you're so great, that you know everything, but—*

MOTHER: *I'll talk to you when you stop yelling and get yourself under control.*

When daughters still do not cease their attacks, mothers are forced to put a stop to them. Sending her to her room may or may not work. Even if she complies, it is likely she will continue her barrage along the way. A more immediate and effective tactic may be simply to walk away from her. If she follows you into your bedroom or bathroom, try closing the door (gently, of course).

These are some guidelines for responding to your daughter's wrath. For many mothers, however, knowing the "right" words to say doesn't automatically make it easier when their daughters explode at them. It's still unnerving, off-putting, and even infuriating. Words that seem all fine and good in the abstract may in the heat of the moment seem absurd. Or in the throes of emotion, all thought may simply evaporate from your mind. Most likely, after the fact you'll think of precisely what you *could* have said. All these experiences are the norm. With time, practice, and loads of patience, you will eventually change the way you interact during your daughter's outbursts.

In the following scenarios you will take a closer look at some of the behaviors that most frustrate mothers, as well as the push buttons that frequently set off their daughters. Strategies based on the general steps above will be described in more detail. As you learn what you can do when you find yourself being screamed at, blamed, and accused by your daughter, remember that you might feel comfortable starting with only one or a few of these suggestions.

WHEN HER ANGER HAS NOTHING TO DO WITH YOU

What's truly baffling and infuriating, mothers often say, is that their daughters' attacks often come out of nowhere and seemingly lack justification. It is hard to predict not only what is going to provoke their daughters' wrath but whether they will serve as unwilling targets. Whereas one day a teen girl may work through her bad mood by talking to friends, the next day she may yell at her mother for rolling her socks incorrectly.

Said Celia, mother of Lee: "At least with an enemy you know you're going to get attacked, and you can prepare for it. With a fifteen-year-old daughter, you never know if she's coming over to start an explosion or to plant a kiss on your cheek. I really resent feeling so on guard, and I'd like to know how to change things."

What makes your role as mother that much more challenging is that you somehow have to contain mounting resentment over being attacked while figuring out how to defuse the situation. If you're not careful, you'll end up only adding fuel to your daughter's fire. It takes supreme strength to stay cool and collected during these times, refusing to be abused, but at the same time making your daughter aware of your accessibility for further discussion. Below are situations that mothers say leave them most resentful when it comes to their daughters' outbursts, along with steps you might take to help defuse, rather than ignite, your daughter's anger:

She Explodes at You for No Good Reason

MOM: *Hi, what's going on?*

DAUGHTER: *What do you mean?*

MOM: *I mean, how are you? How was your day?*

DAUGHTER: *Why do you always have to know every little thing about my life?*

MOM: *What?*

DAUGHTER: *Leave me alone! You're always butting in!*

Whether or not they can describe their mood, girls often admit—after the fact, of course—that their explosion at Mom "felt kind of good." If you are finding that your daughter has taken to instigating fights with you lately, consciously or otherwise, and you know of no underlying reason, she may simply be releasing tension. In many cases these provocative episodes have less to do with you and more to do with the fact that she needs to get rid of pent-up, uncomfortable feelings she's been accumulating all day.

Think back to her world. Maybe she woke up with a "huge" pimple, missed the bus, did poorly on a pop quiz in English, or dropped her lunch tray in front of the whole cafeteria. All day her frustration mounted until she was ready to snap. Then the second she walked through the door, you did it again! Just what she was afraid you were going to do. You looked at her funny. Or didn't look at her at all. Or smiled weirdly. Without even trying, you provided the perfect reason for your daughter to release her feelings.

It would be ridiculous and dismissive to tell mothers not to take these attacks personally. What could feel more personal than being assailed by your own child? But there is something you can do. You can recognize the situation for what it is. This is your daughter venting her adolescent frustrations and hardships. Repeat to yourself, almost like a mantra, that this outburst has nothing to do with you. Vow that you will not get sucked into an argument by yelling back or even attempting to defend yourself against her accusations. At these moments your daughter is probably unable to have a rational discussion. You can tell her that you can see she's upset but that you will not be treated like this and that you'd be happy to talk to her when she is ready. To maximize the effectiveness of this strategy, you might try matter-of-factly leaving the room.

She Won't Even Admit She's in a Bad Mood

MOTHER: *That was unnecessary.*

DAUGHTER: *What?*

MOTHER: *Kicking the dog's dish across the floor.*

(DAUGHTER: mumbles halfhearted apology.)

MOTHER: *So do you want to talk about what's wrong?*

DAUGHTER: *Nothing's wrong. Why don't you get off my back?*

MOTHER: *Nothing?*

DAUGHTER: *No, I was fine until I came home.* (She slams door to food cabinet.) *How come you didn't buy any good snacks again?*

Although it may seem your daughter is playing mind games with you, it's probably the last thing on her mind. Teens simply aren't good (or even adequate) at defining, much less admitting, why they are moody, irritable, or belligerent. Your daughter may not even know what emotion she is feeling. She simply knows things are not going her way; she feels bad. It could even be that nothing specific caused her outburst; she's just experiencing a strong mood shift. It would be a rare teen indeed who could acknowledge that her outburst was provoked not by you but by ordinary frustration, disappointment, or sadness.

So when you ask your daughter, "Why are you in such a bad mood?" and she stares blankly, shrugs, or says, "No clue," she is probably being truthful, not trying to get your goat. Still, there is no harm done in your asking her about the problem. You are interested because you care about her, and she knows that deep inside (in spite of the disgusted look on her face). As you well know, continuing to question her will likely backfire, but as a last suggestion you can try this:

MOTHER: *You look and sound upset. If you change your mind, I'd be happy to listen anytime.*

Although it is exquisitely frustrating not to be able to get to the bottom of your daughter's distress, it is important not to overreact to her nonanswer. You can gently check in with her, but giving her space and time alone usually works better than demanding to know what is wrong. The best you can do is make sure she knows you are available and encourage her to think through on her own what may be bothering her.

She Insults You and Then Accuses You of Overreacting

DAUGHTER: *It's so unfair that I can't go out tonight!*

MOTHER: *I told you. You cannot go out the night before a test.*

DAUGHTER: *You're so mean! I hate your guts!*

(Hours later)

DAUGHTER: *Mom, what's for dinner?*

MOTHER: *There's sandwich meat in the fridge.*

DAUGHTER: *You're not making me stuffed shells? You said you would.*

MOTHER: *You expected me to spend hours preparing your favorite dinner? You just told me that you hated me.*

DAUGHTER: *God, you know I didn't mean it. I hate it when you overreact.*

This most common of situations really irritates mothers. After provoking you to absolute fury, your daughter professes that she has no idea why you are so enraged. She didn't do anything wrong; she only said thus and such. Despite her real or feigned innocence, you know your daughter knows exactly what to say, and which tone to use, to push your buttons.

As difficult as this is to believe, her surprise at your hurt feelings does not mean she has taken a temporary break from reality. Your teen's mood is changing by the moment; what was bothering her earlier is apparently the barest of memories, much less a concern, at the present. She is on to other matters. Sure, the insult she hurled at you was meant to sting, but only temporarily. Moreover, since her anger fully dissolved, she expects the same from you ("If I'm not mad, why should you be?"). This kind of exasperating self-centeredness, for better or worse, is simply part of being a teen.

When your daughter asks what you're planning for dinner as if nothing had happened, take a deep breath, and explain in your most neutral tone that what she said earlier—be very specific—hurt your feelings. Even if she "didn't mean it" or the statement was "nothing" to her, it still felt awful and wasn't "nothing" to you. Eventually your daughter will come to understand the obligation of taking responsibility for her own actions. She doesn't get to dismiss the hurt feelings she caused just because she herself is no longer angry. She needs to learn that the hurt lingers for the other person.

WHEN IT *IS* SOMETHING YOU DID . . .

In the situations above, mothers can at least console themselves with the fact that they were in no way responsible for their daughters' outbursts. While it is terrible to be used as a target for any reason, it softens the blow at least a little when mothers can tell themselves that they truly haven't done anything wrong. Then their goals are refusing to engage and getting some distance while their daughters control themselves.

But sometimes daughters have valid reasons for confronting mothers with what made them angry. Although you might object to how she's expressing her feelings, you can no longer discount what your daughter is saying. Because the truth is, you have acted in some way she found objectionable, and now, at least in some way, you're accountable.

When you hear some truth in your daughter's accusations, you do have an obligation to listen more carefully, even if it's partial truth. That doesn't mean you have to tolerate abusive expressions of anger. But it's no longer okay to tell her to come back at some later point, without first acknowledging that you understand she has a legitimate gripe. As she's screaming at you because you humiliated her in front of her boyfriend or went through her private journal, you're not going to get away with a "Come back when you can speak without yelling." Such a response would feel dismissive of her understandable reactions to whatever you did and probably incite her further. Instead, you might acknowledge your responsibility while emphasizing your right to be treated decently.

> DAUGHTER: *You had absolutely no right to do that to me. You tell me not to do that all the time, but then you can do it? You're a liar—and a hypocrite!*

> NOT

> MOTHER: *Just one second there, young lady, who do you think you are?*

> BUT

> MOTHER: *I definitely want to discuss what happened when you're ready to talk without screaming at me. I'll be downstairs.*

> OR

> MOTHER: *You're absolutely right. I'll apologize as soon as you can talk without calling me names. Please come and get me.*

> OR

> MOTHER: *Yes, I blew it. But I still will not have you treat me disrespectfully. Let's both cool off, and we'll talk this over in a few minutes.*

What kinds of things can you do that are so terrible anyway? As acknowledged throughout this book, teen girls can come up with a thousand and one reasons to be angry at their mothers in any given week. But what makes daughters angriest at their mothers, and most likely to lash out against them, are several specific issues. Below are descriptions of these issues, clarifications of why they so infuriate girls, and suggestions for what mothers can do to handle them.

Understanding these teen perspectives may help you empathize with your daughter's underlying feelings, especially when she lashes out uncontrollably.

Having No Sympathy When Things Are Unfair

"It's not fair!" You've probably heard these exact words from your daughter's lips countless times, right along with its companion, "You're being so mean!" These ubiquitous statements of outrage can address everything from divine circumstances ("Why didn't you make me the oldest child?") to specific crimes ("You had no right to laugh at me!"). How you handle an accusation of course depends upon the veracity and seriousness of the complaint. When daughters are furious about their birth order or other circumstances beyond anyone's control ("Why do we have to live here?" or "Why can't you work for a fashion designer like so-and-so's mother?"), you might feel frustrated. Fair or unfair, you could well be thinking, "That's just the way things are."

When your daughter spews out these frustrations, you find yourself defending your actions ("We have to live here because this is where my job is, and I have to support a family!") or throwing such quips at her as "Who said life was fair?" or "You'd better get used to things' being unfair." After the fact, of course, you realize these retorts are hardly helpful. Your daughter is not interested in hearing you make a brilliant argument for your case, nor does she need further reminders that life can be unfair. What she needs from you is much simpler, really, and in many ways easier to give: It's sympathy. You don't have to be philosophical or come up with a clever reply. All your daughter wants to hear is "Yes, that's unfair, and I understand you're upset." In other words, she would like you to acknowledge and validate her feelings.

Here is an example of how it can work. Jenna, fourteen, was self-conscious about the dark facial hair on her upper lip and had made it her goal to keep her head down as much as possible so no one would notice it. When a boy on the school bus taunted Jenna about her "mustache" in front of all the other kids, she could barely contain her tears. When she got home and her mother asked her what was wrong, she immediately began to cry and yelled, "This!" pointing to her upper lip. "It's so unfair. I got this ugly hair from you! It's all your fault!"

Clearly, Jenna's mother's first impulse may have been to defend herself by saying it wasn't her fault or asking Jenna why she was letting one foolish bully upset her. But she didn't challenge her daughter in any way. Instead, Jenna's mother asked her to tell more about what happened, she empathized with her daughter's embarrassment and fury, and she even suggested a couple of practical solutions, such as bleaching her facial hair. Jenna was not only grateful that there was a solution (there won't always be one) but relieved that her mother was sympathetic to her ordeal. Her mother had taken the episode, as well as her reaction, seriously.

Statements mentioning the issue of fairness frequently include references to sibling competition. Many, if not most, children are extraordinarily sensitive to the possibility of uneven distribution of family resources: money, material possessions, and, especially, parental love ("She sat in the front last time" and "He always gets to lick the cookie batter first"). The best tactic is to avoid becoming embroiled in such rivalry. Instead, from the outset you might take the approach that goodies are almost never distributed equally. At various times your daughter might get something she wants; at other times her sibling(s) will.

Similarly, when issues of injustice arise within the mother-daughter relationship, it is wise to pay keen attention. Is your daughter feeling that you crossed a boundary of propriety? Betrayed her confidence? Intruded upon her privacy? Acted hypocritically? These are the accusations that can make mothers uneasy. Your daughter is viewing your character as if under a microscope, your flaws magnified and scrutinized. A part of you thinks, "How dare she!" while another asks, "Is she right?" Talking it through with her is usually the best reaction. Even if she is blowing things out of proportion, you can still acknowledge her legitimate feelings.

DAUGHTER: *Why won't you let me do anything? Do you always have to treat me like a baby? It's so unfair that you're so overprotective!*

NOT

MOTHER: *What are you talking about? There's no reason to get hysterical.*

BUT

MOTHER: *I know how frustrating it is not to be able to do what you want. I'm interesting in hearing how you feel I am overprotecting you.*

Listening carefully and patiently without losing your self-control is a wonderful skill to model for your daughter. This, rather than a panacea, may be all she is looking for.

Not Keeping Your Promise

"But you promised" are three words mothers are almost guaranteed to hear over and again. A cousin to fairness, being disappointed often makes girls enraged at their mothers. This is true even if you did not in fact promise anything. Somehow an idea merely mentioned becomes carved in stone in teenagers' minds. If plans happen to change, your daughter concludes that you have intentionally lied to her. Again, what you have failed to deliver could be inconsequential (e.g., you mentioned going for ice cream but later couldn't) or monumental (e.g., you had no intention of remarrying but changed your mind). In some way your daughter feels let down or mistreated. Her expectations were not realized. In addition, her outrage may be based in part on the fact that the contended issue is beyond her control. She is angry about having to depend on you when she would rather feel autonomous. She would prefer to take control rather than to leave decisions up to you and run the risk of disappointment.

If her disappointment is unavoidable or simply part of everyday experience, your daughter will have to learn to cope with these feelings. While you cannot make everything "better," you can identify for her (if she cannot do it for herself) that she feels disappointed and possibly angry.

> DAUGHTER: *You lied to me! You said you'd take Kerry, Deena, and me to the movies, and then you didn't. Now I can't trust you!*

> NOT

> MOTHER: *How dare you call me a liar! Now I'll never take you to the movies!*

> BUT

> MOTHER: *I don't blame you for being upset. I'm sorry that it didn't work out this weekend and I had to disappoint you.*

Your daughter will therefore learn that you understand her feelings and can validate them even if you cannot change the situation. When she gets some perspective, you will be able to address the difference between hoping to take her somewhere and promising to do so as well as the difference between disappointing and lying. It is crucial at this stage to be most reliable and honorable. If you take seriously the promises and commitments you make to your daughter, she will benefit immeasurably and probably recall this in her adulthood as well.

Taking Advantage of Her

There are situations in which teenage girls realize and become resistant to unhealthy patterns within your relationship. Maybe she simply feels dumped on ("It's not fair to scream at me every time you have a bad day at work!") or physically overburdened ("I spend my whole weekend taking care of the animals!"). Or it may be a matter of your daughter's giving too much within your relationship. For example, is she investing too much time and emotional energy making you happy? Are there circumstances in your lives that encourage your daughter to take care of you?

When there are stresses, such as serious illness, divorce, and trauma, girls often feel they have to protect mothers, cover for them, or compensate for earlier suffering or hardships. Examples include daughters of alcoholics and Holocaust survivors, who often strongly articulate these sentiments. When daughters effect a role reversal, when they take care of their mothers' needs more than their own, or when they walk on eggshells to avoid upsetting mothers, girls may be giving too much in the relationship. Their own needs go unmet because they deny them or feel unjustified in asking for what they need.

In some cases girls ultimately rebel, expressing rage that knows no bounds. After many years of struggling silently with her mother's drinking, Gwen, seventeen, said this about leaving home: "I've had it with my mother's moods. What does she think, I don't know what she's doing every afternoon? Why else would she 'take a nap' every day while I take care of my half sisters? It's sick that that bitch drinks herself into oblivion and I have to do her dirty work. I'm out of there."

It is hard to hear the kernel of truth in your daughter's complaints without reacting furiously to the way she is articulating them. Although you won't always be successful, you might make up your mind to try a different way of responding the next time such a situation arises. If she tells you that you are always grouchy, for example, resist jumping to the defensive. Instead, you might ask her to explain why she feels the way she does, and really listen to her reasoning.

> DAUGHTER: *You know, Mom, I really hate when you pick fights with me just because you and Dad had a fight.*

> NOT

> MOTHER: *What are you talking about? You're way out of line and absolutely wrong.*

> BUT

> MOTHER: *Is that how you feel? Can you give me an example of how you've gotten that idea?*

A few things will happen. One, your daughter will know that you take her feelings seriously. Two, she will get to practice expressing herself effectively. Three, you might learn something about what you are contributing to the relationship. Somewhat to your dismay, your teenage girl can be an astute observer about *your* behavior.

Not Allowing Her to Be Herself

Eager to retain their mothers' love, girls may struggle desperately to please their mothers. They may fulfill mothers' wishes (spoken or not) that they do certain things or be certain people. Girls may pursue hobbies (competitive swimming, cooking) or goals (a specific college, class president) because they believe their mothers want them to do so. More subtle expressions of this dynamic occur when girls believe mothers desire specific personality characteristics or traits more than others. Girls report with conviction that their mothers want them to be docile or hardworking or unemotional or aggressive. All is well, unless these qualities happen to conflict with girls' inborn tendencies, with who they really believe they are. When there is a poor fit between mothers' and daughters' personality styles and goals, some girls give up too much of themselves to keep their mothers' approval and love. At some point estrangement from themselves or resentment toward mothers may build.

Deedee, sixteen, expressed some of these feelings. "I am not the little perfect girl my mother expects me to be," she said. "I like to run around and play sports with the guys. But my mother is always trying to buy me dresses and get me girly haircuts. She can't stand that I'm different from other girls." Deedee added she hadn't talked about this issue with her mother because "She'll just get mad and tell me how unfeminine I am. It's easier if I just wear what she wants me to, and whenever she's not there, I put on what I want to so I can be myself."

Many girls are exactly like Deedee in that they would rather dress the part and play the role expected by their mothers than risk facing their disapproval. Some are not as self-aware. Instead of learning to define who they really are, these girls learn to play parts that make others happy. Unfortunately many never get to see the benefits of standing up for themselves and being comfortable in the mother-daughter relationship. Worse yet, this dynamic of being as they imagine others would like them, rather than being themselves, tends to spill into other serious relationships (i.e., friendships and marriages).

You will know that your daughter recognizes this bind when she screams at you, "I can't do it! I can't be you!" or, "That's how you would do it, but I'm not you!" Even if you think she is making no sense at all (you don't expect her to be like you), you need to be aware that she feels this way. Maybe you are inadvertently giving her strong messages about your expectations for her. Maybe she is simply misinterpreting what you are saying.

> DAUGHTER: *I'm sick of competing. I'm never going to be the gold medalist you'd like!*

> NOT

> MOTHER: *Don't blame this on me. You're just quitting because you can't take the pressure.*

> BUT

> MOTHER: *I didn't realize how tired you are and how much this is upsetting you. Let's talk about how much of this you're doing for me and what you want to do.*

By addressing your daughter's core message, you make it clear to her that you care about what she's thinking and feeling. She understands that you would like her to be her own person and that you will encourage her in this. Ultimately she needs to be convinced that you are proud of who she is, despite different traits or preferences, and confident in how she's growing up. If there is some truth to what she is saying, it also gives you the opportunity to clarify your concerns.

Not Trying to Understand Her

Your daughter may be angry because she is not getting something she wants. It could be something concrete, such as different privileges (a later bedtime or curfew), or something less tangible but more consequential, such as more attention, support, or respect. Because she is not getting what she wants, your daughter may accuse you of not understanding her. If you did, her thinking goes, you would do exactly as she says. This is where mothering gets challenging. The critical questions are: Are you listening to her, and are you showing respect? Of course, listening isn't merely hearing her words but truly appreciating her feelings and motivations. Are you being empathic? Are you treating her with the regard you would give a friend?

For Bessie, thirteen, this desperation to be heard was at the heart of her lack of self-control and feelings of shame. She and her mother had a long history of terrible arguments, some of which escalated into physical battles. In therapy Bessie explored the consequences of her "blowups." As she put it, "Yeah, I get grounded, but at least my mother stops her lecturing long enough to listen to me. I think when I start screaming or cursing at her, it sort of shocks her into being quiet." Although it caused distress and resulted in further problems, Bessie's explosive behavior served its purpose within the relationship.

If you believe that your daughter is feeling heard and understood but simply wants to get her way, then you will react to her accordingly. Regardless of whether you grant her wishes, you will still be validating her right to ask assertively for what she wants. If you decide, instead, that perhaps your daughter is valid in asking for more respect or understanding, this is a crucial discovery. Your apologetic response and attempts to correct your behavior will speak volumes to her about how important she is to you.

> DAUGHTER: *You're so clueless! Every other mother understands how important this party is!*
>
> NOT
>
> MOTHER: *I am not clueless. I know exactly what you're doing, but I wasn't born yesterday. You're not getting away with this!*

BUT

MOTHER: *I know you want to go so badly because all your old friends will be there, but I can't allow a coed sleepover. Can we come up with a compromise?*

OR

MOTHER: *Okay, so what is it you feel I don't understand? Please tell me about it.*

These responses will show your daughter that you do care what a big deal the event is to her. You want to understand her viewpoint. Yes, she is likely to continue sulking and feeling frustrated; after all, she is not getting her own way. But at least she may better appreciate that you seriously considered her feelings and empathized with her. Asking for her input, whether it be suggestions for a compromise or an explanation of her disappointment, will further demonstrate that you respect her. The bonus is that she will get practice in successfully articulating her needs and wishes, which will benefit her greatly in all her relationships.

THE GRAY AREA

Sometimes, as you know, things aren't black and white. In the above examples the hostility daughters felt toward their mothers was elicited by altogether unrelated issues or by very specific complaints about their mothers' behavior. At times, however, this distinction is not so clear-cut. For example, disagreements over seemingly trivial matters often lead to major altercations. When you begin debating the relative merits of skim versus 1 percent milk and end up screaming about lack of freedom and privacy, you wonder what is going on. Only later does the "real" issue surface. What your daughter is truly upset about comes out in the end. But is this for real? Or is her ultimate issue merely an excuse or justification for her outburst?

Similarly, you may feel she is justified in being irritated by something you did or didn't do, but she is overreacting. Yes, she might be annoyed that you scheduled a dental cleaning for her. But the ferocity of her response makes you wonder if she is perhaps more perturbed by her lack of plans for Friday night or the fact that her best friend just got asked out on a first date. It may be difficult to pinpoint the relative importance of your daughter's complaint.

This is when you, her mother, the responsible adult, have to use your judgment. Do you allow the possibility that she has a valid point? If your soul-searching suggests your daughter is right, what will you do about it? Sometimes your daughter will be crystal clear: It's you! You are the one who is making her miserable—ruining her life, to be exact. How you react will depend on many things, particularly your openness to her having strong, negative feelings and the manner in which she expresses them. It is crucial, however, to distinguish the content of her message from her manner of delivering it. You may not like how she says it, but she may still be right. It is important you deal with each aspect separately. For example, it is one thing to admonish her for yelling or swearing at you, but another to discount the message she was trying to convey.

Now you have some additional tools to use when you find yourself the target of your daughter's anger. Some responses may feel artificial at first, as if you were reading lines from a script. You may find that others don't work for you at all. But at least you may feel better knowing that you have some choices in how you respond to your daughter. Having a repertoire of things to say and do may make you more confident that you can keep your daughter from being abusive and resist lashing back at her. You have thereby encouraged her to express herself appropriately and kept open the possibility of resolving your differences. Above all, you and your daughter stayed connected in the face of anger.

Behind the Closed Bedroom Door

WHAT YOUR DAUGHTER IS REALLY TRYING TO TELL YOU WHEN SHE SHUTS YOU OUT OF HER ROOM. At some time or other it would be safe to say that all mothers experience the sudden cold, hard reality of a slammed door between them and their daughters. As one woman put it, "It feels like a slap in the face." As always, your strategy will depend on your analysis of the situation: your daughter, her typical reactions, and what this behavior means. Here are some of the messages underlying girls' closed doors.

"I'M GROWING UP!" At the very least your daughter's closed door is a symbol of her need to feel autonomous. She is in charge of her door. There is a heady power in her opening and closing it at her will. As the door closes, she is establishing a physical barrier between you that reflects her need to feel emotionally separate from you. It helps her feel less childlike when she keeps a part of her life private from you. It is in fact this act of doing something you're not aware of, or sharing a secret with a friend rather than with you, that makes her feel more mature. Her room has become a sanctuary, its door her savior.

"I NEED AN ESCAPE!" Girls also seek out their bedrooms to avoid the occasional tumult or fracas of family life. When siblings bicker, pets escape, televisions blare, or parents argue, teenage girls can feel overwhelmed. Their closed doors are much-needed guarantees of respite from chaos. They simply need their own space. You can respect your daughter's ability to get her needs met, to soothe herself, and to make herself more comfortable, in a relatively harmless fashion.

"I CAN'T DISCUSS THIS ANYMORE RIGHT NOW!" When, in the middle of an argument, your daughter suddenly disappears into her room, it may be that she is seeking a self-imposed time-out. Perhaps she felt a surge of emotion that made her feel uneasy, or she struggled to contain an expletive teetering on the edge of her tongue. She sensed she was losing control. Fleeing to her room and putting a closed door between the two of you may have presented the ultimate safety net. Her door was a physical substitute for the self-control she could not yet muster. Again, her avoidance of more unpleasant scenarios should be congratulated. When she regroups and reemerges, you two can finish your discussion.

"I'M FEELING DESTRUCTIVE RIGHT NOW!" Some girls are so uncomfortable with their anger, so fearful that they will destroy someone with their rage that they routinely barricade themselves behind closed doors as soon as they are cognizant of this emotion. Each time your daughter senses the possibility of unpleasant words, the threat of a harsh exchange, or evidence of a brewing conflict, she may hibernate. She may need to gather her thoughts and clarify her feelings before she can express them. Alternately, her slamming her door may be a direct communication that she is clearly angry. Again, she is also saying she is uncomfortable with more verbal expressions of hostility. As long as your daughter is able to discuss the issues in time, there is little harm in her brief retreat.

"I'M WORRIED OR UPSET ABOUT SOMETHING!" When girls uncharacteristically flee to their rooms and close the doors behind them, they are communicating that something out of the ordinary made them upset. If, say, your daughter returns from school or a friend's house in tears and secludes herself, you will want to speak with her immediately. If she refuses to have a discussion with you at that point but seems not to be in danger, you can give her the time or privacy she needs. But an unprecedented slammed door can only be interpreted as a distress signal that should not be ignored.

"I NEED HELP!" It is the rare situation in which girls may actually be in danger in their bedrooms. If your daughter is severely depressed, possibly suicidal, or prone to self-mutilation, you must gain entry immediately. Similarly, if she is so upset, distraught, frustrated, or impulsive that she may inadvertently harm herself, you must assure her safety. When girls take potentially self-injurious items (e.g., a kitchen knife, a grandparent's heart medicine, etc.) to their bedrooms, they are pleading for parents to intervene. As discussed in Chapter 5, this is one of the red flags for seeking immediate professional help.

In responding to the silent communication of a closed door, you can usually assure yourself that your daughter is safe while respecting her privacy. Just knock on her door, and without opening it (unless she invites you in), ask if she is okay and wishes to talk. It is good to establish some norms around this behavior. Do you have a household policy about locking bedroom doors: when and if this is permitted and under what circumstances? Most important, unless there is a potential emergency, always, always, always show your daughter the respect of knocking before entering her room.

Chapter Ten

Staying the Course

There are many times when your interactions with your daughter will not go as planned. Sometimes you will be blindsided by her precipitous outbursts, as discussed in the previous chapter. Occasionally, if not often, you may be troubled by the fact that you were unable to resolve a conflict with her truly or completely. Or you may be disappointed that despite your best efforts, confronting your daughter failed to accomplish what you wanted, such as altering her attitude or behavior in the manner you suggested. For example, instead of her acknowledging your point, apologizing, and changing her ways, as you wished, perhaps she minimized or dismissed your concerns or reacted with bristling hostility and defensiveness. Or maybe she listened, seemed to absorb most of what you said, and even agreed to make the necessary changes. You were relieved and hopeful that peace would finally be restored. Except, instead, your daughter failed to follow through ("She's doing it again!"), deteriorated further ("Now she's even angrier and slamming everything in sight!"), or inflicted retaliatory punishment on you ("It's taken me all afternoon to get her to speak to me").

Whatever your daughter's particular behavior, it surely wasn't the positive reaction you had in mind. In fact, you may have even wondered what you accomplished by confronting her, other than having caused more problems. By withdrawing her affection or making you feel guilty, your daughter may have skillfully deflected your attention from her behavior to your own, thereby getting herself neatly off the hook. Besides feeling disappointed, you were probably frustrated and confused and possibly propelled into a fit of second-guessing: Could your approach have been wrong? Did you expect too much of your daughter? Were you "overreacting" or "making a mountain out of a molehill"? Perhaps you questioned whether it was even worth confronting your daughter in the future if the only outcome would be another round of skirmishes.

But instead of judging your efforts by how receptive and responsive your daughter was, it is important to focus instead on your increased self-awareness and constructive channeling of feelings. Once you are assured your approach was correct, it is incumbent upon you, as the responsible mother, to stay the course. It is crucial to resist getting sidetracked by your daughter's failure to respond as you desired or by her efforts at intimidation or emotional blackmail. It is important to withstand backsliding into a sea of self-doubt, and do whatever you must to accomplish the goals you set forth to raise her. This is the time when you must trust in yourself to know that you have done what is best for her and that you are continuing to do what is best for her (even if her immediate responses make you feel anything but sure of your actions). Staying strong not only conveys to her your commitment to her and to the relationship but provides a model for her to emulate throughout her own life.

How mothers are manipulated

Pam, mother of sixteen-year-old Julia, knows how frustrating it can be when daughters react in less than desirable ways to mothers' well-executed confrontations. As she explained, "Whenever Julia's friend Deb was over, she would treat me horribly. Julia would cut me down with sarcastic comments and act exceptionally bratty. I was anxious about talking to her about it, especially since she and Deb are soul mates and extremely protective of each other, but I finally did it, and furthermore, I told her I would no longer tolerate that behavior. It was a big step for me."

In fact, Pam did all the "right" things to address this injustice. She pinpointed exactly what upset her (the fact that Julia was callously hurting her feelings) and decided what she needed to do to set things right (ask Julia to treat her more courteously and respectfully). Pam considered carefully what she wanted to say and how she wanted to say it. She planned an ideal time to confront Julia (just before bedtime). "I even remembered to speak politely, using 'I' statements and not accusing her," Pam said. "I was thrilled when Julia apologized and said that she would make a conscious effort to change her behavior. We even talked a bit about the power Deb seems to have over her. Not a week later, though, she came home from being with Deb and started insulting me right away! I couldn't believe it. Clearly our conflict accomplished nothing. She had just yessed me to death and then acted as if we had never spoken at all."

Besides noncompliance, some mothers experience more immediate and blatant negative reactions from their daughters. Perhaps your daughter becomes defensive when confronted, saying that you "over-react to everything" or "just don't get it." Worse yet, she may blast you with hostile counterattacks that leave you stunned ("You're the worst mother!" or "You've been abusive ever since Grandma died" or "I'd rather live with Dad any day"). Perhaps the fallout from your conflicts typically includes days of smoldering resentment, cruel barbs, and high-wired tension. Any of these repercussions may have convinced you that your daughter's main mission in life is to make you both doubt and regret your decisions.

As a result of these disappointing reactions from your daughter, you, like Pam, may have questioned the wisdom of maintaining your posi-tion. As she put it, "Julia's behavior made me wonder if my point was really all that important. Maybe I could've survived without making a big issue out of Deb's influence on her. Besides, tomorrow it'll be something else. I feel like one of those big plastic dolls that keeps pop-ping right back up after someone knocks it down. I finally recover from a struggle about homework, and I think we're in a good place, and then—wham!—two days later we're into this thing about her atti-tude and—wham again!—she will tell me how many girls in her grade are getting tattoos or whatever the next thing will be. She doesn't let up! Sometimes I just want to give up and say, 'Go ahead. Do whatever you want. I don't care anymore.' "

Many mothers are tempted to accept daughters' undesirable be-havior or cave in to their unreasonable demands because things don't improve immediately after a confrontation (and sometimes, even worsen) or because their daughters' reactions seem too unpleasant, provocative, or threatening. If they are going to risk the discomfort of a confrontation, these mothers figure, tension should at least start to abate once they get their message across. Discussion finished, case closed. When daughters cause them to go over the same problems and issues again and again, mothers come to believe it may not be worth the energy required.

GIVE YOUR DAUGHTER TIME

Your desire to get closer to your daughter, or to stay connected, is only part of the compelling motivation to keep "bothering" to confront her with important issues and to resolve conflicts in your relationship. You also know that when it comes to children, some things take time. Remembering your daughter's early development will help you keep her present behavior in perspective.

Take the saga of getting the baby to sleep, an all-too-familiar hurdle and unforgettable time period for many mothers. Perhaps your growing baby girl continued to interrupt your sleep far longer than necessary. Night after night you made sure she wasn't hungry, wet, or hurting. Night after night you realized she merely wanted your company. At some point in your increasing sleep deprivation, you decided the situation was intolerable. So you consulted the experts (e.g., pediatrician, other mothers, the books) and developed a game plan. Maybe, for argument's sake, you decided to follow advice to pat your baby's back once and then let her cry.

You will probably never forget night one of this plan; your baby girl probably screamed for what seemed like hours. "How is this supposed to help?" you no doubt asked yourself as you lay tense and wide-awake long after your daughter had gone back to sleep. But although you got little or no sleep that first night, chances are you did the same thing the next night and the one after that. You had faith in your approach and confidence that it would ultimately succeed. You hadn't really expected success that first night, and you knew in your heart of hearts that the results would be gradual and cumulative. So when your daughter didn't fall back to sleep immediately, you weren't too discouraged. In fact, each night she probably cried half as long, until one morning you realized she hadn't awakened once until the morning. You also anticipated she might take a step backward occasionally, such as when she wasn't feeling good or was sleeping in unfamiliar surroundings. When it happened, you didn't let regression erode your confidence that you were on the right track.

Just because your daughter is older doesn't mean you can now expect her to make instant or lasting changes. As you well know, because she is still developing into the adult she will become, her ability to comply with your requests hinges on the unpredictable but inevitable day-to-day influences of her hormones, emotions, and daily experiences. Until she matures, she will not have reliable or complete control over what she says and does, despite her good intentions. Knowing all this, you continue doing what you believe is right, what is in your daughter's best interest anyway; you stay the course.

BEWARE OF SIDETRACKING ATTEMPTS

This is one of those cases in which being forewarned is being forearmed. It helps to be aware of teens' favorite tactics so that you can pinpoint exactly what your daughter does that shakes your confidence and undermines your resolve.

- **BADGERS.** Many teens try to get their way by annoying and pestering long after their mothers believe an issue has been resolved. But you know that part of being a good mother requires setting limits and sticking to them. If you give up and let her have her way, your daughter will come to view you as a pushover and anticipate directing your decision making in the future. Although you may gain short-term respite from conflict, you will lose your daughter's respect. More important, any headiness she might gain from holding power over you will be overshadowed by a loss of the security that comes from knowing you provide a firm and unwavering ballast during her adolescence.

- **QUESTIONS THE FACTS.** Sometimes girls insist that mothers reconsider previous decisions, claiming they either lacked information or "misunderstood" the situation. Such comments, which catch you off guard, provoke second-guessing. Your daughter is appealing wisely to your sense of reason when she baits you to respond to the "facts," even when they are irrelevant ("I've been so nice to you all month, why can't you show me some appreciation by letting me go to the party?") or when they are employed as creative loopholes in your argument ("I know her parents aren't going to be at the party, but what you don't realize is that her neighbors live about two feet away"). If you have already listened carefully to her arguments and made your final decision, you might have to say, "This case has been closed." In fact, unless she has a truly valid point, it is best not to consider reconsidering.

- **TAKES YOUR VIEWS TO EXTREMES.** Sometimes teenage girls successfully undermine their mothers' confidence by distorting or exaggerating their viewpoints until they seem ridiculous. For example, Pam reported the following conversation between Julia and her: "When I confronted her again about her bad behavior, she initially accused me of disliking Deb. It was partially true, I guess. But then she said things like 'You don't want me to have any friends. You want me to stay a little girl and hang out with you all the time. That's why you always criticize my friends.' Now I know that's not true, but I couldn't get it out of my head."

- **SENDS YOU ON A GUILT TRIP.** After a confrontation your daughter can pout, sulk, or otherwise evoke your guilt over making her miserable ("I can't help moping around the house; every single one of my friends is out doing something fun"), thereby sending you into a tailspin of self-doubt. You might ask yourself whether the conflict is worth seeing her so unhappy and whether your decision merits depriving her of some opportunity she desperately longs for. But it is wise to remember that this is exactly what your daughter wants you to be thinking so that you will renege on your limits. One of you has to be the parent, and for that she's counting on you.

- **BARGAINS.** Perhaps you assertively spoke your mind and informed your daughter of the consequences of her actions. Afterward, rather than accept her punishment, she tries to make a deal with you. She asks to trade her punishment for another so she doesn't miss a special event. Or she reminds you of some special favor she did that she believes more than compensates for the present misbehavior and asks that you nullify the punishment. Unless you're strong, you could find yourself going around and around about the relative importance of this versus that behavior. Before you know it, you're well into another conflict that seems to go nowhere. It's usually best to limit the debate that girls often initiate when you make a decision they find undesirable.

- **MAKES YOU SUFFER.** One of girls' most effective strategies in getting you to change your mind or relent on limits is to try in some way to make you suffer. Perhaps, as a result of your punishment, for example, your daughter is forbidden from using the telephone. When she brings home a zero for a particular homework assignment and you ask what happened, she nonchalantly states, "Well, I didn't know what I was supposed to do, and you wouldn't let me call anybody." In effect, she's saying, "So there!" or "Take that!" It's your fault that she failed. Her behavior is designed to make you regret yours.

STAND YOUR GROUND

Whether she employs the tactics above or others to get her needs met, it may be difficult for you to remain focused on your original point, to maintain your convictions, and to hold fast to your decisions. Imagine what happened after Brigid attempted to set a clear limit for her sixteen-year-old daughter, Toby. After reading Toby's report card, she was appalled by the teachers' nearly unanimous comments about Toby's sloppiness, indifference, and lack of effort. "Although her grades weren't terrible," Brigid said, "everybody knows that Toby could do much better. I'm very concerned about her attitude toward her schoolwork; she needs to take more responsibility." In an effort to convey how important this was to her, Brigid decided to withhold permission for Toby to get a learner's permit for her driver's license until she improved her school performance.

"It was a hard thing to do," Brigid admitted. "If she had been failing her classes, it would've been more straightforward. But I didn't want to condone her procrastination and sloppy, halfhearted efforts. The license seemed to be my only trump card, so I played it."

After confronting Toby with her reasoning, however, and especially after experiencing the fallout from her daughter's professed devastation, Brigid became less and less sure of her decision. For one, "Toby made my life miserable. She's barely looked at me, ignored me as much as possible, and generally made our days unpleasant. I thought she'd stop eventually, but she became hell-bent on making her fury known. She's good at it." Two, "Toby started getting rides with people she knows I'm not comfortable with. She was clearly trying to show me the fallacy of my decision." Three, "Toby took to twisting my words. She went around telling everyone in my earshot how I push her to be perfect. We both know this was not the issue; this was about responsibility and effort rather than straight As, but she made me out to be Mommie Dearest."

As can be imagined, Brigid's resolve was sorely tested by Toby's tactics. She described vacillating by the moment—from congratulating herself for standing her ground, on the one hand, to chastising herself for being too punitive and controlling, on the other hand. "I kept asking myself, 'Wherein lies the truth?'" Brigid said.

HOW TO STAY ON TRACK

As Brigid can attest, it isn't always easy to know when daughters actually have a valid point. Sometimes you will decide to reconsider. But for the most part you are wise to focus on staying the course. Developing the mind-set to do so is the first hurdle. The critical component seems to be how you decide whether your course of action is correct. If you rely on your daughter's reactions, your conviction in your efforts is more than likely to be undermined. This makes sense intuitively. Your daughter has a stake in getting you to see the situation her way. It is far better to trust your own perceptions and judgments.

Part of developing strong conflict resolution skills is maintaining sufficient self-confidence to stay on track regardless of the strategies your daughter employs to derail you. Although she may be ignoring you, attacking you, or acting as though you were certifiable, you must remain firm in your belief that what you are doing is correct. This will allow you to persist.

One thing that will make this easier is to get support from at least one person whose values and perspective you trust and who can act as a sounding board when you are faced with just these sorts of dilemmas. These are the times you need to rely on a spouse or friend for invaluable feedback. Many fathers can play an invaluable role in such situations. Because they are less frequently used as scapegoats by daughters and often remain outside mother-daughter conflict, they can offer more neutral opinions. Sometimes mothers may not want to hear such objectivity; you might prefer that your daughter's father felt as strongly as you did about the issue. But whether it is a spouse, an ex-spouse, or a friend from whom you ask feedback, you will learn the most if you are willing to risk your opinion's being questioned.

Brigid told of doing just this when Toby was pressuring her to give in to a driver's permit. "First I spoke to her father, who supported my decision but said he didn't think it would work. He felt Toby would have to learn her lesson from the consequences of having teachers think poorly of her. So then I spoke to my sister, who had had a similar issue with one of her children, who's now grown. Just hearing her laugh when I told her about Toby making me out to be Mommie Dearest made me feel better. She reassured me that our relationship wouldn't disintegrate, and that encouraged me to stand my ground."

In addition to learning from others' wisdom and experiences, you will often gain new insights just by telling the story and hearing your-

self speak. You may realize something only after you've said it aloud.
Verbalizing frequently allows you to view the situation from a new and
helpful angle. Each time you discuss a troubling adolescent situation,
whether it pertains to your daughter or another girl, you will usually
learn something valuable. Here are other specific strategies to help you
stay the course.

- **RESTATE YOUR FEELINGS.** When daughters reemerge after a confrontation, armed with counterattacks, defensiveness, or other sidetrack-
  ing techniques, it is important to refocus the discussion. Simply
  repeat your initial core statement. Let's take the example of Julia,
  who kept being "bratty" to her mother after spending time with her
  friend Deb:

  > JULIA: *All I said was that you've been kind of annoying lately.
  > You don't have to flip out. You have to admit you're pretty tense
  > about your job, and you overreacted.*

  NOT

  > PAM: *What do you mean I've been tense?*

  OR

  > PAM: *Have I really been out of line?*

  OR

  > PAM: *Has it been that obvious? I'm sorry if I've been irritable.*

  BUT

  > PAM: *I am upset and disappointed that you've not changed your
  > behavior despite knowing that it hurts me.*

  OR

  > PAM: *It hurts my feelings when you treat me disrespectfully,
  > Julia.*

  In these ways, Pam resists getting sidetracked into discussing her own
  behavior or defending herself. She remains focused on her goal by
  repeating her concerns about Julia's actions.

- **KNOW WHEN TO STOP RESTATING YOUR CASE.** You do not need to
  repeat your feelings and requests ad infinitum. If you believe your
  daughter understood what you said, despite her protests that "you just

don't understand," then you need to end the discussion. You will not be damaging her or your relationship if you say, "You know what? We're done with this topic." Here is how Brigid did just that with Toby:

> TOBY: *Why won't you listen to reason, Mom? You're wrong if you think that not letting me get my driver's license is going to make me want to study more. I'll just get madder and won't be able to concentrate. Why do you think your punishment is going to help?*

NOT

> BRIGID: *Because, in my opinion . . .*

BUT

> BRIGID: *You know, we've been through this before, and I know you don't agree, but that's my final decision.*

OR

> BRIGID: *Let's change the subject before we get into a fight that neither of us wants.*

OR

> BRIGID: *I think we both realize that we're not going to see eye to eye on this.*

In these ways Brigid is acknowledging that they must "agree to disagree" and not allowing herself to get sucked into yet another go-around with Toby about the merits of her decision. If Toby continues, this is what Brigid can say and do:

> TOBY: *But just tell me why you're doing this. It's so unfair!*
>
> BRIGID: *Let's not get into this again.*
>
> TOBY: *You're being so mean!* (Brigid exits.)

- **SELF-COACH.** When your daughter tries to convince you that what you said or did was wrong, remind yourself actively of the valid reasons for your feelings and your right to make decisions for her. Tell yourself to continue doing what you believe is right, much as a coach would encourage you to persevere in reaching your goal. Remind yourself that since you are the expert on your daughter, you are capable of working through this conflict with her. You can also cue yourself to stick to the path of effective communication, rather than stray into irrelevant territory.

- **TAKE RESPONSIBILITY WHEN IT IS APPROPRIATE.** The desperate need to feel good about themselves prohibits many teenage girls from acknowledging any and all imperfections. If your daughter is feeling "blamed for everything," she will be that much more resistant to accepting responsibility for her actions. Ironically, when you can acknowledge that the problem is not "all" her fault, you encourage her to claim the part that is hers. Even more effective, when you admit your own contribution to the situation, you give your daughter both permission and a viable model for taking responsibility herself. Getting back to Julia and Pam, this dialogue may have occurred:

> JULIA: *I think you're overreacting. You've been kind of tense about your job lately.*
>
> PAM: *Well, maybe you're right. It's been pretty hectic at work, and I may be touchy. I'll give that some more thought. But I'd like you to think about your part, Julia. We seem to have this conversation about your attitude and tone whenever you've been with Deb.*

In this way Pam acknowledges the part of Julia's statement that she believes to be true without becoming sidetracked or letting her daughter off the hook.

- **PRACTICE PATIENCE.** Realize that your daughter may merely need time to digest your words, consider your message, and attempt to apply your concepts to her behavior. That doesn't mean you have to tolerate mistreatment or disrespect. But it does require you to give her some time and space to process most effectively what you said. For instance, Brigid may need to give Toby more than one reminder or opportunity to change her ways. Julia may need to experience being with Deb repeatedly before she connects her behavior toward her mother with what Deb may be stirring up in her. Rather than punish her or continue to berate her, simply pointing out the continuation of her behavior may be helpful. Better yet, ask her if she has noticed the pattern. Give her the room to figure out how she can be different. In the meantime, practice all your strategies for being patient and maintaining your cool.

It is also critical to remind yourself—over and again, if necessary—of your particular goal in each situation. For example, if you wanted your daughter to change her behavior (e.g., to stop insisting on a daily basis that she's "too tired" to do her chores, to come in by curfew, to study for her midterms), it shouldn't matter whether she put up a fuss, whined, or retaliated in the process. The bottom line is, she did what you asked: She changed her behavior. So, when you evaluate the success of your conflict, it is crucial that you overlook the static and focus instead on the end result.

If, however, she failed to do what you insisted on her doing, remind yourself of the goal, ignore her distractions and rationalizations, and insist, "There is no discussion. This is nonnegotiable." This of course is what Brigid ended up demonstrating to Toby: "No matter how much or in what ways you protest, you are not getting your learner's permit until you show me you're more responsible."

At other times, however, the goal of intervening with your daughter might not be a specific behavioral change but rather a dialogue or discussion about a situation you find troubling. You cannot say for certain what you think should change, but you believe you and your daughter should discuss the subject together. This approach pretty much guarantees and even invites her to express her views, arguments, and rebuttals. Although you may know this in your head, when your daughter responds by challenging, questioning, and negotiating— saying anything except "Sure, Mom"—you still might have a negative visceral reaction. This is when it will be helpful to remind yourself of your ultimate goal.

SHED UNREALISTIC EXPECTATIONS

Similarly, you may sometimes need to do some soul-searching after the fact to figure out why you're disappointed; what had you *really* expected from confronting your daughter? Deep down maybe you were hoping that when you pointed out her error, she would say something on the order of "Oh, so that's what I'm doing wrong, okay!" or "You're so right, Mom. I'll fix that right away" or "Even though you're not letting me do what I want to do, I know you're just being a good mother." Although these responses sound silly, there is still probably a part of you that wouldn't mind hearing them and feels disappointed when you don't. Consider the following unrealistic expectations mothers often have about how teenagers will respond when confronted.

An Immediate Positive Response

Although this would be wonderful, no teen likes being told she is doing something "wrong" or displeasing her mother. It is only natural your daughter may need time to mull things over, even sleep on new information, before it sinks in. It may take her awhile to overcome her initial defensiveness or tendency to counterattack. So if you don't get an initial apology or remorseful look, don't lose hope or assume you failed.

A Complete Turnaround

When one speaks of such substantive issues as teenagers' character, judgment, or trust, it is unrealistic to expect monumental changes all at once. Your daughter may need additional years of maturity to develop greater control over impulses, as well as the ability to handle emotions and think abstractly. Your interventions are necessary, though not sufficient, to produce desired changes.

A Compliment

Although this may sound far-fetched, it is perfectly normal and common for mothers to harbor some hope that daughters will notice and compliment them for their new assertive and communication skills. Despite teenagers' developing astuteness about others, however, they may easily overlook or choose to ignore their own mothers' admirable new ability to speak their minds—especially when it gets in the way of their desires. It's easy for mothers to be hurt and disappointed when daughters fail to acknowledge or even denigrate their growth.

Gratitude

Perhaps all you would like in return for everything you do as a mother is a little gratitude. What is wrong with that? Nothing, unless you expect appreciation within the next decade or so. Although teenage girls are honing their ability to empathize, your daughter cannot begin to appreciate fully your experience, needs, and vulnerabilities in being a mother. Although you may be fortunate if she thanks you for specific favors or gifts, the soonest you can realistically expect true gratitude or appreciation for your efforts to be a good mother is when she has a child of her own.

By staying the course during confrontations with your daughter, you demonstrate your commitment to her and to your relationship. You are not caving in to her demands, avoiding conflict, withdrawing in frustration, becoming immobilized by helplessness, or rejecting her out of anger. Will you always be right? Hardly. In the course of parenting your teenager, you will make hundreds, if not thousands, of decisions, some of which you will regret. All you can do at this point is base your choices on the best information available to you and on your own gut feelings.

Even if she rails and protests to the contrary, it is reassuring to your daughter to know that she can count on you to do what you think is best. So when her responses to your parenting limits and confrontations are less than desirable, your love and concern about her well-being keep you hanging in there. Regardless of her complaints, objections, or outright campaigns to have her way, you stay the course. You trust in the belief that over time you will accomplish your ultimate goals: instilling values, encouraging behaviors, teaching skills, and building self-confidence. By acting on your convictions and using your skills to the best of your ability, you know you have done your best for your daughter. In this process she will learn how worthy she is, a prerequisite for her experiencing other healthy relationships in years to come.

Chapter Eleven

Dealing with Stressful Events

As you have no doubt discovered, it is hard work to improve your relationship with your daughter. Daily stresses, frustrations, worries, and disappointments threaten to get in the way of your choosing battles, expressing yourself, and responding to your daughter ideally. But these everyday issues pale in comparison with major life circumstances—especially, serious illness, death, divorce, and residential moves—which intrude upon the mother-daughter relationship.

Because these events are an inevitable part of life, no book on the mother-daughter relationship during the teenage years would be complete without attending to their impact. It is not that major changes or tragedies affect only mothers and daughters or even that they affect mothers and daughters more than other family members. It is that both mothers and daughters, as well as their relationships, are profoundly affected by such crises.

You are forced to cope with your daughter's intense, painful reactions at a time when you yourself are experiencing similar feelings. Moreover, she is apt to use you as a scapegoat when she struggles to manage these disturbing emotions, making these life events doubly stressful for a mother. Given that at some time you will likely face a move, an illness, or a death in the family, this chapter aims to help you develop a better appreciation for how these events affect teenage girls and how you might handle them in ways that are consistent with your goals for parenting.

THE MAJOR ISSUES FOR GIRLS

Although every individual copes with upsetting or traumatic life events differently, it is certain that your daughter will have to do much mental work to deal with whatever happens. As girls grieve for losses and adjust to major events in their lives, the following salient issues are generally stirred up.

Not Being in Control

During adolescence, when girls are struggling to gain more autonomy, when their emotions and bodies feel out of control, they are distressed by having to deal with yet another challenge that is not their choice. When they are informed their families will be moving, for example, many are incensed by the total lack of say they have in the matter. Their initial reaction is often based not on feelings about the new location but on the sense that the rug has been pulled from under them.

In a sense that's true. Chances are you made the decision to move independently or with another adult (e.g., a spouse or partner) without consulting your daughter. Regardless of whether she is ultimately in favor of the move, being told she is moving reinforces her irksome dependency and highlights her most dreaded message: You are still a child who must obey your parents. Being told to do anything is hard enough, but if your daughter is asked to say good-bye to friends and leave behind all that is familiar, she may well resent being unable to refuse. Even later, as she is adjusting to her surroundings, this sense of lacking control may recur whenever she experiences awkwardness, insecurity, or desire for acceptance.

Similarly, daughters have no say (and shouldn't) when parents decide to separate or divorce. Not only is this news anxiety-provoking and devastating, but it underscores their feelings of not being in control of their world. Although they are the ones being affected, they reason, they're not the ones making the decisions. Adina, thirteen, described her reaction to her parents' splitting up like this: "I was so shocked I thought I'd die. I was beyond mad at them. I couldn't believe they'd do this to my little sister and me."

Illness is the ultimate loss of control to teenage girls. They are often enraged by having to endure the indignity of poking and probing by doctors, the intrusion on their privacy, and the betrayal of their own bodies. Plus, adults, such as parents and physicians, restrict teens' all-important ability to come and go, attend school, and play sports. Kelly, seventeen, who had Epstein-Barr virus her senior year of high school, said, "I felt so crappy just when everything was supposed to be so great. It was so unfair. Instead of doing all these fun things, I had to miss school, get tutors, and be away from my friends."

Feeling powerless is common when someone dear to your daughter gets sick or dies. When her grandmother became terminally ill, said Heidi, sixteen, "I hated a lot of things about it, but most of all, I hated that there wasn't a thing I could do about it. The timing sucked, and I was worried the whole summer something would happen to her." Again Heidi felt helpless to affect the situation. Not only was she unable to make her grandmother well or prevent her impending death, but she had no control over when this event would take place. She felt powerless to do anything but worry about her grandmother's imminent death.

The flip side, however, is that sometimes girls do take responsibility even when situations are not their fault. This is especially true when the stress of the event triggers regression to magical thinking and other behaviors typical of younger ages. Jenn, eighteen, said she was racked with guilt after her maternal grandfather died. "When I was younger, he made me really nervous. I think he intimidated me a lot. I guess a few times I wished he'd just disappear—as in, drop dead. So when he suddenly died from a heart attack, I felt awful, as if I'd killed him." The more ambivalent or conflictual your daughter's relationship to the ailing or deceased, the more vulnerable she is to feelings of self-blame and guilt.

In the same vein, girls may know in their heads that a divorce is not their fault. Yet many harbor unrealistic guilt about their contributions to parental conflict. Kara, sixteen, articulated what many teen girls think when she said, "If only they didn't argue about me all the time, maybe they'd still be together." Girls imagine that any misbehavior or problems they presented were responsible for their parents' discord and separation.

Coping with Change

During adolescence, which is all but synonymous with transformation, coping with yet another change is often perceived as tragic. For a teenage girl who has to adapt to new bra sizes, fleeting moods, and an ever-changing body shape, moving to a new house can be the ultimate blow. Tell her she needs to get used to a new school, make new friends, and assimilate into an unfamiliar neighborhood and town, and you may have perceived trauma on your hands. As Taylor, fourteen, aptly put it, "It's horrible having different teachers and bus routes at the start of every year, but now I find out I have to deal with a new apartment, new room, new kids, new place—I hate it!"

Change is also a typical consequence of parental divorce. Wendy, eighteen, had this to say when her parents told her the news: "Even though I'm going off to college, it feels as if they're destroying my life. When I come home on vacations, I'll be going to a whole different house and a new room. Holidays are going to be different too. Everything will be so strange."

Losses of All Kinds

Life events also result in losses of what used to be. Whether teenage girls undergo losses of health, intact families, or people dear to them, they mourn. As part of the mourning process, girls experience an enormous range of feelings, some predictable, others surprising. Elisabeth Kübler-Ross, author of the classic *On Death and Dying,* describes five stages of dealing with death that are now widely used to understand the mourning process stimulated by all sorts of losses: denial, anger, bargaining with God, depression, and acceptance. Prevailing thinking is that not everyone experiences all five stages or at least not necessarily in a particular order. Your daughter, for example, may simply fume as opposed to denying or bargaining.

Permanent and irreversible losses caused by death are often the worst. When a loved one dies, adolescents mourn the deceased, all future opportunities with a person, and their own inability to have eased pain or prevented suffering. When adolescents are asked about traumatic experiences in their lives, however, they frequently mention the deaths of beloved pets. Their intense pain and grief when a pet dies are understandable. These favorite animals not only love them unconditionally but listen to them faithfully and attentively (without so much as a word of disagreement). They are loyal and affectionate regardless of teenagers' moodiness, surliness, or rebelliousness.

Although not to the same degree, perhaps, teenage girls who move also grieve—for losses of important people, familiar places, and comforting routines: "my best friend since I was five," "the soccer field where I played since kindergarten," "the restaurant where we always went to celebrate stuff." Sometimes they experience the loss of hopes they have held for the future: "starring in the senior class play," "going to the prom with Dave," "making varsity swimming."

Parental divorce too is often accompanied by tremendous losses: of the family unit, time spent with noncustodial parents, financial resources, and sometimes a family home or lifestyle. Emma's parents divorced during her middle school years. In her early twenties she said: "My entire life changed dramatically after that one short announcement. My mom sold the house and moved my brother and me to a tiny town house. Being thirteen, I was most furious about not being able to get as many clothes as I had before; that was how I felt the loss. But later on I came to realize I had lost not only my father, who moved away and barely saw us, but my mother, who became preoccupied and overworked and wasn't ever the same person again."

Keep in mind that these events often reevoke painful feelings from other losses that occurred earlier in girls' lives. Moreover, loss is cumulative. Ruthann, fourteen, was brought to therapy by her mother after a disastrous seventh grade. In the prior two years she had lost two grandparents, moved cross country, and suffered a serious illness. Each event alone would have precipitated grieving, but together they contributed to a profound sense of loss, helplessness, and despair of which Ruthann was largely unaware. Unless she recognized the importance of these events and worked through the issues, she would continue to act out her feelings self-destructively.

HOW GIRLS REACT

Just what do girls do with these intense feelings? Because they are often unaware of their feelings and apt to act them out unconsciously and uncontrollably, you are likely to see any of the following.

She Gets Angry at You

First and foremost, of course, girls take out their feelings on their mothers. As you have clearly seen, you make a convenient target for all of your daughter's frustration, sorrow, and impotent rage. Although this is hardly unfamiliar, when you yourself are in crisis, often faced with the very same feelings, you may feel even less prepared to deal with your daughter's wrath. Labeling this phenomenon for what it is and understanding its cause are your best strategies.

Sometimes your culpability is not clear-cut. When Jan was forty-five, her company offered her a promotion that required her and her daughter to move to another state. "Selena was fifteen at the time," she said, "and I knew it wasn't going to be easy for her. But I had to weigh all the factors. At my age I thought it was probably my last chance to move up to that level, and miraculously there was an opening in the division I wanted. As a single parent, financial security has always been important to me. I also figured Selena would have over half of her high school years in the new school. All in all, I felt it was worth it to move, but for a long time I thought she'd never stop hating me."

Rather than accept what they cannot change, teenage girls often battle and rail. Furious about having to move, Teri, seventeen, found a way to blame her mother. As she said, "I know it isn't fair to be ticked off at my mom. She doesn't want to move either. So why doesn't she just say no to my dad? Every time he gets transferred, we all have to pack up. Why is she letting him ruin my life?" Teri was angry because her mother did nothing to prevent an unwelcome move. This unreasonable behavior is redolent of your daughter's past, when she protested vehemently if her wishes were unmet. Even now, as she declares that she can take care of herself, she still harbors a kernel of hope that you will magically fix all her problems.

This same dynamic is responsible for yet another reason girls express anger at their mothers. When someone close to a girl dies, especially a father, the importance of her mother becomes even greater. This is a scary thought to a teenage girl. Rather than thinking perhaps, "My mother is the only one I've got now. What am I going to do if she dies too?," she thinks, "My mother is such a jerk; who needs her?" This shift allows her to keep frightening dependency needs, vulnerability, and resultant panic out of her awareness.

Whether it is the mother or the daughter who is sick, girls typically blame their mothers for whatever discomfort or inconveniences they must endure. For example, if physicians order blood tests, girls may be furious with their mothers for taking them to the doctors' and forcing them to be stuck with needles. When mothers are ill, girls are equally apt to express apprehension about their needs being met (e.g., essential shopping, preparation of meals, chauffeuring to and from activities) as concerns for their mothers' recovery.

Many mothers are surprised, if not appalled, by their daughters' apparent insensitivity. In fact, teenagers' typical self-preoccupation and tendency to evaluate all events in terms of personal consequences are often perceived as proof of their "selfishness." Edie, forty-seven, reported that when she was recuperating from back surgery, "My daughter, who was fifteen, constantly asked questions like 'Who's going to drive me to volleyball?' and 'How can you not come to my game?' as if I had any choice! She was clearly angry at me for being laid up and not doing all the things she needed me to do."

When Alexis was fourteen, her mother underwent a hysterectomy, which required two weeks of bedrest. "I knew it wasn't my mom's fault. She didn't even want to have the operation. But I was ticked off when she missed my choir recital. I had a solo and everything." Although girls are mostly distressed by any inconveniences, it is true that they also express hostility toward the sick person—much to their mothers' chagrin—to disguise discomfiting fears and guilt.

Parental divorce is yet another life event that typically provokes girls' anger toward mothers. Perhaps your daughter simply needs someone to blame. Or she resents the changes in her life caused by your decision to divorce. At the very least she is unlikely to welcome you into the singles dating scene. As she struggles with her own attraction to and acceptance by the opposite sex, as well as burgeoning sexual feelings, she is probably uncomfortable with the mere thought of yours. Carrie, fifteen, spoke for many girls: "I couldn't imagine my mother going out on a date and kissing. It's totally disgusting." Becoming single and beginning to date bring you into her world, forcing her to face the fact that you are a sexual being and likely intensifying her uncomfortable competitive and ambivalent feelings.

She Tries Too Hard

When girls are shaken up by disturbing or frankly devastating life events, they frequently feel intensely dependent on their mothers. To assure themselves of their mothers' continued emotional availability, some girls unconsciously but tirelessly try to prevent their mothers from being upset, bothered, or stressed. They become desperate to ensure their mother's well-being, perhaps their good moods. After her father died in an auto accident, for example, Allison, twelve, stopped being argumentative or challenging with her mother. "She became too good," said her mother, Ellyn. "She does her chores without being asked, offers to make me tea in the evenings, and has even become protective of her younger brother. I know this isn't normal, at least not for Allison. She seems determined to make sure I'll be okay." Girls like

Allison are so intent upon maintaining the status quo that they often keep all negative feelings locked away inside. Thus, they steadfastly avoid conflict with their mothers.

She Gets Angry at the World

When girls can't blame their mothers for unfortunate life events, they often try to find other targets for their rage. Perhaps they turn to medical staff ("They screwed up," "They killed my grandmother with their experimental treatment," or "They didn't bring her the pills in time"). Or they blame other loved ones ("My aunts made too much noise," "My father hardly ever visited him," or "My pesky cousins are always interfering"). Some girls blame God ("How could this wonderful person be allowed to suffer?" or "Why did she have to die when all these horrible people in the world are still living?"). Others even become angry at the person who died ("Why was he driving so fast?" or "Why did my mother have to want another baby?").

In part, such angry feelings actually help girls say good-bye to important people. Just as teenage girls often use hostility unconsciously to separate emotionally from their mothers, so it can help them detach from those they lose through death, divorce, or residential moves. A.J., age sixteen, realized that this happened when she and her family moved cross country two years earlier. "Since first grade my best friend and I were always together, and I couldn't picture being somewhere without her. The closer I got to moving, though, the more annoying she seemed to me. Everything she did got on my nerves. Finally we had this huge blowup, and I remember thinking, 'Good, now I don't care if I move.' Being mad at her took my mind off how much I'd miss her." Thus, your daughter may suddenly devalue relationships she feels she will be losing.

She Needs You More

At the same time that your daughter is angry and pulling away, she is likely to become needier and more demanding. With the hectic pace, disruption of schedules, and preoccupation accompanying a crisis, she needs that much more reassurance that you will be there for her. Some of these demands may seem capricious or even ridiculous unless you understand their roots. As Mimi, fifty-two, told it, "When my mother was sick, my daughter seemed to revert back to the way she was as a little girl. Suddenly she couldn't seem to do things for herself that she used to. I had to make her breakfast or she wouldn't eat. We would laugh about the fact that she said French toast didn't taste good unless I made it."

When mothers are caring for their own parents, girls can become particularly resentful. Why isn't she paying attention to us? is their outlook. As much as your daughter wants to feel grown up, she also wants to know that she can count on you to nurture her if and when she needs it. Monica, fourteen, said: "I got so sick of my mom's going to my grandma's house. Every day she'd be gone for hours, doing stuff for my grandma and not us. Then, when she'd get home, she'd be tired. I know my grandma needed her, but give me a break."

Similarly, when your daughter's sibling is ill, she may overlook her stricken brother's or sister's suffering, focusing instead on all the "unfair" attention he or she may be getting. Said Laney, sixteen: "When my sister went through a couple of kidney operations, I was definitely mad. My mother was always talking to her doctors or going to the hospital or taking care of her. I felt invisible." Trish, fifteen, was resentful when her brother became seriously ill. "He was sick for a long time," she said, "and my mother spent every minute she had with him. It was like she cared about him a lot more than me."

There is almost nothing girls abhor more than feeling dependent upon their mothers. So if your daughter becomes clingy, demanding, or envious of the time you spend with others, she is likely to compensate by becoming belligerent, provocative, or off-putting—just to convince herself that she doesn't need you. These mixed messages, at a time of significant stress, can be particularly challenging and frustrating for mothers.

A MOTHER'S STRATEGIES

Although your daughter's already complex feelings and needs will be further complicated by these life events, you can apply some of the same tools you may have used already for everyday situations. It is probably even more essential to focus on resolving conflicts and strengthening communication during crises. Not only do you prevent further pain at a most inopportune time, but you maintain a potential source of support and solidify your relationship in the process. During a crisis you may need to remind yourself of the following basic strategies.

Take Time for Yourself

Your own feelings are a formidable factor in determining your ability to help your daughter through a crisis. Give yourself time to adjust to new developments, to grieve, to be by yourself, or to seek comfort from others. Unless you take care of yourself, you will be less available emotionally to your daughter. It is also important that you demonstrate to your daughter that it is not a luxury to take care of herself in a crisis; it is a necessity.

Decide What to Tell Her

In thinking about what information you will share with your daughter, as well as how and when you will do so, consider the following suggestions.

- **SPEAK DIRECTLY AND IMMEDIATELY TO YOUR DAUGHTER.** As hard as it may be to give her bad news, it is far better to speak directly to her rather than through an intermediary or, worse yet, allowing her to find out inadvertently. Whether you must tell her about a death, an illness, a divorce, or a move, try to say it face-to-face and as soon as possible after you find out. Delaying serves no purpose; in fact, since girls almost invariably know "something's up," without information they conjure up devastating possibilities that incite even greater apprehension.
- **TELL THE TRUTH.** Many mothers circumvent facts or tell daughters half-truths to protect them from distressing news. Throughout any crisis, however, it is critical that she knows she can come to you for straight answers. It is especially important to be truthful about the medical conditions and probable recovery of loved ones who are ill. Telling your daughter that someone close to her "will be fine" is a good strategy only if it is true. Giving her false reassurance will undermine her trust in you. Moreover, pretending someone will recover prevents your daughter from finishing her "business" with the dying person and engaging in preparatory grieving.
- **GIVE ONLY NECESSARY INFORMATION.** During crises mothers may forget that teenage girls are not yet adults. Regardless of how bright or mature she is, your daughter is apt to become confused or overwhelmed by too much information. If you are unsure precisely what she is asking, try: "What is it exactly that you want to know?" In addition, be sure you have a good reason to give her information of a

sensitive nature. If possible, do not ask your daughter to keep secrets; it is too much of a burden. When she asks questions that you feel are inappropriate or intrusive, rather than become evasive or lie to her, you might express directly how you feel: "You know, I'm uncomfortable discussing that with you. What I can say is . . ."

- **CONSIDER TIMING ISSUES.** As previously discussed, use your knowledge of your daughter to time upsetting discussions. Be sensitive to what else is going on in her life.

Facilitate Her Acknowledgment and Expression of Feelings

During a crisis some of your strategies may be the same as, but others may be different from, those you would employ under everyday conditions.

- **PERMIT ANY AND ALL FEELINGS.** If your daughter is inclined to speak, allow her to express her thoughts and emotions, whatever they are. This is particularly true of feelings associated with grieving. Because of increased longevity today, many youngsters are spared the experience of a family death until they are teens. This may be the very first time your daughter has faced mortality. She may be frightened by the intensity of her emotions or embarrassed by experiencing things that she is "not supposed to feel." Or your daughter may be ashamed of what she perceives as lack of feeling. Some girls say, "I loved him, so why am I not more upset?" or "Why didn't I cry?" News of parents' divorcing also may elicit strong negative, unsettling, or confusing feelings. Your empathetic response will help your daughter believe that whatever her emotional reaction, she is not abnormal or bad but simply human. You emphasize this by communicating her right to feel as she does, regardless of how incomprehensible her reaction may be to you. Coming to terms with her feelings directly will enable her to avoid coping with them in unhealthy ways, such as drinking or taking out her frustrations on others.

- **EMPATHIZE WITHOUT MINIMIZING.** It is important to walk that fine line of acknowledging your daughter's feelings, while providing realistic reassurance of what the future is likely to bring. Many mothers, eager to reassure daughters that painful feelings will be brief, insist that daughters will, for example, adjust to a move or "get over" the loss of someone dear "in no time." Since teenagers have difficulty focusing on anything but their present pain, these well-intended words can feel dismissive of their very real fear, sadness, and anger.

- **ENCOURAGE CREATIVE EXPRESSIONS.** Especially if your daughter is reticent, encourage her to get in touch with her feelings through creativity. She might write in a journal, compose songs, create stories or poetry, or play music.
- **VERBALIZE YOUR EMOTIONS.** Although mothers often hide their own feelings in fear of upsetting their daughters, girls can and should realize that mothers have feelings too. Whether you feel sad, anxious, angry, guilty, or whatever, expressing emotions aloud can offer your daughter possible labels for her vague angst. Moreover, this gives her tacit permission to speak up about her feelings; in short, you're saying, "It's okay to talk about these things." Having a good cry together can help you comfort each other. Sharing special memories of better times and healing laughter can also bring you two closer.

Empower Her

To counteract feelings of helplessness, empower your daughter to take whatever action she can. Doing things, rather than merely reacting, will help her feel more in control and capable of coping with crises. Consider the following actions.

- **REMIND HER OF HER STRENGTHS.** Your daughter may need to be reminded that she has coped successfully with other firsts and transitions in her life. It may be reassuring for her to hear stories of her entry into preschool, that initial kindergarten bus ride, a solo visit to grandparents. Sharing your own stories about adjusting to life changes can also be helpful.
- **SEEK HER INPUT.** Whenever possible, give your daughter the chance to participate in making decisions. Although she cannot choose whether or not to move, for example, she may be able to give her opinion about when would be the best time to move, which of several possible new homes she would prefer, and which bedroom she would pick. She might be invited to go along on your initial visits to check out the town, the schools, or the homes. When someone dies, elicit your daughter's wishes regarding her participation in any memorial service or cemetery burial. Many mothers, again in an attempt to protect daughters, forbid them to attend such events. However, teenage girls often express resentment at having been "ignored," "babied," or "excluded" from ceremonies long after they occurred. When she herself is sick, permit your daughter to take as much control as possible of her treatment. Respect her comfort level with and opinions about her doctors.

- **TEACH HER TO GET INFORMATION.** Empower your daughter by helping her become educated about her illness, its course and treatment. But draw the line at noncompliance. Impress on your daughter that you will insist she go to doctor appointments, take prescribed medication, and recuperate as directed to make sure she recovers and stays healthy. When you move, encourage her to write away for information about what interests her: sports facilities, organizations, music centers, etc. Help her find sources of current events and cultural offerings in the new community.

- **GIVE HER COPING STRATEGIES.** Facing difficult life events for the first time, your daughter may be at a loss about what to do. When she learns that someone she cares about is dying, she may be particularly anxious. Discuss this openly with your daughter, perhaps finding age-appropriate books that would be helpful. You might also encourage her to use whatever time remains. She may come to see that talking about her feelings with the dying individual is a gift to both of them, that talking, crying, laughing, and comforting each other are healthy coping strategies. If your daughter acts, she will be able to look back and remember the closeness she shared with that person, without regrets about what she failed to do or say. Similarly, help your daughter to maintain ties to old friends after a move by supporting her efforts to write, phone (within reason), E-mail, and plan a summer visit.

- **ENCOURAGE PROBLEM SOLVING.** Help your daughter generate potential solutions to overcome obstacles to her goals. A family crisis can therefore have a positive result: spurring growth in adolescents. For example, girls can learn to be more resourceful about finding other avenues to get their needs met: learning public transportation routes; using alternate school buses; getting after-school jobs to earn money. Some adolescents, after experiencing serious or life-changing illnesses, have become involved in organizations devoted to fundraising for research or the dissemination of information to others.

As a result of dealing with stressful events, your daughter will gain powerful evidence of her coping ability. As she faces innumerable changes and stresses through the years, she will benefit from your guidance during her earliest experiences. This mastery is an investment in her future, the resulting self-confidence a seed that will grow into her ultimate ability to leave home for college, work, and adult life.

When to Intervene

A common dilemma mothers face in the event of divorce, illness, or death is differentiating normal grief reactions from those signaling a deeper or more urgent problem. It is often difficult to predict how long it will take your teenager to recover from such stressful events. Personality, previous experiences, inner strengths, and complicating stressors all are factors. You can expect an exacerbation of grief around holidays, particularly the first ones after a move, divorce, or death, as well as the birthdays, anniversaries, and special occasions reminiscent of the deceased.

As a general guide, it may be necessary to seek further help when your daughter's grieving appears prolonged (more than, say, six months), worsens in intensity, or interferes with her everyday functioning. For example, if she stops experiencing pleasure in her usual activities or withdraws from friends or family members, if she becomes anxious or avoids certain activities or places, or if her school performance deteriorates, seeking further help may be warranted. Although this is more difficult to ascertain, you might read your daughter's stories and poetry to see if she has become preoccupied with death or morbid thoughts. Observe her closely to determine any changes in sleeping or eating patterns that may result in significant gains or losses of weight. Especially when teens bury intense feelings, they may suffer from persistent physical symptoms (e.g., headaches, stomach pains) for which no medical explanation is found. Also, as you know, whenever girls engage in risk-taking or overtly self-destructive behavior, immediate consultation with a professional is wise.

In addition to individual work with guidance counselors and mental health professionals, many bereavement or "coping with divorce" groups are offered for this age-group by communities (e.g., outpatient hospital services, clinics, religious organizations, schools). You might do some research on available resources to decide which setting would be best for your daughter.

Chapter Twelve

Gaining Perspective, Giving Forgiveness

By this point you may have experienced rewarding changes as you interacted with your daughter. Perhaps on one or more occasions you reacted differently to her behavior, tried a fresh approach, or said something out of the ordinary. You may have purposely decided *not* to make your typical comment or refrained from reacting impulsively. Whatever the change, you were pleasantly surprised, even amazed that there was a notable improvement in your interaction with your daughter. You two were not stuck in a deteriorating relationship after all. You might even survive her teenage years.

Of course these thoughts may have lasted for all of two minutes. Despite the progress you have made, mothers and daughters revert back to old, self-defeating patterns occasionally and make frustrating errors both deeply regret. Your daughter, for certain, will continue to test and retest your patience, frazzle your remaining nerves, and err so severely sometimes you'll be alarmed about her judgment. She is in the end a teenager.

Just one awful fight can instantly rekindle the feeling that you are incapable of saying or doing anything right. Out of sheer frustration and anxiety, mothers are often too quick to think in these extreme or catastrophic terms ("Obviously, it hasn't gotten any better" or "She's hopeless" or "We'll never get along!"). After all, if you're still having fights even after using all those great communication strategies, you reason, there's simply no hope. This is when it is time to bring in "big picture" thinking.

TAKING A FEW STEPS BACK

The big picture can be appreciated only by your taking a few steps back and reviewing the total of your shared experiences. It involves the conscious act of focusing on the forest rather than on any individual tree. Just as you acknowledge anger, frustrations, and disappointments, so it helps to remember intentionally the joys, the laughs, the times you've swelled with pride, and the moments of palpable gratitude.

What is hard for mothers to keep in perspective at these times is that one blowup—no matter how off-putting or upsetting—does not obliterate all the hard work they and their daughters have accomplished. Nor will the incident cause the relationship to dissolve, explode into pieces, or unravel at the seams. It's important to see an upsetting incident for exactly what it is: a single upsetting incident. Even several fights, no matter how disturbing, will not define an entire relationship, which consists not of a particular day or even several unpleasant incidents but of a succession of moments and hours and days and months and years spent together.

Admittedly, keeping your relationship in proper perspective is no easy task when your daughter blatantly breaks your cardinal rules, lies shamelessly to you, or purposelessly insults you without mercy. As you stand there thinking, "Oh, no, just when I thought we were beyond all this," it will be difficult to see past her utter disregard for your authority, cold-hearted insensitivity, or absence of common decency.

This is not the time to generalize about your daughter's adult character or the quality of the mother-daughter relationship in years to come. Since your relationship, like all relationships, has its natural rhythms, its ups and downs, you might use these occasions to focus on the here and now. By working through the incident and saying what you have to say, you find the resources to forgive her so you two can move on.

THE ART OF FORGIVENESS

Forgiveness is the key to action and freedom.
—Hannah Arendt

How rapidly and successfully mothers recover from hurt and anger depends mainly on their ability to forgive. For many mothers, the word "forgive" is troubling and burdensome, perhaps because of the meaning they assign to it: specifically condoning or forgetting their daughters' mistakes. But this is not the case. Forgiveness, which is about letting go of anger and hurt *in spite of* being mistreated, is often the result of a well-thought-out, conscious decision. It is a gift you give to yourself, one that frees you from becoming consumed and immobilized by anger. In fact, forgiving your daughter is often more about allowing yourself to let go of your own painful feelings than wishing to absolve her. By allowing you to take care of yourself, forgiveness in turn enhances your relationship.

Susan learned this lesson after catching Lexy, her fifteen-year-old daughter, drinking: "I had just come home from work, and planned to throw in a load of laundry. When I got down to the laundry room, I found Lexy drinking beer with her friend. I screamed at her to march her behind upstairs and told the friend to get out. Worse yet, I found out Lexy had gotten the money to pay for that beer from my pocketbook! When I calmed down enough to see straight, I went up to talk to her. She apologized over and over and said her friend had dared her to do it, and she was sobbing hysterically. She kept begging me to forgive her, and she obviously felt horrible. But the truth is, at the time I didn't know how I could ever forgive her."

After the incident Susan admitted she couldn't sleep for several nights. She found herself walking to and from work with her fists clenched, as she replayed the scenario in her head. At that point she honestly believed she would never be able to forgive Lexy. Or if she did, it would never feel sincere. But then, one day, it happened. "It wasn't that I stopped thinking about what she did," she said. "It was more that I couldn't stand being so angry anymore. It was not only painful for me, but draining." The emotional cost of harboring anger is as valid a reason as any to forgive your daughter. Susan was relieved to find that the intense feelings no longer accompanied her memory of the incident with Lexy.

EMPATHY AS A FIRST STEP

When you've reached the boiling point or perhaps your "absolute limit," it is easy to tell yourself you will never forgive your daughter. There are dozens of things she may do that will fall into your category of "unforgivable." When they happen, it is best to decide to take your feelings one day at a time. Allow yourself the opportunity to feel different after dinner, next week, or whenever.

One strategy often helpful in hastening this process is to drum up some empathy for your daughter. According to Michael McCullough, Ph.D., director of research at the National Institute for Healthcare Research in Rockville, Maryland, empathy is proved to motivate forgiveness, and people who feel empathy for the person who offended them are more able to forgive than those who don't (see sidebar, page 222, for more information). Putting yourself in your daughter's place will allow you to imagine what may have prompted her to do or say what she did. For example, imagining how Lexy felt trapped into her friend's dare that day in the laundry room might not lessen Susan's condemnation of her daughter's action, but it is likely to abate her anger.

You can also achieve perspective by reminding yourself of all the "unforgivable" things you did as a teen and what a relief it was when your mother finally forgave you. Even when you pretended not to care about her reactions, you waited anxiously for the moment when your mother would pardon you for that antic you pulled or that episode of particularly bad judgment you used. As you reminisce about your own adolescent experiences, your resentment toward your own daughter may well begin to ebb.

HOW TO FORGIVE

When it comes to offering forgiveness, daughters are usually grateful when mothers make it short and sweet. Chances are, she already knows full well what made you angry. Reiterating her bad behavior will probably backfire; you will rekindle the embers of resentment. Exacting her promise never to do that again is likely to be equally fruitless. As well intentioned as she is, your daughter probably cannot honor a vow not to be hurtful or sneaky or irresponsible again. Better just to let her know you forgive her and feel ready to put the incident behind you.

Real forgiveness means truly letting the matter go, once and for all. When you forgive your daughter, you relinquish the right to rub her nose in her mistake, make sarcastic or mean-spirited comments, or elicit any guilt. It is especially bad form to bring up the issue in future arguments. Lastly, holding the issue over your daughter's head when you are attempting to get your way, a type of emotional blackmail, is also out of bounds. Forgiving means truly letting go!

WHEN SAYING "I FORGIVE YOU" DOESN'T SIT RIGHT

After your daughter knocks you for one of her countless loops—telling you what she really thinks of your mothering ability, refusing to follow house rules, humiliating you in public, or fill in numerous other possibilities—you use your repertoire of strategies to find some healthy perspective. You spend countless hours determining what made you so upset in the first place, trying to pinpoint the most likely possibilities. Next, you explain your thoughts and feelings to your daughter, choosing your words carefully to make sure your message is crystal clear and to the point. As you voice your concerns, you experience relief that comes from releasing your accumulated emotions. If you are especially lucky, you might receive from your child an actual apology along with a promise to change. That is when you will be able to say precisely what you've wanted to all along: "I forgive you." You will have the closure you desperately want; life can return to normal. Except sometimes it doesn't.

At some point you may realize that your anger or frustration or disappointment didn't dissipate as fully as you believed. Despite the fact that you said everything on your mind—perhaps you even expressed yourself better than you'd expected—you can't seem to put aside your negative feelings. Despite your conviction that there is truly nothing left to do or say, when you think about what happened, your resentment lingers or, worse, festers. You're wondering what's preventing you from putting the incident to rest; perhaps there is something wrong with you. She's your child, and you love her, so why can't you forgive her? If you are familiar with these troubling thoughts, you are hardly alone. To figure out which factors may be impeding your forgiveness, consider the following possibilities.

You Characteristically Have Trouble Forgiving

Every mother has a different style. Some are quick to anger but equally quick to forgive. Someone says, "I'm sorry," and the memory of the offense vanishes instantaneously. It may take a lot to get mothers at the other extreme angry, but once they are, the people closest to them know to take cover. These are the quintessential grudge holders who never forget. In between are mothers whose patterns depend more on the circumstances of what made them angry and the responses of those who were responsible. Often, the greater the intensity of one's outrage, the longer the healing process.

Regardless of where you fall on this continuum, it is important to be aware of your personal style, to know what typically prolongs your anger, and to accept your individual responses. If you know you'll need extra time to feel ready to forgive your daughter, give yourself permission to seek it. Though your daughter may have an inkling about whether or not you're holding a grudge, she undoubtedly would benefit from your explaining that you will need a little time to get past the incident.

There's More to the Issue Than You Originally Suspected

Unresolved issues also prevent mothers from feeling ready to forgive their daughters. During a confrontation you may have neglected to address a larger issue. For instance, while your daughter's electric blue mascara provoked a brief screaming match, the issue that continued to simmer afterward was that she never asked for your permission to wear makeup. It wasn't the mascara itself that irked you as much as her failure to consider your input and authority.

When Diana's fifteen-year-old daughter, Alicia, announced during dinner that the swordfish "tasted like an inner tube," Diana was furious. She knew she shouldn't take this relatively inoffensive comment so seriously, but it was definitely a thorn in her side. In an effort to rationalize her feelings, Diana decided she was angry simply because she'd paid good money for that fish, and Alicia was "acting like an ungrateful brat."

When she explained to her daughter how she felt, Alicia shrugged, apologized, and said she was "just kidding around." Said Diana: "I could see that Alicia thought I was blowing things out of proportion, but I accepted her apology anyway, just to be done with the incident." Days later, however, Diana realized she still felt angry, and worse, she couldn't figure out why.

"It took me a couple of more days to think it through," Diana said, "but finally I realized what it was that had made me so angry. I've been feeling pretty useless in Alicia's life lately. It seems like I can't help her with any of her problems or that she even wants my help anymore. One of the few things she counts on me for are meals, as pathetic as that sounds. So when she told me I couldn't even do that right, it made me feel terrible."

If you are feeling you can't seem to move on even after hearing your daughter's apology, there may be more to the situation than you originally suspected. Until you figure out the bigger issue(s), it's easy to feel stuck in a rut. The best thing to do is to step back and reflect on what's really upsetting you. Ask yourself what feelings have been stirred up and what else they might connect to beyond this one scenario. You may discover that something in your relationship has been bothering you for a long time. Rather than berate yourself for being unaware of it beforehand or for letting it slide this long, you can do something about it. You can always talk to your daughter again about the "real" reason you were or still are so angry. Alternately, you might figure out a way to come to terms with the problem by yourself. Either way, you will do what you must in order to move on.

You Were Left Unsatisfied with Her Response

Perhaps you can't let go of your resentment because when you confronted your daughter, you didn't get the response you were hoping for. Maybe you took the plunge and bravely revealed your vulnerable, hurt feelings. But instead of expressing genuine remorse, she denied anything happened ("It's totally in your head"), became defensive ("I did not!"), or got accusatory ("It's your fault!"). Maybe she avoided your discussion by informing you she had important things to do, such as calling her boyfriend or watching a sitcom, as if your pain were of such little significance that she couldn't be bothered to hear about it. In the same vein, maybe she gave you a halfhearted apology to put an end to the conversation as quickly as possible.

As one mom put it, "I was expecting tears and an expression of humiliation from my daughter when I confronted her about blowing off my birthday dinner. Instead, she rolled her eyes and told me she didn't realize it was such a big deal. What could I even tell her? Of course, it was a big deal!" Feeling dismissed by your own daughter is enraging.

As discussed in previous chapters, your teenage daughter may be too preoccupied with matters that directly and immediately concern her to empathize with your experience. It is not that dismissing your feelings is in any way acceptable; it's just typical. In fact, don't be surprised if you have to remind your daughter that you even have feelings! While an apology is often the preferred goal, and punishment may or may not be warranted, what is most crucial is expressing your limits for what you will and won't tolerate in your relationship. Only when you clear the air—all of it—will you truly be able to forgive your daughter.

Your Daughter's "Crime" Was Serious

Just because you want to put negative feelings behind you doesn't necessarily make it so. Another important factor in forgiveness is the gravity of your daughter's "crime." No two ways about it, there's a huge difference between a teenager's making an obnoxious comment or spilling cereal on the floor and a teenager's leaving her two-year-old brother alone in the driveway. Forgiveness becomes a much greater challenge when she crashes the family car, swears at a teacher, "forgets" to show up at her SAT testing, or shoplifts from the local drugstore.

Take once again the example of Susan, who found her daughter drinking after stealing money from her pocketbook. The first thing Susan did was tell Lexy that she would pay back every cent for the alcohol and be grounded for the next four weekends. The two of them had a long discussion about alcohol, why Lexy was not allowed to drink at age fifteen, and how she could say no to friends and refuse dares in the future. "I told Lexy that I understood she was sorry and of course, I still loved her, but that I was not ready to forgive her just yet. That was the hardest part," Susan said. "I knew how desperately Lexy was looking for my forgiveness, and I wanted to give it to her so we could just move on. But I didn't feel it. She had lost my trust on so many different levels."

You Worry About a Bigger Underlying Problem

There are other times when mothers are unable to let go of an incident—specifically, when they are fearful it signals a more significant underlying problem (e.g., teenage alcoholism, truancy) that may recur in the future. When her fourteen-year-old daughter, Shelly, returned one evening thirty minutes after curfew, with her T-shirt inside out, Rhoda became alarmed. Although Shelly denied having the slightest idea about the state of her shirt, she did acknowledge her responsibility for her lateness and accepted her punishment. "Still," said Rhoda, "I had this lingering uneasiness. It wasn't quite anger, but I couldn't let the incident go. I guess I really was afraid that Shelly was being sexual in ways I would oppose, and that opened the door for a thousand worries." It is easy to understand why Rhoda was unable to put the incident behind her.

There will be times you are not ready to forgive your daughter. While it's important to keep yourself open to the possibility, you cannot force yourself to say words you do not feel. If you do so, your daughter will see through your untruth. Realizing that you are still angry, she will no longer trust you when you forgive her in the future. Because it is part of women's role to be "nice" and have "pleasant" feelings toward everyone, they tend to reproach themselves or become consumed by guilt if and when they can't "find it in their hearts to forgive." It is important, however, that you be true to yourself. When your daughter hurts you, you will forgive her when you can. In the meantime, you can let her know that you continue to love her unconditionally and will always mother her.

FORGIVING DOESN'T MEAN FORGETTING

Again and again mothers ask themselves: "If my daughter tampered with my trust, how can I forgive and forget at the drop of a hat?" Shouldn't girls have to deal with repercussions? Do daughters really understand the amount of damage they've done? Will forgiving them let them off the hook? If you forgive your daughter, does that mean you are expected to forget all about what happened?

Said the mother of one fourteen-year-old daughter: "I am trying to forgive my daughter. I really am. But she went too far this time. She actually forged a letter from me to my ex-husband, asking him for money. This is the man who up and walked out of our lives to be with another woman! I am ashamed of her, stooping to that depth. Although I love her, I don't know when I'll be ready to forget about that!"

Another mother asked, "Am I really supposed to forget about the fact that my daughter practically destroyed the value of the house after throwing a party while I was away? I don't think so!"

No, you are not supposed to forget. Although you can and probably will forgive her, it is probably wise that you not forget the incident. Forgiveness means letting go of the emotional force. It does not mean disremembering the cause of your pain. In fact, there are good reasons for not forgetting when your daughter has wronged you—namely, you want to make sure she doesn't make the same mistake again. It's one thing to forgive your daughter for taking the car without permission and causing you endless worry. It's another thing to overlook the need to reinforce the rules and consequences of such potentially dangerous behavior.

Forgiving your daughter makes you and your relationship strong; forgetting what she's done makes you someone with bad judgment and puts her at potential risk. Again, this doesn't mean you throw the incident in her face at every opportunity. It means that you use her mistakes to guide you in making future decisions about her welfare.

LEARNING TO TRUST HER AGAIN

Even after you have relinquished your resentment and forgiven her, there is sometimes an unwelcome, smoldering residue of your conflict, the remains of your trust. When your daughter violates your trust, you feel as if something huge has been lost. Moreover, you wonder how it will ever be regained. It is this issue that often lingers in your mind longer than the emotion or even the memory of the incident.

It is important to be honest with girls about your feelings regarding trust. Daughters must learn to differentiate their mother's love, which is unconditional, consistent, and forever, from trust, which must be earned. As she learns life's harder lessons, you will want your daughter to know that you will stand by her even when she makes mistakes. Although mothers have varying levels of comfort saying the words "I love you very much, and that's never going to change," it would help your daughter if you found some way to demonstrate that her mistakes will never cost her your affection.

Of course, it doesn't mean your daughter won't be punished or forced to suffer consequences for her actions. In fact, loving her may compel you to ensure that she learns from her mistakes. Telling her, "I can't just forget that you violated our trust," and keeping this message consistent and clear will help reinforce your values.

Once your trust is lost, your daughter will have to work hard to regain it. It is critical that she knows you will allow her to earn back your trust, as well as the specific ways in which she may do so. Otherwise, girls who believe they can never do so figure, "Why bother?" and continue or even escalate their inappropriate behaviors. It is always helpful to reiterate to your daughter how much you value and want trust restored between the two of you.

WHEN YOU ARE THE ONE ASKING FOR FORGIVENESS

As you very well know, there are times when you will hurt, disappoint, or even fail your daughter. This scenario often challenges mothers. While some believe it unnecessary to admit wrongdoing (i.e., "The mother is always right"), others find it awkward or embarrassing or disturbing to apologize. When you have done something to upset your teenage daughter, however, understand that she is watching carefully, waiting to see how you will behave under these circumstances. In a sense it is a test.

As always you have an opportunity to model a behavior you would like your daughter to emulate. As hard as it may be, you must acknowledge that what you did was wrong. This action tells her that you respect and value her, that you take seriously your own unfortunate or regretted behavior, and that apologizing does not diminish you but enhances both your own dignity and the relationship.

Ask Directly for Forgiveness

Maybe you've humiliated your daughter inadvertently, reneged on a promise, or pushed her too hard. Or nagged her, forgotten to ask about something important to her, or acted unfairly toward her. Marilyn, for example, was caught rifling through her stepdaughter's desk drawers. "It was the worst feeling in the world. I had this sinking sensation in my stomach. I knew a simple apology wasn't going to cut it for Jenna," Marilyn admitted. "I didn't even have a good reason to be going through Jenna's things. I was just feeling bad that she had stopped telling me about her life, and I was curious. It's a horrible excuse, I know!"

Marilyn immediately tried to explain to Jenna why she had invaded her privacy, but Jenna told her she didn't want to hear it and her stepmother had "better get out!" Several hours later Jenna told Marilyn that what she had done was "totally unfair" and "the most disgusting thing." Marilyn listened quietly, said she understood completely, and apologized for her "unacceptable behavior." Jenna told her she needed some time apart from Marilyn. After a while everything returned to normal.

Marilyn handled the aftermath of her error exactly right. She attempted to talk to Jenna right away but respected her stepdaughter's request for time away. Later she listened to Jenna's perspective without interrupting ("even though a lot of it was very hard to hear"). She told her stepdaughter she had heard every word Jenna had just said, explained why she had done what she had, apologized sincerely, and vowed never to do it again. The only remaining task was to stick to her word, and Marilyn did.

Sometimes you will have to work hard to initiate the conversation with your angry daughter, especially if you are in the midst of a silent treatment. It takes courage and self-confidence to admit you've done wrong. This is when you might want to use some of the alternative techniques set out earlier in the book or to get creative, such as tape a note to her door, give her an "I'm sorry" card, or find a small token of apology to make your point. Whatever method you use to communicate, be honest and to the point. You might tell your daughter that you regret what you said or did and you wish you could undo it (if that's the case). Even if you cannot promise not to do "it" again, you can assure her that you will try your best.

Let Her Respond Without Interruption

It is likely your daughter will want to take this opportunity to explain in great detail how she feels about what you did. You might allow her a little leeway, even if she is informing you how "obnoxious" or "rude" your behavior was. Bite your tongue, if necessary, if she uses this occasion to remind you of your numerous other "crimes." It may be difficult to resist the temptation to correct her exaggeration or to assure her your intentions were good. No doubt it will be hard to endure her obvious pleasure in watching you on the hot seat for a change, squirming uncomfortably. No one said it was easy to ask for forgiveness.

If, however, she becomes abusive, screaming at you, insulting you, or using unacceptable language, you are certainly justified in breaking in. "What you did stank!" may be perfectly reasonable; "You suck!" is not. Although it is her right to be upset, it is not her right to attack you. You can tell her that she needs to express her feelings in a more controlled, respectful manner. After setting this limit, you may have to give your daughter some time to collect herself before she can deal with the issue productively. After figuring out what she needs to say, she can approach you and try again to resolve the problem. It may be an hour, it may be three days later. If you are uncomfortable with the silent treatment, you can always pull her aside and say, "I see you're still upset, and I'd like us to resolve this as soon as possible. Let's talk whenever you feel ready." Although many mothers describe the impulse to shake their daughters at these moments and scream, "Talk to me!" or "You can't ignore me forever!", there is great consensus that pushing girls only backfires.

Give Her Time to Heal

Your daughter may continue to hold a grudge, reminding you at every opportunity of your heinous crime. "Enough is enough," you may think. Even worse than having to face up to your error is to have it rubbed in by your teenager. Ignoring her snide remarks is probably a good initial strategy. At some point, however, you may have to say quietly that you have apologized, have made amends, and would like to move forward; your daughter's dwelling on the subject is no longer constructive.

You may have to remember, however, that if your unfortunate action eroded your daughter's trust in you, the healing process may well take longer. Trust works both ways. Although mothers may like to gloss over their own errors, it is understandable that daughters are unforgiving when their confidence in mothers is compromised.

As always, it is important to allow teenage girls to find their own ways of reacting to others' mistakes, accepting apologies and handling resentment. Whether your daughter's anger is burning or lingering, she will come around to forgiving you eventually because she loves you. In the long run your acceptance of her feelings and respect for her individual style will go a long way to build her self-confidence and desire for closeness.

Empathy Promotes Forgiveness

In a study of 239 college students, including 131 females and 108 males, Michael McCullough and his colleagues assessed whether people who forgive are more conciliatory toward and less avoidant of their offenders. Participants completed questionnaires in which they described events in which people had hurt them, how hurt they were, how wrong the offenders were, and the extent to which the offenders apologized. The researchers then measured the degree of empathy participants felt toward the offending persons and the degree to which participants had tried to reconcile with or avoid the offenders. They concluded that an apology does indeed lead to empathy, and empathy mediates forgiveness. People who were able to forgive were also less spiteful and avoidant of the persons who had hurt them.

Part 3

═══════════

Putting It All into Practice

Chapter Thirteen

Standing Up to Her Peers

When your daughter was younger, you protected her from hot toasters, sharp knives, electrical outlets, and other potential household hazards. On occasion she got burned, cut, or stung, but it was always a quick, fixable problem that ended with a hug and succeeded in teaching her a lesson. These days, however, the hazards in her life are far more severe than a mere toaster or outlet. Out there, in the world of teenage angst, lurks the dark and hovering potential of your daughter's getting burned by others—those who betray, dump, ridicule, or ignore her—and there is rarely anything you as her mother can do about it.

The average girl, sometime during her teen years, will experience friends, male and female, backstabbing, pressuring, abandoning, or lying to her. At some point these relationships may make her question her worth. Whether your daughter is a relative loner or voted most popular senior in high school, she will probably learn the pain of being excluded from a desirable social event, "blown off" by a date, or shunned by a clique. She will find herself alone on at least one Saturday night. She will face an intimidating boyfriend, intoxicated driver, or emotionally blackmailing friend. She will feel the hopelessness of not being pretty enough, cool enough, thin enough, smart enough, or sexy enough. Or equally disconcerting, she will be told by envious peers that she thinks she's too smart, pretty, cool, sexy, etc.

In this third part of the book you will apply the communication and conflict resolution skills you have been learning and perfecting thus far to help your daughter deal with such issues. As she approaches the time when she will move beyond the home, it is important to think through your role in assisting her in her struggles with peers, authority figures, and even herself.

WHAT YOU KNOW ABOUT HER SOCIAL LIFE

As your daughter progresses from childhood to adulthood, the degree to which she shares her irritations, her spats and battles, and even her joys with friends varies dramatically. At some points, when she considers every nuance sacrosanct, your pipeline to her social life may be abruptly cut off. Conversely, she may have a need to give you her perspective on every conversation and intrigue with her peers, whether she wants your input or not. Occasionally she may be willing to share with you brief updates on her social life: friends she feels closest to, those who upset her, who did what to whom. But as described previously, as soon as you ask the gentlest question, she is likely to clam up and resent your "nosiness."

Most likely, you will know when something is up socially the same way you often learn about other important news: by finding yourself the target of your daughter's frustration and despair. When a teenage girl is on the outs with her group or feeling miffed at a close friend, she is more prone to sulking, snapping, or provoking her mother. Your keener appreciation of your daughter's social pressures enables you to interpret these signals. Although you know she needs to deal with what or whom is causing her unhappiness, it is not so easy to ascertain your role. Deciding if, when, and how you should intervene in your daughter's peer conflicts is the focus of this chapter.

THE INVITATION THAT NEVER COMES

To test yourself, imagine your reactions to the following scenarios, all of which are variations on the all too common theme of your daughter's being excluded from a teen party.

- **UNBEKNOWNST TO YOU, A CLASSMATE OF YOUR DAUGHTER'S HAS TALKED ABOUT SENDING OUT INVITATIONS TO HER PARTY.** All you know is that for three days straight your daughter checks and re-checks her E-mail, replays the answering machine, and peeks inside the mailbox. You watch her fly upstairs when she gets home from school, immediately posting a Keep Out sign on her door. Or when you return from work, you sense the same warning from her tone of voice. Something is obviously going on, and this time you are pretty sure it has nothing to do with you, so you stand outside her door wondering what you should do. Do you ask her what's wrong? Or do you back off and let her bring up the problem?

- **YOUR DAUGHTER HAS BEEN DESPONDENT BECAUSE SHE WAS ONE OF ONLY A FEW GIRLS NOT INVITED TO A CLASSMATE'S PARTY.** You sympathize with her disappointment and suggest she make other plans for that evening. As the night of the party approaches, however, your phone begins to ring incessantly, and you overhear your daughter whispering frantically. The day before the event she announces casually that she has been invited to this particular party and asks you for a ride. You're concerned. Why did she get included at the last minute? What, if anything, did your daughter do to secure an invitation? Are you comfortable with her accepting a last-minute invitation when she wasn't invited from the start? Do you ask for an explanation? Do you call the parents who are hosting the party? Do you allow your daughter to attend?

- **A FEW DAYS AFTER A PARTY TO WHICH SHE WAS NOT INVITED, YOUR DAUGHTER ASKS TO HAVE THE GIRL WHO GAVE THE PARTY SLEEP AT YOUR HOUSE.** You're wondering why she is doing this, and you're concerned that she is putting herself in a less than desirable position. Do you say anything of the sort? Do you forbid her to have the person over? Do you come up with some other reason for her not to invite this person?

- **A FEW DAYS AFTER A PARTY THAT YOUR DAUGHTER DID NOT ATTEND, SHE IS DISTRESSED AND DIVULGES THAT SHE WASN'T INVITED BECAUSE SHE'S PERCEIVED AS "NOT COOL ENOUGH."** You wonder what that means. Do you ask her whether those who were invited are using substances or doing other things you don't permit? If she admits they are, do you take further action? Do you tell your daughter to take action? Do you forbid her to see them?

- **AFTER THE FACT YOUR DAUGHTER IS DEVASTATED TO LEARN THAT HER FRIENDS WHO WERE INVITED TO THE PARTY FAILED TO SPEAK UP FOR HER.** Do you speak to her about what true friendship is all about? Do you encourage her to address her concerns directly with her friends? Do you convey your feelings about these friends through your actions or words?

Your daughter's social difficulties precipitate dilemmas for you that may feel like obscure games with unwritten rules: Are you supposed to bring up problems directly or hint around? Are you supposed to look sympathetic or act as if nothing were out of the ordinary? If she doesn't respond, are you supposed to ask what's wrong more than once? Do you help her come up with solutions, or are you expected to do this for her? In other words, when your daughter is having difficulties with her peers, what is your role? How can you help your daughter feel better, learn from the situation, and move on?

USE YOUR SKILLS

Fortunately the skills you have learned thus far can be applied directly to just these sorts of dilemmas your daughter and therefore you face during her adolescence.

Confront Your Own Fears

As you know, until your own feelings, memories, and biases are clear in your mind, you cannot offer your daughter the most objective and effective help. It is only natural that you will react emotionally when you see your daughter hurt by her peers. So rather than deny, minimize, or act out these feelings, reflect on how they may be affecting your responses as a mother. Here are some of the fears mothers commonly express.

"I WON'T SAY THE RIGHT THING"

Pressure to come up with precisely the "right" response makes many mothers anxious. In fact, because they feel so unprepared, some attempt to overlook or avoid social topics. However, your daughter rarely seeks from you the perfect words or sage advice. She is well aware you cannot make things better for her. So reassure yourself that no degree of wisdom would enable you to give her what rarely exists. What your daughter does need from you are empathy and the knowledge that you are always emotionally available for her. These you are more than capable of providing. Your interest and concern demonstrate emphatically that she can always count on you to be a sympathetic sounding board, a source of "reality checks," and ever-ready compassion.

"MY DAUGHTER IS UNPOPULAR"

It is only natural to worry if your daughter is socially awkward or alienated from her peers. You want her adolescent experiences to be as healthy and happy as possible. But if you are unduly invested in seeing your daughter achieve the popularity you previously desired, you may be putting unnecessary pressure on her or even allowing your own social insecurities to spill over onto her. Worse, you might become angry, depressed, or withdrawn because unconsciously you feel that she failed socially. Your personal reaction prevents you from helping your daughter figure out what's right for her socially. If you find yourself reacting emotionally to your daughter's social situations, it will help enormously to revisit these issues from your own life.

"MY EXPERIENCES WILL CLOUD MY JUDGMENT"

This worry demonstrates psychological savvy about how your own issues potentially impact on your daughter's. Your insight is invaluable in helping you separate your social experiences from hers. Because you recognize the importance, you will make every effort to encourage your daughter to do what is in her best interest: to take chances, even if you want to protect her from the hurt you endured; to be selective in friendships, even if you wanted to be everyone's friend; to speak her mind, even if you were frightened of rejection.

"MY DAUGHTER WILL BE HURT"

You may well be heartbroken for your daughter, infuriated at whoever caused her distress, and determined to help her avoid such situations in the future. But by now you realize that conflict can be healthy and constructive. Sure, some of your daughter's social experiences will be painful—for her and for you. But through these encounters she will hone her skills in negotiating complex relationships and develop self-confidence both to get her needs met and to tolerate inevitable disappointments. She will become more empathic toward others who undergo similar social encounters. These experiences, which are a necessary part of her growth, will contribute to her repertoire of coping skills, making her stronger and more resourceful. Because of these convictions, you support your daughter in working through her social dilemmas despite the possibility of her being hurt.

When she addresses issues of trust, intimacy, and criteria for healthy relationships, she benefits now and in the future.

Encourage Discussion

You can use the active listening and communication skills you've been working on with your daughter to help her through peer difficulties. This means being alert to the clues to if, how, when, and where your daughter is most likely to open up about what is bothering her. Here is a review.

- **RESPECT HER PRIVACY.** This is one of the times your daughter may need to sort out her feelings privately before she can speak to you about the situation. She may choose to spend hours on the phone with a friend, withdraw into her room to cry, or escape into a video. As outlined in previous chapters, you can approach her, letting her know you care and are available, then back off if she clams up.
- **READ HER CUES.** As you bring down the emotional temperature and strengthen the underlying bond with your daughter, you'll naturally become more sensitive to her unique nonverbal cues. Although she may not announce the problem and ask outright for your opinion, she may, for example, begin appearing in your vicinity looking as if the weight of the world were dragging her down. She may shoot a gloomy, sullen expression in your direction as she glances to see if you're noticing. You'll read this accurately as your invitation to bring up the issue and start a conversation.
- **LISTEN ACTIVELY.** When she is ready, encourage your daughter to speak by not interrupting, contradicting, or questioning her as she shares the incident.
- **VALIDATE HER FEELINGS.** As we all know, the quickest ways to cut short discussion are either to downplay the problem ("It probably won't be a good party anyway" or "It's not as bad as you think" or "There will be plenty of other parties") or to exaggerate its seriousness ("Oh, my gosh, that's horrible!" or "Your weekend is ruined!" or "That girl should be shot!"). Although you long to ease her pain and bolster her fragile self-esteem by speaking about how fabulous she is, you realize she is unlikely to be receptive to your reassurance ("You're supposed to say that; you're my mother" or "You're wrong; it's never going to get better"). When your daughter is in this state, nothing you say may seem right to her. But instead of contradicting, minimizing, denying, or rationalizing her reactions, simply acknowl-

edge her perspective ("You're feeling left out/disappointed/hurt/
lonely"). You are thereby validating your daughter's right to have
these feelings.

Help Her Seek Information

Sometimes you'll want to encourage your daughter to get more information to solve her problem or resolve a conflict. This would
include being aware of both her own and the other person's perspectives and feelings. Your neutrality enables you to encourage your
daughter to put herself in the other person's shoes ("How do you
think she felt about it?" or "Why do you think she might have done
that?"). In this way she learns to empathize and to view the situation
fairly. It is probably wise to wait until your daughter is less angry and
agitated, however, or she may interpret your approach as a betrayal
("Why are you taking *her* side?"). As discussed in Chapter 12, facili-
tating her empathy for others will enable your daughter to forgive them
and move on.

Facilitate Her Problem Solving

Your efforts to communicate effectively and resolve mother-daughter
conflicts constructively pay off when your daughter is faced with social
difficulties. The same skills can be applied here.

- **LET HER TAKE THE LEAD.** Despite your understandable anxiety, resist
  the temptation to take it upon yourself to right your daughter's social
  wrongs. To empower her, allow her the opportunity to work through
  conflicts on her own. So instead of intervening yourself, for example,
  by calling the mother of the girl who excluded her from the party or
  by forbidding her to socialize with that girl, you encourage your
  daughter to think through the situation—with you, by herself, or with
  another confidante. By allowing her the opportunity to deal with the
  situation herself, you communicate your confidence in her ability to
  handle and grow from social challenges.

- **REMIND HER TO PICK HER BATTLES.** Help your daughter realize that she
  has a choice about which social issues she confronts. Support her in
  deciding which battles she believes are truly worth taking on. If she
  responded to every slight with equal passion, she would be emotionally exhausted. Conversely, there are injustices she cannot and should
  not tolerate. As you listen to her interpretation of the problem, assist

her in articulating and clarifying what exactly upset her and how important that issue is.

- **ALLOW HER TO GENERATE A PLAN.** Because the larger aim is to teach your daughter to rely on her instincts and problem-solving skills, resist the urge to dispense immediate advice. Instead, ask her what she thinks she needs to do to resolve the conflict or to feel better. If she says, "Nothing," or, "Let's just drop it," you can gently remind her that there are many options she can consider. It is possible that even after your well-intentioned suggestion, your daughter will still not be ready for this discussion—now, next week, or until she is nineteen. All you can do is make her aware that alternative solutions exist and that you'd be happy to help her think of them when she is interested.

- **HELP HER BRAINSTORM.** If your daughter is willing to think of alternatives, encourage her to imagine as many solutions as possible. At this point it's important to avoid critiquing each of these strategies, just to list them. Also, it's wise to be alert to subtle efforts on your part to manipulate your daughter into handling the situation as you yourself would ("It's pathetic to call her up now" or "You're too smart to say something like that"). She needs to know that this is her problem, and although you might not choose her particular solution or may even disapprove of it, you would never reject or abandon her because of it. Better to demonstrate clearly and directly how your daughter can get what she wants.

- **ENCOURAGE HER TO CONSIDER CONSEQUENCES.** Occasionally, because of hurt or desperation, your daughter may suggest tactics you hardly favor ("I'll spread a mean rumor about her" or "I'll butter her up with compliments" or "I'll tell her if she invites me, I'll get her tickets to that concert" or "I'll ask her if I did anything wrong"). Rather than condemn these ideas, encourage her to think through their probable consequences. Prompted, your daughter can imagine what would happen as a result of carrying out each of those options. Yes, the girl might invite her out of greed or regret or guilt, but how would your daughter feel about her own behavior? Yes, the girl might be devastated by the rumor, but how would your daughter ultimately feel about that?

- **GUIDE HER PLANNED CONFRONTATION.** If your daughter decides to confront a peer who she believes wronged her, help her speak her mind directly but respectfully, using "I" statements and asking succinctly for what she would like. Help her avoid inflammatory tactics that will provoke a full-blown fight. Perhaps you might remind her of how she has been effective in resolving situations that have arisen within your own relationship.

- **ENCOURAGE HER TO STAY THE COURSE.** Your daughter may be apprehensive about how friends will react when she sticks up for herself. Knowing how reluctant teenagers are to hear they made mistakes or were hurtful, you appreciate this fear. Your daughter is being realistic when she expects some friends to deny their actions and others to twist the situation to blame her instead. Your experience maintaining your stance within the mother-daughter relationship, despite her protests and recriminations, will bolster your efforts to encourage her to do the same. The message she has learned is that a committed relationship can withstand, and grow from, resolving differences. She can be reminded that a true friend genuinely cares about her and their relationship. She will therefore be more likely to appraise her actions according to what she herself believes than to how others react. Rather than depend on others to satisfy her or rather than derive esteem from whether she accomplishes social goals, your daughter's self-worth will come from within.

- **ALLOW HER TO FAIL.** No matter what her social expertise, there will be times your daughter's best efforts won't succeed. Perhaps she is unable to make her point heard, to get someone to respond to her request, or to change a situation to her liking. She may have contributed by misinterpreting the problem or mishandling the solution. Regardless, it is important to allow her to fail. This of course is more easily said than done. What might help is to tell yourself that the worst that can happen is that she will realize where she went wrong. Maybe she will learn something about a friend, or maybe she will recognize something about herself. If she was misguided, this is an ideal time for her to learn such important lessons. Most important, your daughter's capacity to cope with disappointments and mistakes will strengthen her and bolster her inner resources.

- **STEP IN FOR SAFETY REASONS.** It is one thing if your daughter isn't invited to a party or gets stood up at a dance, quite another if her boyfriend has been getting drunk before driving her home or has been pressuring her sexually. Similarly, if you find out that her clique is threatening her with social ostracism if she refuses to try the latest recreational drug, your sympathy and understanding are not sufficient.

If your daughter shares this information, she is asking you to step in and be her "great protector." She wants you to take a stand and help keep her safe—even if she manages to issue vociferous, obligatory protests to the contrary. This is when you want to support her by encouraging her to listen to her instincts and exit uncomfortable situations. Even if it is not your preferred role, you may be called upon to be the heavy, forbidding her from social situations in which you believe she is at risk. Your daughter is relying on you to take the blame, however, so she can complain to her friends, "I really want to go, but my mom is being such a jerk about this, and she just won't let me."

In a similar vein, before daughters begin to face teen pressures, many mothers establish a system by which girls can signal that they are uncomfortable with a situation (e.g., a friend's house, a party, a ride, etc.). They might call home to say they feel sick or need a favor or forgot to turn on their answering machines. Your daughter should be reassured that when you hear the prearranged message, you will gladly pick her up—no questions asked.

When Friends Are Mad at Her

Maybe your daughter was the one who committed the faux pas, betrayed a friend, cheated on a boyfriend, blurted out gossip, used the brainy girl in class. Part of the teenage experience is learning what it feels like to hurt someone—intentionally or not—and then having to live with the error and its backlash.

Because you hurt for your daughter, you may be tempted to assuage her guilt by assuring her that what she did was "no big deal." However, not only would you be teaching her that she doesn't need to feel responsible for her own actions, but you would be undermining her trust in you. She knows that she did something wrong and that she should feel remorse when she hurts someone.

On the other hand, you may find yourself wanting to hammer the point home that what she did was reprehensible. After all, you can't believe you could have raised such an (insensitive/thoughtless/uncaring/cruel) child who would do what she did. Therefore, you will make sure she understands that what she did was wrong. If you can see that your daughter is regretting what she did, however, she is already punishing herself. This if far more effective than anything you can do. Teens are adept, and rarely need adults' help, in tormenting themselves when they make mistakes.

Another possibility is that you believe your daughter may have wronged a friend but is not taking responsibility for her behavior and in fact may even be blaming the friend for the conflict. What do you do then? Many mothers, fearing altercations with their daughters, choose simply to stay out of the situation. Others, believing they should teach daughters about being a friend, will intervene. Of course, this is when choosing battles comes into play. While you won't get involved in every little spat your daughter has, you might decide that when she does something you consider truly reprehensible, you will speak your mind. Strategies for effective communication will enable you to get your point across without alienating your daughter in the process.

The stronger the connection between you and your daughter, the easier such conversations will be. When you remain loving toward her, she experiences you as critiquing a particular action rather than as issuing a general condemnation. She is reassured that her "crime" did not make her unlovable. Empathizing with her is almost always appreciated (e.g., "I can see you feel really terrible about this"). You might ask her what she needs to do to make herself feel better, and talk to her about the beauty of apologies. If you find that she is chastising herself without relief, you can step in with the idea that this approach benefits no one. Moreover, since teens often assume their mothers never made these sorts of errors, she might welcome a well-timed tale, complete with sordid details, of one of your worst social gaffes. Finding the humor in the situation is always a plus. At the very least you can reassure your daughter that this is one mistake she is unlikely to repeat.

PLAYING OUT A SCENARIO

Below is a typical dialogue you might have with your own daughter that puts into practice some of the ideas discussed in this chapter.

YOU: *Hi, honey. What's going on?*

SHE: *Nothing! (Stomps off to bedroom, slams door.)*

YOU *(after waiting for about a half hour, venturing up): You are clearly upset. Do you want to talk about what is going on?*

SHE: *NO!*

YOU: *Okay. Well, if you change your mind, I'll be downstairs. (Hours later she approaches you.)*

SHE: *I hate Amy!*

YOU: *Oh?*

SHE: *She is such a jerk!*

YOU: *Really? What happened?*

SHE: *She basically left me alone at the party tonight with all these people I didn't know, just because I refused to go outside and get drunk with her!*

(You look at her with a concerned but neutral expression, not saying a word.)

SHE: *I can't believe she was pissed off with ME! I'm the one who sat there like a loser all night by myself. Well, forget it, I'm not hanging out with her anymore. I hate her!*

YOU: *Well, it's obvious why you're so upset. What're your options?*

SHE: *Kill her.*

YOU: *Well that's definitely one solution. . . . How about another?*

SHE: *I want to go to a different school. I hate Amy and everyone she hangs out with.*

YOU: *Okay, changing schools. What else?*

SHE: *There's nothing else I can do.*

YOU: *Well, it seems to me that you do have other options.*

SHE: *Like?*

YOU: *Have you considered talking to her?*

SHE: *She won't change; she doesn't care about anyone but herself.*

YOU: *How do you know? Have you tried to talk to her?*

SHE: *What would I tell her?*

YOU: *Let's see if we can come up with some ideas. Start with what you'd really like her to know.*

SHE: *That what she did was totally rude. If you go to a party with someone, you don't just leave them by themselves—especially if that person doesn't really know anyone else. You stick together.*

YOU: *Sounds reasonable.*

SHE: *She probably won't listen.*

YOU: *She might not. But maybe you can think about how you could say it so Amy would be able to hear it. Then at least you'd feel better for speaking your mind.*

SHE: *Yeah, but what if she says I'm being stupid or something?*

YOU: *Do you think you're being stupid? You know you're not. She might not come right out and apologize right away, but you've still got a right to tell her how you feel.*

SHE: *She'll probably try to make it like I did something wrong.*

YOU: *It might help to imagine what Amy might say, and then you'll feel more prepared with what you could say back to her. Why don't you think about it some more?*

Even after all your expert guidance, your daughter may remain indecisive or may choose an alternative that doesn't seem right to you. She may think through the situation and decide it's in her best interest to confront Amy. Or she may come to you again and talk about the situation further, asking for more ideas about how to go about it. Ultimately she may decide to let the situation blow over, postpone confronting Amy, or handle the situation in an entirely different manner. It can be especially frustrating for mothers when daughters solicit their opinions, decide on a course of action, and then do nothing of the sort. But before you express disappointment, discouragement, or anger, remind yourself that your daughter has the right to choose whether and how to handle her own social situations. Her style and preferred tactics may simply be different from yours. Also, if you listen carefully to her reasoning, you may find she came to a thoughtful and logical conclusion that you hadn't considered.

You also have no control over how Amy or any other of your daughter's peers will react to her efforts to stand up for herself. Sometimes she will feel gratified by her efforts, sometimes not. She can always be reminded to stay the course when she's acted according to her feelings and convictions.

Part of what makes mothers' roles so confusing is that there is rarely any consistency in girls' ever-changing and complex social situations. On one occasion you may have considered all the available facts and found an approach that seemed to work like a charm. Soon afterward, however, another predicament arose that presented a whole new set of problems you'd never before encountered. Your previous strategy now seems inappropriate. Similarly, at various points your daughter may be more or less receptive to your input about her social life. While she's visibly grateful for your help one moment, she's declaring you "totally clueless" the next. For all these reasons, it is nearly impossible for mothers to feel completely confident in dealing with their daughters' peer issues.

What helps perhaps is knowing that the outcome of any given conflict is less important than your daughter's realizing the importance of sticking up for herself and recognizing that there are viable strategies for her doing so. As you help her develop a better appreciation for her options, she becomes empowered instead of feeling victimized. Though she may not behave assertively on one occasion, the process you have gone through together has given her tools—specifically, an internal template for effective decision making—to use in the next situation. The better your daughter can handle conflicts with her peers, the more confident and safe she will be in the future.

Telephone Tyranny

Because of all the time teenage girls typically spend on the phone, chances are good that at some point your daughter will experience telephone abuse. Sometime when she least expects it, she will be blasted over the phone by an infuriated friend or boyfriend. She will pick up the phone anticipating a friendly voice, and in response to her innocent hello, she will be bombarded brutally over the wires. Never mind if she actually did anything wrong. Or she may receive repetitive phone calls from peers who are playing jokes or being cruel. Girls often tolerate such verbal abuse over the phone because they don't realize that they have other choices.

Teach your daughter a straightforward two-part solution to this problem: (1) Say, "I will not be screamed at like this. Call back when you're ready to talk," and (2) hang up.

If the person calls back speaking more respectfully, your daughter can have a rational discussion about whatever she supposedly did. But caution her that if the person calls back behaving just as irately or abusively, she should repeat steps 1 and 2, as often as necessary.

It is more difficult for your daughter to handle unwanted, especially middle-of-the-night calls. Despite her protests, her caller may continue to dial at all hours. In such cases she may need to know it is acceptable to take the phone off the hook temporarily or turn off the ringer. You may have to get involved when calls are continuous despite your daughter's requests and especially when they are threatening or sexually inappropriate in nature.

Chapter Fourteen

Contending with Authority Figures

As comfortable and competent as mothers become in their ability to model conflict management for daughters, one area frequently continues to rattle their confidence: standing up to authority figures. For many women, the very idea of taking on someone powerful, particularly an older male, can be intimidating, if not overwhelming. Even when women are certain their frustrations and grievances are justified, they often feel inadequate to verbalize them. Sometimes they even fear that doing so will cause them to go to pieces. If you can relate even slightly to these feelings, you surely want things to be different for your daughter. You want her to feel entitled to stand up to authority when she feels she has been wronged, disrespected, or otherwise mistreated and then to feel good about herself for doing so. You have already taken the most critical steps by teaching her she is worthwhile and has every right to be treated with dignity and respect. Now that she is on her way to moving beyond the family, your role is a matter of supporting her as she increasingly contends with authority figures. Before you do this, however, it is important to examine whether you yourself (like many women) harbor conflicted feelings about taking on powerful people.

"RESPECT YOUR ELDERS"

As children many women had this message drummed into their heads, based on the carved-in-stone rule that well-mannered girls don't "talk back" or "sass" grown-ups. Even when adults said or did something you knew was clearly wrong, you may have been taught to stifle your protests, swallow your remarks, and behave "respectfully" toward elders. Early on you learned that age somehow earns adults the right to treat children however they wish.

In an era when children were safe roaming neighborhoods and playing unsupervised in parks, when kidnappings, carjackings, child porn, and pedophiles were far more distant fears than they are today, parents taught their children to put adults' rights and feelings before their own. Expressing irritation or resentment, much less anger, toward an adult practically guaranteed a swift spank or another punitive response. As a result, you may have learned to keep your feelings and comments about adults to yourself. These attitudes are often passed on to the next generation. Unfortunately this contributes to children today allowing harmful incidents to slide by, everything from their being slighted, patronized, and belittled to their being emotionally or physically harmed.

As your daughter grows up in this culture and deals increasingly with such authority figures as instructors, employers, and coaches, you are compelled to reevaluate what you want her to know about confronting adults. It is not that mothers should discontinue teaching teens respect for their elders but rather that they need to emphasize as well girls' rights to be treated with dignity and fairness. Women must convey to their daughters that it is more than acceptable to assess adults' motives, to set limits when they feel uncomfortable, and to take action when they are wronged.

FEAR OF BEING PUNISHED

For many girls, the thought of confronting an adult is enough to send them seeking refuge headfirst under blankets. When they imagine facing adults and expressing convictions of being mistreated, teens often feel "horrible," "sick," and sometimes even "terrified." Because girls rarely see women (much less girls) confronting authority figures, the process is virtually alien to them. Also, because girls rarely know how to approach an adult or what to expect if they do initiate a confrontation, they almost always imagine their worst fears.

Despite their protests to the contrary, teens often cling to the notion that adults know best; after all, they are the adults. Girls' fear of confrontation is further heightened when the adult in question holds some type of power; there is simply too much to lose for them. Specifically, a girl may worry that she will instantaneously make a bad situation worse. What if her coach benches her for refusing to try a dangerous maneuver? Or a salesperson ignores her when she tries to return merchandise? Or the couple for whom she baby-sits bad-mouths her because she reminds them of a forgotten payment? What if instead of respecting her thoughts and ideas, the person she confronts disparages her for having the audacity to speak up? Because there is no guaranteed payoff, be it an apology or a promise to set things right, it is no surprise that many girls would simply rather not take the risk of confronting adults.

So how can you convince your daughter that it is in her best interest to stand up for herself in spite of the intimidation? How should you teach her to go about it?

ESTABLISHING THE MIND-SET

First things first. Before your daughter can practice her skills and allay her anxiety, she must be convinced that there are times when it is necessary and absolutely in her best interest to confront adults in powerful positions. She must understand and truly believe that she is entitled to do so. She needs to know that she has a right to stand up for herself when she is being mistreated. Age and status do not entitle anyone to disrespect her. Although you have undoubtedly taught her that she deserves to be treated with decency and civility, as an adolescent she may need to hear straightforwardly that there is no excuse for adults to trample on her dignity, lie to her, offend her, make her question her worth, or hurt her.

Your daughter may not yet realize that the biggest benefit she will derive from speaking her mind to an adult who has wronged her is a sense of worth. You have been working hard to instill this in her since infancy. Nevertheless, hearing over and again why your teenager is so special and valued fortifies her as she faces the fear and intimidation of confronting an adult for the first time. This self-worth is what she takes with her as she goes out into the world, the indelible stamp you leave on her that enables her to speak out, make good choices, form healthy relationships, protect herself, and live life fully.

To combat your daughter's fear of confronting authority figures, you might assure her that she can use the very same skills she is learning within your relationship to think through carefully what she wants to accomplish and to communicate her thoughts and requests clearly.

The mistakes your daughter will make in her efforts are not necessary "evils," but essential learning tools. You may want to remind her once again of her learning curve in sports and school when she anticipates the likelihood of making mistakes in the process of mastering new skills. The same applies to her confronting authority figures. She would likely welcome hearing that you do not expect her to conduct herself perfectly but that with practice you are confident she will continue to improve. More important, you support her efforts because you know they will help her become stronger and more capable.

Using your own skills, you can listen actively to your daughter's worries and fears about confronting authority figures without assuming you know what they are, cutting her off before she finishes, or dismissing them. Asking about her worst fears often helps diminish them. Probing your daughter's assessment of the situation and clarifying her thinking facilitate effective problem solving. To elicit her reasoning, you might play devil's advocate or encourage her to generate as many alternative solutions as possible to the problem. Sharing anecdotes in which you or other adults faced similar dilemmas is often helpful. As always, avoid making her feel tested by helping your daughter to recognize that there is no one right answer. Both of you should come away from the discussion feeling as if you had learned something.

PRACTICE THE PROCESS WITH HER

Below are examples of circumstances your daughter may well have to deal with sooner or later, if she hasn't already. There are dozens of authority figures—relatives, restaurant owners, guidance counselors, etc.—but the sampling below best represents those whom teens say they deal with most often. As you read through, you might ask yourself and possibly your daughter how you both would handle each conflict; discuss your thoughts on how they were resolved. Listening to her reactions will help you pinpoint which areas might need further work in the future. As she talks through the possibilities, your daughter will realize she is capable of analyzing situations and thinking through good decisions.

- **THE TEACHER.** Considering the number of teachers with whom your daughter interacts during the course of her education, it is no surprise that she may have her share of clashes. No doubt she likes some of them, dislikes and distrusts others. The question is, What is your daughter supposed to do when she feels she's being treated unfairly by teachers and her grades are at stake? Take the case of sixteen-year-old Naomi, who had this story to share: "I had taken off two days of school for a Jewish holiday. The day I came back, my math teacher handed out a huge test. When I told her I didn't know anything about it, she told me that she'd told the class about the test two days before. She said, 'If you were going to be absent, you should have called someone in class to find out what was going on. It was your responsibility.' I don't even have any friends in that class! So I asked her if I could make up the test the next day, and she said, 'Absolutely not.' She wouldn't give me even one day!"

Naomi's mother, Ilene, felt that the teacher was clearly being inflexible about the situation, especially given the fact that her daughter had informed her beforehand of her planned absence for religious observance. As she put it, "Naomi offered to make up the test the following day, and still this teacher refused. Frankly that infuriated me." As incensed as Ilene was, she initially felt lost about how to help Naomi handle the situation. "I guess I was afraid that if we made a fuss with the teacher or took the issue to an administrator, Naomi and I might alienate the teacher further, and she had to be in this class the rest of the year. Plus, what if the teacher penalized Naomi by lowering her grade point average?"

Because she wanted to avoid making a big deal, Ilene at first encouraged Naomi to take the test and see what happened. Naomi got a sixty-two, effectively reducing her hard-earned A average.

Here's what Ilene had to say: "Maybe that was my wake-up call. I realized that I was doing what I always tend to do, going along with things because I'm afraid to rock the boat. I never want to be militant about issues or come off as demanding because I suppose that's how I saw my own mother, and that embarrassed me, especially as a teenager, to no end. But when I saw Naomi devastated because she had failed a test she had not had time to prepare for, it spurred me to rethink the situation. Talking to my husband and some close friends, and hearing their outrage, gave me courage to act on mine. I didn't want Naomi to get the idea that teachers are always correct or that she had to accept such injustices."

Speaking to her mother, Naomi made it clear that she wanted to handle the situation herself. So the two agreed the next course of action would be for Naomi to approach her teacher again. Ilene helped her daughter think through what she wanted to say. Essentially, there were several points they identified: (1) Naomi felt she had a right to observe the religious holiday without being penalized; (2) had she known of the test earlier in the week, she would have made different arrangements; (3) she had worked very hard in this class and was asking to retake the test to show what she had learned.

Said Ilene: "Naomi's teacher did in the end rethink her policy and let Naomi take an alternate version of the test. There's no question Naomi felt great about standing up to the teacher and making a change on her own behalf. I was glad that I was able to work through my own fears so I could allow her the chance to do that and feel stronger. But if the teacher hadn't changed her mind, I was also prepared to follow through by seeing her guidance counselor or the principal, if need be."

- **THE COACH.** This is the person who trains girls to challenge their limits, work through their self-doubts, and strive to achieve their peak performance. Girls and their parents trust coaches to know how far to push and when to pull back. They put faith in coaches to bring out girls' best. So what should a girl do if her coach pushes her too hard, makes her feel like less instead of more, or diminishes her esteem? Fifteen-year-old Chanelle told of the time this happened to her: "I was on my third lap around the track, remembering to pace myself, and I heard my coach scream, 'Push it! Come on, move!' So I gave it everything I had, and I knew I'd never run that fast in my life. When I passed through the finish line, I was so psyched. I came in second and broke my own record. When I went over to my coach, he said, 'Three seconds faster, and you would have had it! What a waste!' I couldn't believe it. I mean, he's always been a tough coach, but I couldn't believe he was yelling at me for coming in second. I burst into tears and said I was quitting."

Chanelle's coach tried to push her to run faster, but his strategy was too costly. She interpreted his message as: "Your effort doesn't count unless you take first place." Thus, she believed that he failed to appreciate that she had reached a personal victory by breaking her own record and that he believed only that she had failed for the team and for him. It was this perception that her coach had dismissed her effort, achievement, and personal goals that devastated her.

Observing what was happening on the track, her mother, Lucia, became enraged. She said: "I knew my hot temper was about to get me—and my daughter—in trouble again. All at once I was so furious I wanted to do him bodily harm. I nearly ran down those bleachers to give that coach a piece of my mind. I'm not even sure what stopped me. I actually did get up, and either someone grabbed my arm or I got hold of myself. Anyway, I figured we'd deal with it later."

Like her mother, Chanelle first wanted to tell the coach "what a jerk he was and that he sucked as a coach. And I would've said that too, but I was too busy crying." What she did do was impulsively quit, at that moment seemingly her only option. However, when she learned of this, Lucia became even more irate and determined that this coach would not get the best of her daughter. She insisted that Chanelle confront him and demand back her place on the team—or Lucia threatened to do so herself. When Chanelle refused, saying she wanted to "forget the whole thing," the conflict that started between her coach and her then became a problem between her mother and her. "After two days of going around and around," Lucia said, "I realized how ridiculous this was. The coach behaved horribly, Chanelle was out of a sport she loved, and we were the ones fighting!"

Taking a step back and thinking more clearly, Lucia recognized that it was simply not Chanelle's style (at least not as a fifteen-year-old) to "tell the coach what she thinks of him." Cajoling, pressuring, or threatening her daughter would be fruitless. She realized that she was inadvertently giving Chanelle the wrong message that there was only one right way (her way) to handle the situation. Ultimately she decided to help her daughter figure out what she wanted to do about the track and field coach.

Because she felt overwhelmed by the memories of the incident and the continued intensity of her feelings, Chanelle decided she was most comfortable writing her thoughts in a letter to the coach. Essentially, she told him that (1) she was proud of what she had done at the track meet because she had tried her best, (2) she wasn't going to feel bad about not taking first place, and (3) although she loved being on the team, she had a hard time with the coach's idea of success.

Much later Chanelle admitted to hoping that her letter would prompt the coach to ask her to rejoin the team. This was not the case. Also, although she regretted impulsively quitting, Chanelle refused to ask the coach if she could return. "Still," Lucia said, "I'm glad Chanelle feels good that she spoke her mind. Of course, we both got another lesson in how important it is to stay in control when you're upset, and I hope in the future she won't cut off her nose to spite her face."

- **THE PHYSICIAN.** Confronting, even questioning medical doctors has always been a hurdle for people, especially females. Viewing doctors as too all-knowing and powerful to be wrong, many allow themselves to be rushed through exams or spoken to condescendingly or rudely. Girls need to be reminded that they are paying for the physician's time and that they deserve to be treated respectfully. Eighteen-year-old Dana, about to leave for college, described an incident that challenged her in this regard: "I'd been tested for HIV, and I was in the doctor's office, waiting for my results. I was so nervous I thought I was going to throw up, and all I could think of was, What if I tested positive? What would I do? When the nurse brought me into the room, the doctor sat at his desk, holding my lab results. 'That's it,' I thought, 'he's going to tell me I'm HIV positive.' But before he said a word, the phone rang on his desk, and he picked it up and started chatting. Something about a restaurant and meeting spot—the guy was making dinner plans! I wanted to kill him. He talked for a few more moments, and just when I thought I was going to yank the paper from him, he hung up and told me I was negative—in the clear. I was so relieved I felt ecstatic. It wasn't until I got home and thought about his behavior that I wished I'd told him what a jerk he was. How dare he sit there chatting on the phone while I was waiting to hear if I had AIDS!"

Why hadn't she addressed the doctor's behavior? In part Dana was so relieved to hear the good news that at least for the moment she was not even aware of her anger. It was only later that she began to think about what had occurred and labeled the doctor's actions cold and insensitive. But Dana also admitted that even had she known in his office how she was feeling, she would have been speechless in the doctor's presence. She said, "Afterward I was telling my mother about my clean bill of health and then how badly the doctor had treated me. It was only when I started talking about it to my mom that I realized how mad I was."

Dana's mother, Joan, confessed that initially her daughter's anger was the last concern on her list. "I was so shocked that she had gotten an HIV test that I couldn't focus on Dana's anger toward the doctor. I was thinking, 'Why is she worried about AIDS?' and just those words made me shake." It took all her self-control not to blurt out, "What's wrong with you? Are you sleeping around?" but "Somehow I told myself just to stop and take a deep breath. I knew if I'd said those things, the trust we'd been building would fly out the window. Dana was leaving for college soon, and I was determined not to let that happen."

Although she attributed her ensuing silence primarily to being speechless, Joan later decided it was the most effective thing she could have done. For one, it encouraged Dana to continue talking. "I think I learned more about my daughter's ideas in that one conversation than I had in a long time. Dana's views about the doctor led into a discussion about other situations she had been in that I had never known about. I also understood better her motivation to be tested before she went to college."

Ultimately Dana and Joan did speak about options to deal with the doctor. After the fact, of course, it was far easier for them to be Monday morning quarterbacks, thinking of the perfect response, the exact right words, to express how Dana was feeling. Basically, Dana decided that she really wanted him to know that his insensitivity was hurtful, that telling her the test results quickly would have been kinder, and that she hoped he would never make patients wait for life-and-death results while he talked casually on the phone. She wrote down her thoughts in a letter and sent it out the next morning.

Joan was pleased about how she handled the situation with Dana. "For once," she said, "I was able to separate my feelings from hers. I got past the sexuality issue enough to be somewhat neutral, and that is what she needed. Next year she's going to be living on her own and can do whatever she wants, so I hope our talks will stay with her." When Joan could help Dana convey her feelings to her doctor, her daughter felt stronger and less victimized, and both came away from this experience feeling closer.

- **THE EMPLOYER.** Many teenage girls take on part-time jobs after school, helping out in offices, working cash registers, baby-sitting, or bagging groceries. Perhaps your daughter has been flying high after beginning a job, reveling in newfound independence and the thrill of her first paycheck. One thing is for sure, though: At some point, if it hasn't happened already, the boss who pays her wages is going to do or say something that upsets her. In certain situations (the employer asks her to put in extra hours or tells her that she can't take a certain day off) she will have to do as her employer wishes, despite her feelings. Still, when bosses abuse their power or take advantage of teens, it is imperative that girls speak up. Thirteen-year-old Margarite found this the case in her baby-sitting job: "It was the first time I had ever baby-sat for the new neighbors. I was really excited. They were supposed to be home at ten-thirty, so by eleven I started getting nervous. They didn't call or anything to say they'd be late. What if something bad had happened? What if they'd been in an accident? Of course, my mother called to see what was up, and she didn't sound happy. When the parents finally showed up, all they said was 'Sorry, we ended up going out for coffee.' I couldn't believe the lame excuse! When they paid me, I figured I wouldn't ever be baby-sitting for them again."

Margarite knew she had every right to be upset. She always counted on adults to be home when they said they would, and by their not calling to say they would be late, she felt completely taken advantage of. They had put Margarite in a situation that made her worry needlessly. On top of that, they had made her late getting home, and to add insult to injury, they had barely acknowledged their behavior. Despite all these justifications for her anger, it never occurred to her to do anything but keep quiet and politely thank the parents when they paid her.

Rosa, her mother, admitted she was ambivalent herself. "I don't think my daughter should be treated that way, but I don't want her to grow up disrespectful either. Besides, what could she say that would make a difference to these people? I know it's not my way to speak up. It's something I've been working on myself." Because she was aware of her own misgivings and troubled by a need to resolve the situation for Margarite, Rosa made it a point to discuss the situation with her sister. "I especially wanted to get her opinion since she's known in the family for saying exactly what she thinks." According to Rosa, her sister was vehement that Margarite may have been only thirteen, but she had earned that money. It wasn't a gift or charity; it was owed to her. And it was separate from how the parents treated her.

This feedback fueled Rosa's resolve to address the situation. But the solution seemed less clear-cut. She considered whether Margarite or she should call the parents. After much discussion Rosa and her daughter decided that if the parents called again asking her to baby-sit, Margarite would say to them something to the effect that she'd like to keep baby-sitting for them, but she would need to know that they'd be home as planned. Further, because her mother worried if she were not home on time, the parents would need to call in advance if they were going to be late.

The husband did in fact call to ask Margarite to baby-sit again, and Margarite said she could accept only if they were okay with her mother's conditions, which she promptly explained. Although he offered no profuse apology, he did promise to return on time in the future or, at the very least, to call if they were delayed. The couple stuck to their end of the bargain, and Margarite continued to baby-sit for them. Had they not agreed to her terms, Margarite said, she was prepared to tell them they'd have to find another baby-sitter. Either way she felt good about her sense of control. Speaking up prevented her from smoldering about her mistreatment, berating herself for doing nothing, or imagining all the things she could have said. Both Margarite and her mother felt better that they had not passively accepted the situation or avoided a confrontation out of fear.

- **THE POLITICIAN.** These days girls are aware of social issues, often finding causes that stir them and push them to get active. Your daughter, for instance, may feel strongly about recycling or protecting endangered species, helping the homeless, or making sure girls have the same opportunities as boys to play sports. Although girls want to contribute to causes, they too often decide that they are too young or powerless to do anything of real value. Here's what happened to seventeen-year-old Leslie: "Our local government was getting ready to approve plans for a huge new development in the community that would mean hundreds of trees were going to be torn down, not to mention add tons of traffic to the area right by our house. It made no sense at all, and I was furious, but I didn't feel there was anything I could do. I wasn't even old enough to vote or anything. It stinks knowing you have to be at least eighteen to have any real say."

When Leslie's mother, Donna, heard her daughter complaining about the town development plans, she found it difficult to be sympathetic. After all, Donna supported the development, which promised many conveniences: "It will make my life a whole lot easier since the closest place to do errands right now is thirty minutes away." Therefore, whenever Leslie talked about how horrible the change was, Donna poured her energy into convincing her daughter that the development was a town improvement that would make all their lives better. The more Leslie resisted, the more adamant Donna became about persuading her daughter that the development was a good idea.

In the middle of Donna's defense, Leslie suddenly yelled, "Why do I have to agree with you? What makes your opinion any better than mine?" It was at that moment, Donna said, that "it clicked. She was right. I had spent years encouraging her to stand by her own opinions, and here I was telling her she had to agree with mine. I felt horrible, like a hypocrite, and I knew what I had to do next. I had to put my feelings aside and encourage her to do what was right for her."

That's exactly what happened. After apologizing to her daughter for not respecting her opinion, she told Leslie it was wonderful that she wanted to make a difference about a situation she felt strongly about. She informed her daughter that as a constituent and future voter, Leslie had plenty of power right now to voice her opinions. Not only wasn't her age a barrier to making her beliefs known, Donna explained, but Leslie had several alternative ways to handle it—namely, she could (1) write a letter to the town government stating exactly what she thought about the project and why, (2) write a letter expressing her thoughts for the op-ed section in her local newspaper, and (3) start a petition, and get as many signatures as possible.

Leslie, excited about this chance to express her views, drafted a letter to the town government that night, explaining her thoughts on why the development was environmentally detrimental. Donna not only praised her but offered pointers on how to make the letter even stronger; within a few short hours both were proud of how the letter had turned out. "We learned a lot from this situation," Donna said. "I can see that she is growing into someone with strong opinions, even if they are different from mine. She now knows I will support her, even if we disagree, and I know it meant a lot to her that I could admit when I was wrong."

- **THE STORE SALESPERSON/OWNER.** For all the time teenage girls spend in malls and stores, you would think they would feel comfortable speaking to sales staffs. But girls have a terrible time standing up for themselves, even asking for help, because they often feel ignored or belittled by salespeople. May, fifteen, was one of those girls: "When I brought back the broken Walkman, I figured I'd be in and out of the store in under a minute. I'd just tell the salesperson that one earphone didn't work and I wanted a new one. So when the saleswoman told me, 'Sorry, final sale,' I was pissed. I told her I had a receipt, and the Walkman was broken when I got it. She sighed like I was making it up and said something to another lady. I was getting madder and madder, so I told her again that I wanted my money back. She rolled her eyes, and at that point I lost it. I told her what I thought about her and that store, using R-rated words I can't repeat, and slammed the Walkman on the counter. Then the manager came out and asked me to leave the store, without even hearing my side of the story!"

Suyin, May's mother, was none too pleased upon hearing the story from a neighbor who had returned from the mall after witnessing the incident. Suyin listened to the story in humiliation and stewed in her anger until she could confront her daughter.

"I was mortified," Suyin admitted. "All I could think of was that my neighbor must see me as an unfit parent and that she would tell other neighbors what she had seen. When I told May that I heard what had happened and that I was furious, she said I was as bad as the manager, who wouldn't listen to her side of the story—and even worse, because I was supposed to be on her side."

Suyin, still infuriated, told May she didn't want to hear another word about it. She then called her own mother to relay the incident and get some sympathy. Instead, she got a whole lot of ribbing. "My mother thought it was hilarious since I used to drive her crazy all the time. She was right, of course, and I remembered how mad I would get when my own mother would chew me out without hearing my side of the story. She even got me to laugh a little, and I realized I had allowed my own embarrassment, instead of the real issue, to become the focus of the situation."

The next morning Suyin told May that she would like to hear her side of the story. She listened and then explained that while May's feelings were perfectly understandable, her behavior was not—not so much because she had made a fuss in public as because it had eliminated her chance of being taken seriously and accomplishing her goal. She told May about her own childhood tantrums and how they had left others thinking she was irrational and therefore not worth listening to. She was then able to discuss with her daughter other approaches to standing up for her rights: (1) asking to speak with the store manager, who could authorize returned merchandise; (2) explaining (without losing her temper) that she had received faulty merchandise and wanted a refund; (3) contacting the company headquarters (by phone or letter), describing the problem, the steps she had already taken, and her realistic request ("I'd like my money back within two weeks" or "I want this product fixed by next week"); and, if all else failed, (5) calling the local Better Business Bureau.

To handle the situation, May and Suyin decided it was probably best to send a letter to the store manager, apologizing for the outburst but explaining the problem. A week later the manager called and told her that a new Walkman was waiting for May at the front counter. Said Suyin: "I'm glad the situation happened. At least when May is in danger of losing her temper next time, she might remember that there are better ways to handle a problem. I wish I had understood how to stand up for myself when I was a kid. It would have saved me a lot of heartache."

ASSESSING THE CONFRONTATION TOGETHER

Once your daughter decides to confront an authority figure, there is nothing more for you to do than perhaps sit back and hold your breath that it goes as she hopes. For many mothers, this is the hardest part. Although you respect and applaud her efforts to handle such situations on her own—indeed, you have been raising her to do so—it is unsettling when she initially goes off on her mission, leaving you powerless to do anything but wait to hear the outcome.

Regardless of whether the confrontation was ultimately satisfying, your daughter will benefit from hearing that what she did was courageous and responsible. If you encourage her to critique her own behavior, instead of your doing it for her, she is more likely to act according to her convictions than to act merely to please you. Of course, she will not always get the strong, positive response she was looking for from the authority figure she confronts. She may need to be warned that some authority figures in fact will not take kindly to a teenager who doesn't "remember who's in charge" or "not talk back." Should the person she confronted respond inappropriately, she must not interpret this as evidence of her failure. Just as you learned to stay the course in your conflicts with your daughter, you are teaching her to act according to her beliefs, regardless of whether she ultimately gets the response she wants. You want her to feel good about herself because she articulated her needs, took steps to protect herself, or attempted to right wrongs. This is true whether the person she confronts is the next-door neighbor, her gym teacher, the clerk at the DMV, or her senator. Through these experiences your daughter will gradually develop a repertoire of powerful skills at her disposal.

Out of Line

•**HOW TO KNOW WHEN ADULTS REACT INAPPROPRIATELY DUR-ING A CONFRONTATION** ... Not only will authority figures not react to your daughter's confrontation positively, but sometimes they may be so unnerved by a younger person's addressing their behavior that they will respond with hostility. It is crucial that your daughter learns to detect when an adult's behavior is out of bounds, especially if it is abusive or nearly so. Here are questions your daughter might ask herself.

IS THE PERSON'S FURY OUT OF PROPORTION TO THE PERCEIVED CRIME?

When adults raise their voices or verbally express emotions that seem unwarranted or extreme, your daughter should rightfully wonder if they are out of control. As she gains more experience, she will be better able to trust her judgment.

DO I FEEL PHYSICALLY THREATENED?

When adults invade your daughter's personal space, coming too close for her comfort, or raise their arms in a threatening manner, she is correct in feeling their expression of feelings is inappropriate.

IS THE MESSAGE CRUEL OR ATTACKING?

It is never okay for adults to use your daughter's vulnerability to their advantage in a conflict. If someone mentions, for example, her disability, religion, family, gender, or race, this constitutes a personal attack; it does not belong in conflict resolution. Such behavior should be regarded as unnecessary, cruel, and perhaps evidence of prejudice.

IS THE MESSAGE ACCUSATORY AND UNDESERVED?

Sometimes, when adults react according to their unacknowledged feelings or issues, they may accuse your daughter undeservedly. She will recognize this phenomenon when adults come out of left field and especially when they're unswerved by the facts of the situation.

DOES THE TIRADE GO ON AND ON?

Your daughter should recognize when adults get carried away, repeating their messages over and again without cessation or going off on tangents. All these times their fury seems to have a life of its own, over and above whatever it is that she may have done.

If your daughter answers yes to any of these questions, she should understand that she is within her rights to protect herself from both verbal and physical threats. She need not listen to an adult's inappropriate or out-of-control tirade. She should also realize that defending herself at that time will most likely fall on deaf ears. If she chooses to set a limit on what she will tolerate, she can say something on the order of "I can see you are upset, but I won't be spoken to that way." Or she may need to separate herself from the person acting inappropriately. Walking away, ending a discussion, and hanging up a telephone are effective strategies. Should she feel the need to confront that person again, it may be in her best interest to ask that she be accompanied by an adult, such as yourself or, in a school setting, a principal, a guidance counselor, or an ombudsman.

Saying It on Paper

Whether your daughter is overwhelmed by the idea of confronting an authority figure face-to-face or she simply expresses herself best in writing, she needs a basic formula for crafting a letter. Knowing how to protest effectively will allow her to feel more powerful and competent and enable her to get her needs met more often. Following are the dos and don'ts you can share with her about writing someone in power.

- **ADDRESS THE PERSON IN POWER CORRECTLY.** It is important to know the official title or position of the person to whom you are writing. This information can be obtained simply by making a phone call (e.g., to find out the position of an employee at a store) or making a trip to the local library (e.g., to see a list of elected officials and their addresses).
- **BE SPECIFIC.** Rather than say you don't like a certain bill, rule, or policy, explain your reasons, and whenever possible, provide evidence for your views. For example, instead of "I don't like bill no. 2014," try, "If you pass bill no. 2014, I worry that the gray wolves will lose their homes and possibly become extinct. That's what almost happened back in 1988 when . . ."

- **BE DIRECT.** Say what you have to say, without rambling; then sign off. People in power typically receive enormous amounts of mail and have little time to wade through mininovels. Briefer is usually better.
- **DON'T BE ACCUSATORY OR MALICIOUS.** Try to mention something positive before saying what you disagree with. For example, you might write, "While I agreed with your decision to [fill in blank], I have a hard time with your decision to . . ." In general, people are more open to your ideas if you don't malign them.
- **DON'T THREATEN.** Telling people they had "better listen" will not encourage them to continue reading the letter or motivate them to hear your message.
- **SUPPORT YOUR OPINIONS.** Enclose with your letter any articles, studies, or editorials relevant to the topic.

Sample Complaint Letter

Your street address
City, state, zip code
Date

President of company/director of customer service dept.
Name of company
Street address or post office box
City, state, zip code

Dear Mr. or Ms._____:

First paragraph: Briefly summarize the facts of situation, including the date of the dispute, what occurred, names of person(s) to whom you have spoken about this problem so far and how they responded.

Second paragraph: State clearly what you would like the person to whom you are writing to do to resolve the problem (send refund, replace item, reconsider employment application, etc.).

Third paragraph: State your expectations about when (by a certain date, within three weeks) and how (in the evenings at such and such phone number, by letter to the above address) the person to whom you are writing may best respond to your letter. Then thank the person for his or her anticipated help.

Sincerely,

Your signature

Chapter Fifteen

Growing from
Her Mistakes

Not only are you teaching your daughter to address grievances, manage strong negative feelings, and resolve conflicts that arise in her interactions with others, but also you want her to exercise the same judiciousness with herself. When teenage girls believe they have committed a heinous crime, however, their reactions may be extreme and unconstructive, perhaps even self-defeating or downright dangerous. Feeling ashamed about something she did or didn't do or becoming disgusted with herself, your daughter may behave in any number of ways that challenge you as her mother to respond helpfully.

What did your daughter do to "screw up royally"? The potential crimes are too numerous to list. On any given day she may disappoint a close friend, fail a final, cave in to drinking temptations, allow her boyfriend to pressure her sexually, or simply say something so "stupid" that it makes her wince to think about it. Whereas you have the perspective to view your daughter's error as just one of many experiences in her life education, the catastrophic thinking of adolescence may cause your daughter to believe her mistake will eliminate all hopes of future happiness—or at least threaten her present social survival. Just as you did in peer situations, you can apply your skills to assisting your daughter resolve conflicts within herself. This chapter will offer some common scenarios that will test your knowledge. But first, take a look at the signals girls send out to indicate their distress after making (or at least perceiving they made) an error.

ACTING OUT HER DISTRESS

As you are well aware, when your daughter is upset with herself, there is not a small chance that she will take out her feelings directly on you. For example, it must have been your asking about her friend's surprise party just before school that made her blurt out the news at the exact worst time. She never even would have thought about the party, much less mentioned it aloud, if you hadn't planted the idea in her head! "It wasn't my fault" is the refrain you may hear, over and over again, whenever there is the remotest possibility your daughter blames herself.

The reason of course is not that she hates you or wants to make you miserable. It is that the alternative—facing up to her own mistakes—is often far too disturbing for a teenage girl. To acknowledge that she erred means allowing herself to feel regret, shame, and tremendous anxiety. It can be terrifying for teens to realize they have the capacity to inflict emotional damage, disappointing and hurting the people they care most about, especially when they didn't intend to do so. Anger directed at herself is just as frightening as rage toward others. What will she do with it? When such strong feelings are channeled toward you, they seem safer and far more manageable.

KEEPING IT ALL INSIDE

Instead of taking out her unhappiness on you or other family members, your daughter may characteristically keep her negative feelings locked up inside. In response to a perceived error she may, for example, hide out in her room, avoid using the phone, and withdraw from close relationships. She may have trouble sleeping or may lose her appetite. When girls obsess about their problems, they often cannot concentrate on schoolwork. In more extreme cases girls may feel so ashamed they blatantly punish themselves or take risks to bring about unconsciously the punishment they feel they deserve. In the worst situations girls feel as if they cannot go on with their lives. Faced with such possibilities, you might prefer that you yourself were the target of your daughter's fury. It is easier than seeing your daughter "beat up on herself."

TYPICAL MISTAKES OF TEENAGE GIRLS

Below are typical situations that instigate teenage girls' self-condemnation. As you read about these crises, imagine how you would apply what you've learned thus far to help your daughter through them.

Being Irresponsible

- Your fourteen-year-old daughter tells the next-door neighbors that she'd love to take care of their cat while they are on vacation. Because she loves their cat, as well as the thought of earning extra money, she convinces the neighbors that they should entrust her, rather than a kennel, to handle the job. The first day everything goes fine, but on the second day the cat sneaks out of the house the moment she opens the door. After searching for hours, your daughter becomes distraught, has trouble eating and sleeping because she berates herself for her "stupidity," and convinces herself that the neighbors will never, ever forgive her. As far as she is concerned, this is her last job.
- While baby-sitting for a young boy, your thirteen-year-old daughter is putting his favorite video in the VCR when she hears an awful scream. Running to the kitchen, she finds that when he pulled his "blankie" off the counter, a glass of lemonade fell and cut his toe in the process. Although she uses the correct first-aid procedures and he seems fine, she spends the next several hours reprimanding herself for leaving the glass on the counter and rehearsing what to tell his parents. She can't stop imagining what would have happened if he had had to go to the hospital.

Letting Other People Down

- During her team's play-offf game your fifteen-year-old daughter's coach puts her in as goalie. Although she thinks she is concentrating, she gives up two goals at the end of the game, and her team loses to their biggest rivals. Your daughter, feeling personally responsible, apologizes repeatedly, but her teammates remain disappointed. Although they reassure her it wasn't her fault, she is certain they hate her. She readily admits that she despises herself.

Letting Herself Down

- During her junior year your daughter becomes so obsessed with a boy that her life revolves around him. Though her friends (and you) try to talk to her about how much she has changed, she refuses to acknowledge it. Then she gets a D on her science midterm, a significant drop from her typical achievement. Although she is panicked about "screwing everything up" for college, she still refuses to get help because it would mean giving up time with her boyfriend. She never does anything to solve her problem and continues to think less of herself.

Being Clumsy or Scatterbrained

- While visiting her favorite aunt while you were away, your twelve-year-old daughter is saying how much she appreciates staying there when she trips on the edge of the rug and knocks over a vase that was a treasured gift from a special friend. Your daughter calls herself vicious names and can't stop worrying even when her aunt tells her not to worry. Your daughter is beside herself, as if she can't let go of the incident.
- Your sixteen-year-old daughter is personally responsible for losing more house keys than anyone else in the family. Despite her promise to be careful with the newest key, she soon discovers she can't find it anywhere. When her father has to change all the locks in the house and make enough keys for the whole family once again, she becomes distressed and verbally abusive to herself.

Giving in to Peer Pressure

- After your fifteen-year-old daughter's friend pressures her to take a drink in front of all her other friends, she caves in and drinks a couple of shots. In her mind, "everyone was looking at me like 'What's the big deal? Just do it!'" To make matters worse, a boy she has liked suddenly acted interested in her, and under the influence of alcohol, she says she got more physical with him than she had ever intended. Afterward she feels humiliated.
- Your seventeen-year-old daughter's friend convinces her that the whole class is cheating and it "isn't that big of a deal." She says she wouldn't have even thought about it except that she needs at least a B— to keep up her average. Although she studies, she knows that cheating would guarantee excelling on the test, and she doesn't want to take any chances. Plus, she figures that so many kids do it and don't get caught that she will do it just this one time and then never again. But she is caught and receives an F, which causes her to loathe herself to no end.

Breaking Trust

- After she and some friends sneak out of their respective apartments at 2:00 A.M. and meet at a downtown club, your sixteen-year-old daughter is caught and punished. She says the worst thing, however, is the way you look at her now. She can tell that you don't trust her anymore and wishes desperately she could turn back the clock. She feels devastated over losing your trust.

- When your seventeen-year-old daughter starts driving to school, she occasionally stops at the local doughnut place for breakfast. Soon friends begin asking her for rides, and stopping for doughnuts becomes the routine. More often than not she is late to her first-period class, but this doesn't stop her. When she gets a detention notice and realizes the teacher holds her tardiness against her, your daughter finally gets upset. Plus, her soccer coach is informed of all this and threatens to kick her off the team if she gets one more tardy notice.

Saying the Wrong Thing

- Your thirteen-year-old daughter is talking with some girls at school when someone makes a comment about a mutual friend. She hears herself saying something about this girl that sounds unkind. Your daughter claims that her comment wasn't meant that way. A few days later, however, it precipitates an enormous conflict because classmates are talking about what your daughter said. The friend she was speaking about finds out and won't talk to her. Your daughter is convinced that everyone hates her and no one wants to be her friend anymore.
- In the middle of a fight with you, your fifteen-year-old daughter yells "No wonder Dad doesn't want to be married to you anymore!" She knows how cruel that is as soon as she says it. Although she apologizes, she can't take it back and now is ashamed at how hurtful she has been.

RESPONDING TO HER SELF-BLAME

If saying or doing the wrong thing is embarrassing for adults, it is nothing short of devastating for teenagers. As you know, regardless of how heartfelt your assurances ("It will be forgotten tomorrow" or "This will all work out"), they will do nothing to alleviate your daughter's agony and shame. She cannot appreciate that tomorrow "everyone" will be focused on someone else's late-breaking story or mortifying moment. If you tried to convince her that her mistake is not as glaring, obvious, and unforgivable as she thinks, your credibility would be nil. This approach would serve only to invalidate her feelings and confirm her worst fears about the deficiencies of your judgment.

Similarly, you know the likely consequences of reacting with hostility. Even if you realize your daughter is angry at herself, it is difficult not to resent her for using you as her target. But she might misinterpret your anger as a reaction to her "crime," rather than to her mistreatment of you. In this way girls often end up provoking from mothers the very criticism and punishment they feel on some level they deserve.

Instead of your reacting negatively, it is important to focus on helping your daughter work through her own internal conflicts: to acknowledge or to deny she was at fault; to remain passive or to take action; to perpetuate or to cease her self-denigration; to maintain a grudge or to forgive herself.

Your daughter needs to know that you expect her to make mistakes and to grow from them. As part of mothering her, you help her through this process. Although you take this seriously, by the same token, you will not allow her to express her disappointment in herself by disrespecting or abusing anyone, including herself. Finally, whatever her course of action, she must learn how to put the incident behind her and move on.

HELPING HER DEAL WITH MISTAKES

Certainly some of the circumstances described above would be considered more your daughter's "fault" than others. But that isn't really the point. What matters is that regardless of their severity, she needs to acknowledge her mistakes, as well as the pain she provoked in others or feels toward herself. Only then can she do what she can to set things right. By fixing her error the best she can, she comes to terms with it and moves on with her life. Of course, expecting your daughter simply to "get over" the incident when it feels tragic and permanent to her is unrealistic. So what can you do to help?

Empathize and Support Her

Your experience allows you to place mistakes precisely where they belong on the grand scale of life's tragedies. But your teenage daughter rarely can. This is frustrating not just for her but for you too. You know that being scolded by a coach for showing up late to practice, getting a speeding ticket, and getting a poor grade are, in the scheme of things, mere bumps in the road—soon to be left behind and utterly forgotten. But your daughter, who believes these errors are tantamount to homicide, has a difficult time getting perspective and moving ahead.

By now you're a pro at empathic listening. So instead of telling her, "It's no big deal," or, conversely, that you agree she has "really blown it," you can acknowledge her guilt and pain about the situation ("I can see how upset you are" or "I know how much you'd like to turn back the clock" or "It's hard to stop thinking, 'If only . . .' ").

Even when it tugs at your heartstrings to hear how "stupid" or "evil" she thinks she is, remember that listening empathically is your invaluable gift to your daughter. You may not be able to fix her problem, but your attentiveness and abiding love are crucial. They are the standard against which she measures her crime. Since you haven't abandoned her, her mistake could not have been as horrible as she thought.

Differentiate the Person from the Behavior

Girls are often at their most vulnerable after admitting mistakes. Your daughter may well believe that what she did was hateful, so you must now hate her. Particularly if you agree that what she did was wrong, she may look for and overreact to any sign of your disapproval. You convey your unconditional love for her by keeping your voice tone neutral and concerned ("Maybe you can think of how to avoid this mistake next time" or "Why don't you come up with a different plan?"), not angry or accusatory ("You're the biggest klutz in the family" or "If you would just think before you talk!" or "When are you going to learn?"). Your daughter thereby recognizes that you wish not to rub salt in her wound but to help her understand what motivated her to make the mistake and how to avoid repeating it. This knowledge will contribute to her developing sense of self-control.

Girls can be demanding of themselves, perfectionistic or self-critical to an extreme. Instead of moving on, some handle guilt by doing self-injurious things. Others assuage anguish by drinking, starving or purging, or "forgetting" to take prescribed medication. If you are concerned about your daughter in these ways, you may want to watch over her more closely when she is angry at herself. For example, rather than isolate or even reject her, you might choose to stay even more connected with her. For this reason, additional punishments such as grounding or restricting her to her room may be counterproductive when she is already regretting her error. If your daughter's discouragement and self-criticism last for more than a few days or interfere with

school or social activities, get a consultation to see if further help is
needed.

Teach Her the Value of Learning from Mistakes

When your daughter does something she regrets, it is an opportunity to
teach her about the potential for learning from mistakes. She might be
surprised to learn that much of society' progress has been accidental:
Someone goofed, and, voilà, a whole new invention, technology, or
medical cure was born. Your daughter may have a hard time accepting
that people learn by doing—and that includes failing. Although she
may roll her eyes when you tell her this, it's important she hear the
message anyway. One day she will experience this powerful phenomenon for herself. Along with the ability to accept responsibility
for her actions, this knowledge will facilitate her becoming a more
resourceful and resilient person.

Guide Her on the Path to Self-forgiveness

Help your daughter through these five distinct steps as she makes her
way from self-condemnation to self-forgiveness.

STEP ONE: ACKNOWLEDGE THE MISTAKE

The first step in setting things right is for her to acknowledge she's
done something wrong. If your daughter has contributed to hurting
someone, for example, you will want her to accept responsibility for
her actions—regardless of whether she says she wasn't "totally" responsible, "didn't mean it," or "wasn't the only one involved." On the
other hand, watching your daughter struggle with guilt and self-
deprecation is so painful you may be tempted to protect her. Some
mothers, for example, rush to reassure ("You wouldn't hurt anyone"),
to minimize the severity of the situation ("It's no big deal"), or to
absolve their daughters ("You couldn't have known better"). These
responses may ease girls' pain temporarily, but at the expense of impeding their growth and preparedness for life.

Consequently, as difficult as this is for both of you, encourage your
daughter to acknowledge her part in hurting or disappointing others.
Undoubtedly you will not accept her excuses for her behavior ("But it
wasn't my fault!" or "The cat just snuck out!" or "How was I supposed

to know there was a glass on the counter?") or blaming others ("I wouldn't have done that if he hadn't . . ."). Through your interactions with your daughter, you have admitted you made mistakes and apologized for them. You can remind her that she can do the same.

Regardless of whether her message is delivered in person, by phone, or in a written note, when she can say to someone, "I'm genuinely sorry. I will do whatever I can to fix the problem, and I'll do my best to make sure it never happens again," she is empowered to move beyond guilt and self-loathing. She can acknowledge her actions and apologize as the first steps in moving on.

STEP TWO: FIX IT WHEN YOU CAN

You can teach your daughter to channel her anger at herself into constructive action. She can make amends for her mistake. Whenever your daughter can replace or fix a broken object, for example, she is fortunate to find a simple and satisfying solution. In other situations she may not be able to set things exactly right but can come up with creative ideas. If the cat got away or a child was hurt while she was baby-sitting, she can't make this unhappen. But she can do her best to repair the damage she caused, such as bandaging the cut or looking for the cat, tacking up reward posters, calling the pound or local vets, and so forth. The cut will heal, and one hopes the cat will return. If she cannot replace what has been lost, contributing money she earns for that purpose is another strategy. Whatever she decides to do, your daughter will learn that doing something, anything, is usually more satisfying than doing nothing. Your support of your daughter's attempts to make things better will demonstrate that effort counts, even if it doesn't completely resolve or erase the problem.

STEP THREE: BUILD SELF-AWARENESS

Rather than dwell on how awful, horrible, pitiful, or pathetic she is as a result of her mistake, ask your daughter if she knows why the mistake might have happened in the first place. In shifting her focus, you empower your daughter to make connections among thoughts, feelings, and behavior.

Sometimes the answer to this is obvious: Your daughter tripped and broke something, didn't study enough, or was too nervous or careless. Other times, however, it may take her a bit of soul-searching to find the real reason. This is especially true when she's hurt someone's feelings. Even if the act wasn't deliberate, you could encourage her to ask herself why it might have happened nonetheless.

Your daughter may not yet realize her part, however unconscious, in choosing to do what she did. She may say, "I have no idea," or, "How am I supposed to know?" Your role may be to encourage further reflection. You might, depending on your daughter's receptivity, suggest several possibilities ("Could you have been feeling a bit jealous?" or "Did you think the others would be impressed?" or "Were you afraid to speak up?"). Although you may not get an immediate answer from your daughter, you may inspire her eventual insight.

Although your daughter may be horrified that she acted out of malice, jealousy, or spite, she ultimately benefits from this realization. First, becoming aware of negative feelings will reduce the possibility of her acting them out in ways that she will regret. Second, she may choose to express her negative feelings verbally or at least to channel them into constructive action. Third, your assurance that these are normal human emotions will teach her to accept them in herself.

For example, if your daughter admits that she started a rumor about a friend, you might go beyond making suggestions ("Why don't you apologize?" or "Call her and ask her to come over"). You can explore the motivation behind her actions ("What do you think prompted you to do that?" or "Was something bothering you?" or "What do you suppose you wanted to accomplish?"). In doing so, you will have the opportunity to discuss such feelings as being threatened, coping with jealousy, or being vengeful.

Sometimes soul-searching compels girls to confront their true feelings about people or circumstances for the first time. Such revelations can open floodgates of emotion and encourage girls to "spill their guts." Many mothers and daughters have experienced the satisfaction that comes from new understanding and closeness after the storminess of discussing a problem. In other words, you and your daughter might anticipate a silver lining in the clouds of conflict.

STEP FOUR: MAKE SURE SHE DOESN'T DO IT AGAIN

Until scientists perfect a nonklutz gene or superorganization vitamin, your daughter will have to figure out how to change the old-fashioned way. Here are some pointers you can give her that have a proved track record.

- **BECOME ORGANIZED.** Have your daughter establish a special place for such important items as keys, money, homework, and so forth. A sensible motto is: "A place for everything, and everything in its place" (although it is not advisable to quote this repeatedly). She should get used to putting away important belongings as soon as she's done with them, as opposed to leaving them under the couch or amid a pile of papers on her desk. She should also have a routine that works, such as storing finished homework in her backpack at night, rather than when she's running around bleary-eyed in the morning. If she's having trouble managing her time effectively, she might develop a realistic schedule and post it somewhere conspicuous.

- **MAKE RULES.** Help your daughter establish reasonable rules for herself and then stick to them. For example, if she's performing poorly in school because she's sleeping through classes, she's going to have to get more rest, maybe even by setting an earlier bedtime. Or take the examples above. If she "screws up" by letting the cat escape while cat-sitting, encourage her to figure out how she'll keep pets safer when she's caring for them. Maybe she'll need to watch them more closely or open doors only when she's holding them by collars. Having these new rules will make her feel more in control and competent and, therefore, safer and more confident.

- **LIVE BY VALUES.** As previously discussed, teens are highly motivated to be liked and accepted by peers. They want to be perceived as attractive, funny, charming, and smart. They desperately want to be seen as gutsy and "cool," and that is why it's so easy for many of them to cave in to peer pressure. For all the lectures on "just say no," at the end of the day they don't want to be the one "nerd" or "baby" who wouldn't take a puff, sip, or drag.

What these girls have yet to discover is the pride in inner strength that enables them to say no. Telling your daughter it's wrong to drink or smoke, when her peers are telling her it's cool, is often less than effective. Besides, as soon as she leaves home, she will have to determine her own guidelines. So encourage her instead to think through her personal beliefs and policies and then to be true to them.

You might ask her, for example, what kind of person she wants to be. What does she think of peers who drink, smoke, shoplift, etc.? You can help her notice what she admires in others, and try to emulate them. What does she approve and disapprove of in others' behavior?

It is crucial to support your daughter in paying attention to her inner voice. Anytime she perceives that voice warning her, "Not right," or urging her to "think twice," instruct her to listen closely. This is evidence she is incorporating the values and principles you have been teaching her. The more she trusts and follows her own inner voice, the safer she will be, and the less likely she is to make and regret mistakes.

- **THINK BEFORE YOU SPEAK.** Your daughter has to learn the value of thinking long and hard before saying something likely to be hurtful. Even as an adult you know that this is one of the most difficult resolutions to keep. To help her, you can remind her of the awful feeling she gets when she says something thoughtlessly and then would give anything to take it back. Although she may not correct her behavior all at once, she will probably learn gradual self-control. If she says, "I can't do it!" or "It's just not me," she needs to know that thinking before speaking is a learned behavior that gets easier with practice and time. Please note, however, that your daughter will probably need you to clarify the distinction between intentionally saying something hurtful, on the one hand, and deciding to confront someone despite the risk of hurting his or her feelings, on the other hand.

STEP 5: FORGIVE YOURSELF

After she's dealt with her mistake as best she could, done everything possible to make amends, and thought long and hard about how to avoid the same error in the future, your daughter needs to know that it is time to forgive herself—even if the person she hurt has not forgiven her. She may welcome a reminder that she can be responsible only for her own actions, not for others'. It may be helpful to point out past incidents in which each of you forgave mistakes in the mother-daughter relationship or when she has forgiven her friends after they have mistreated her. You will want your daughter to be as kind to herself as she would be to anyone who hurt her but then genuinely apologized and made amends. Just as you have previously shown her the connection between empathy and forgiveness, so your understanding of her reactions when she blunders encourages her self-acceptance and forgiveness. The capacity to make mistakes, grow from them, and tolerate imperfections are thereby incorporated into your daughter's sense of self—invaluable tools in her developing repertoire of lifelong skills.

EPILOGUE:
CLOSING THOUGHTS

Throughout this book you have focused specifically on your relationship with your daughter. Yet we are hopeful that the voices you have heard within these pages have also given you a stronger sense of connection with the larger community of mothers. You may have been reassured that your feelings, no matter how uncomfortable, confusing, or disturbing, are actually common among mothers of teenage girls. Like other mothers, you may be comforted by the knowledge that you are not alone, nor are your parenting experiences peculiar or, worse, "abnormal"; rather, they are typical and even expected.

As you put new ideas and skills into practice, it is helpful to continue to seek support from others within your community. Women are increasingly finding ways to reach out for much-needed help from one another. School-affiliated parent councils, informal mothers' groups, and lectures by parenting experts are being formed. Mothers are talking spontaneously at bus stops, in parking lots, and on grocery lines about what is happening between their daughters and them. As they exchange their anecdotes, frustrations, hopes, and dilemmas, they get invaluable validation and plenty of welcome input. Women learn how other mothers handle issues with teen girls, what seems to work best, and, conversely, which comment in which circumstance is a certain lethal combination. Typically, mothers walk away from even the most chance meetings with renewed hope for their relationships' surviving their daughters' teen years.

Meanwhile, daughters are undergoing an almost parallel process. Schools are increasingly recognizing that teenage girls have a similar need to share their experiences, to be heard and to learn from one another. In one coed secondary school, for example, students in seventh and eighth grades are offered a For Girls Only class as a weekly elective. According to the group facilitator, For Girls Only is one of the most consistently popular electives for girls. Thirteen- and fourteen-year-old girls, she says, relish the chance to sit down with one another and be "just girls."

When the most recent session began, students were asked to generate a list of the most important myths about girls. According to the teacher, there was an immediate buzz of voices and a flurry of activity, as the girls threw out ideas excitedly and wrote them down with great urgency.

High on this list of myths was: "Girls don't want to get along with their mothers."

This is especially remarkable because parents were never mentioned in the curriculum, and girls were allowed to raise any issue they wished. They chose to bring up a topic dear to them, their relationships with their mothers. These girls were making an important point: that despite their reputation for being rebellious and argumentative with mothers, they saw themselves as wanting good relationships. (Ironically, the teacher also commented that in order to appear cool and independent, the girls spent considerable time complaining about and criticizing their mothers.) The comforting message here is that in spite of all her outward behavior, the typical teenage girl does not really want discord between her mother and her.

In the spirit of this For Girls Only class, many other schools are offering "lunch bunch" groups to help middle school and high school girls deal with emotional and social issues. There are efforts to teach better social and communication skills to girls who are struggling with peers. Health classes and drug resistance programs—sometimes as early as the kindergarten year—are building self-awareness, management of feelings, and problem-solving skills to enable students to make healthy choices. Across the country, growing recognition of the importance of social and emotional expertise has prompted educators to include these key life skills as components of the curriculum.

It may help to know that schools from the preschool to the high school level support your efforts by teaching your daughter to use her words to handle her anger, to identify her strengths and unique qualities, to use practical strategies to resist peer pressure and substances, and to recognize the impact of the popular media. In one town, for example, an association devoted to offering educational programs, speakers, resources, and reading materials for women and adolescent girls has flourished in the past few years. There are also organizations in which mothers and teen daughters volunteer together for various charities. A national book club for mothers and daughters has been created, complete with a suggested reading list designed to spark a variety of discussions. These are all exciting opportunities, and where they do not yet exist, there is a need for women to take the initiative in creating them.

As these outside forces strive to improve teen girls' esteem and help them resolve conflict, you will be better able to do your part with the new tools you have acquired to help your daughter. Over time you will likely notice your daughter speaking up for herself increasingly and with greater confidence, tackling conflicts directly and competently. She has been enriched by your role in making this happen. Feel good about your part in helping her become the strong, proud woman you always hoped to raise. Someday your investment may be compounded even further, as you see your daughter cultivate these same capabilities in your granddaughter.

Years ago, when your daughter was small and people warned, "You'd better enjoy her while you can," the words probably conjured up thoughts of the dreaded adolescent years. Now that you and your daughter are on your way to a closer, more satisfying relationship, perhaps these words will take on a new, more positive meaning. As you strengthen your bond and enrich your relationship, you may remind yourself occasionally to "enjoy her while you can," savoring your time together before she leaves home.

Index